FROM BATTLES TO VICTORY

FROM BATTLES
to
VICTORY

Standing Strong in Your Call

DEBORAH A. BURD

XULON PRESS

Xulon Press
2301 Lucien Way #415
Maitland, FL 32751
407.339.4217
www.xulonpress.com

Paperback ISBN-13: 978-1-66287-306-5
Ebook ISBN-13: 978-1-66287-307-2

Dedication

$\mathcal{T}$his book is dedicated to the glory of God the Father, Son, and Holy Spirit.

It is also dedicated to all those who inspired the writing of this novel/textbook and to everyone currently in ministry facing their own spiritual battles.

Acknowledgement

I would like to thank everyone who read my manuscript and gave suggestions as it was being written. Your input was a blessing!

Dr. Deborah A. Burd, D.Min.

Endorsements

"Certain challenges in ministry are not always what they appear. That's because Satan skillfully cloaks his schemes in people we know and events we experience. In my nearly fifty years as a pastor, I have seen scenarios similar to those found in *From Battles to Victory* play out in real life and ministry ... sometimes in my own! Since spiritual warfare was not a subject covered in seminary, I was more vulnerable than I should have been, especially in my early years. It doesn't need to be this way for others. I highly commend this book to those who are preparing for Christian ministry, as well as those who are currently serving, because of its practical insights and strategies for turning defeat into victory for themselves and for the kingdom."

Rev. Dennis Barta, Congregational Care Pastor,
Grace C&MA Church, Cleveland, Ohio

"I found Dr. Deborah Burd's novel to be difficult to put down, feeling more like history than fiction. It arouses an awareness of challenges and dangers faced by those of us seeking to serve the Lord, but, also raises hope for overcoming them. I highly recommend this book to all seeking to follow the call to God's service."

Messianic Jewish Rabbi Jeffrey Adler,
Sha'arey Yeshua Congregation, Indianapolis, Indiana

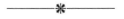

From Battles to Victory is endorsed by *Dr. Mike Hutchings, Christian author and Director of Education for Global Awakening Ministries, Mechanicsburg, Pennsylvania.*

———— ✿ ————

"*From Battles to Victory* shows what happens in real life to real people in ministry when one does not deal honestly with motives and one's own tendency towards self-referential love. . . .

The result is never experiencing the fulfillment of God-given desires nor the fulfillment of one's spiritual gifts."

Pastor Sanford Yoder, Disciple-Making Coach and 30-Year Pastor, Harrisonburg, Virginia

———— ✿ ————

"The book was fantastic and your summary of issues we need to be aware of at the end of the book brought out how they were covered in the narrative portion of the book. I've read at least 200 life-inspired books in my retirement, and, not one held my interest as well as yours. I could not stop reading. I read the whole book in a day and a half because I couldn't put it down. Your use of a narrative to get across major Christian points and doctrines was wonderful."

Rev. Douglas Barnes, Pastor Emeritus, Wallace Street Evangelical Church, Indianapolis, Indiana

Contents

Introduction

Victory in Ministry: A Pioneer Journey

*T*his novel was inspired by the experiences of an actual pastoral couple and their encounters with spiritual warfare while
in church ministry. The lived experiences of other ministry leaders,
including the author's, were also incorporated into the storyline making
it more of an amalgamated account than just one couple's narrative.
Some fictional elements were also woven into the storyline to high-
light certain theological concepts and give the reader a glimpse into
the supernatural realm as it exists and functions simultaneously with
the natural world around us. The vividly detailed visions and encounters the main character, Pastor Steve Hanson, experiences in this novel
were created to help achieve that end.

This book was written with the ministry student and new pastor
or church leader in mind. However, anyone who has dedicated his or
her life to serving the Lord Jesus can benefit from reading this book
for we are all ministers of the Gospel (1 Peter 2: 9) and will engage in
numerous spiritual conflicts of one kind or another during our lifetime.
It is my hope and prayer that this novel will be used in Bible colleges,
seminaries, and Christian universities as an instructional tool to help
prepare ministry students for spiritual battle, a topic often overlooked
or underemphasized in many courses of study.

As for those of us already in ministry leadership positions, we recognize we will continually encounter spiritual challenges until we leave
this earth. How we handle them is what makes the difference. Will we

compromise or relinquish our divine callings for an easier path, or will we pick up our swords and stand firm on the Word, fighting against the powers of darkness, through the strength, authority, and power of Almighty God?

The Apostle Paul well understood spiritual warfare and told the early Church …

> *Finally, be strong in the Lord and in his mighty power. Put on the full armor of God, so that you can take your stand against the devil's schemes. For our struggle is not against flesh and blood, but against the rulers, against the authorities, against the powers of this dark world and against the spiritual forces of evil in the heavenly realms. Therefore put on the full armor of God, so that when the day of evil comes, you may be able to stand your ground, and after you have done everything, to stand. Stand firm then, with the belt of truth buckled around your waist, with the breastplate of righteousness in place, and with your feet fitted with the readiness that comes from the gospel of peace. In addition to all this, take up the shield of faith, with which you can extinguish all the flaming arrows of the evil one. Take the helmet of salvation and the sword of the Spirit, which is the word of God.*
>
> *And pray in the Spirit on all occasions with all kinds of prayers and requests. With this in mind, be alert and always keep on praying for all the Lord's people. Pray also for me, that whenever I speak, words may be given me so that I will fearlessly make known the mystery of the gospel, for which I am an ambassador in chains. Pray that I may declare it fearlessly, as I should. (Ephesians 6: 10-20, New International Version)*

May you be blessed and encouraged by the reading of this book.

Chapter 1

The New Church

$\int$ teve Hanson lifted what he hoped would be the last of the suitcases onto the back of the family's black Jeep Cherokee. He turned just in time to see Sara, his wife of twenty-two years, coming down the steps of the front porch of their white cape cod, which served as the church parsonage, carrying a heavy cardboard box full of Steve's favorite reference books and materials. She looked relieved to be finally bringing what was left in Steve's office to the carefully, but tightly packed, vehicle.

"Is that everything, Sara?" Steve called out to her from several yards away, wiping the sweat from his face with an old kitchen towel. It was already getting warm that late summer morning.

"Yes, I believe so," she responded, somewhat out of breath. "Peter and Mary are going back through the house to make sure. I told them to double-check the windows. I checked most of them myself a little while ago, but just want to confirm they're all locked."

"Good," Steve replied, reaching for the cardboard box Sara handed to him when she approached the Jeep. "I'm anxious to get on the road." He placed the box in the last available spot in the back of the SUV, closed the tailgate, and brushed the dust from his hands.

It was August 1997 in Middleburg, Ohio, and this was moving day. Pastor Steve and Sara Hanson, their teenage son and daughter, and their stout, playful, tricolor beagle, Samson, were on their way to a new calling, a new adventure. In many ways, they were sad to leave the place they had called home for over five years. However, during that time, their once-thriving church congregation of 300 active members had dwindled to just forty people, a third of whom were children. Middleburg was quickly losing many of its residents because of a drastic change in the economic climate. Several companies had pulled out of the county in the last couple of years, moving on to what they believed were better opportunities in other states and overseas, leaving the Hansons' community without the strong tax base the residents had once enjoyed. There was no longer enough money to support a pastor and his family, so Steve and Sara looked to God for a new calling, which came through after several months of intense prayer and searching. To their relief, it was a church connected with the denomination of which they were members. Steve had been ordained in that denomination after graduating from seminary almost twenty years earlier.

Steve, a tall pleasant-looking sandy-haired man in his early forties, stood back from the Jeep to take a last look at the home they were leaving. He would miss summer nights on the screened-in porch on the back of the house. He loved looking up at the stars and marveling at God's handiwork. Sometimes he would look through his telescope, an anniversary present from Sara, to get a closer look at how extraordinary the universe was. Steve had spent many nights praying there and often felt God's presence as he gazed up at the sky. Some of his best sermons were inspired while reflecting on God's beautiful creation from the vantage point of that porch.

Sara, several inches shorter than her husband and two years younger, moved close to him, pushing her curly, dark brown, shoulder-length hair from her face and dark brown eyes. She was a pretty woman with a welcoming smile. She too was taking in her last long look at the house and at the encircling flower gardens she had spent so much time planting and nurturing. They had been her solace, her place to commune with God when she needed to be alone. There, on cool summer mornings after the sun had just come up, she often imagined the Lord walking through them as she tended her plants. She could see Him smile as He bent down to enjoy the sweet-smelling aroma of the variety of types and colors of flowers she had planted with love and prayer. It was as if she had the Lord all to herself as she worked the ground. What peace and comfort her gardens had given her. What spiritual insights she gained from spending time in them.

Sara often took some of her flowers to a local nursing home she regularly visited. That was her special ministry. There her flowers were always welcomed with great anticipation and appreciation. Their wonderful fresh fragrances filled the rooms they were displayed in, bringing a sense of hope and newness to the residents. One of those places was the guest meeting room, which contained an old up-right piano. Sara loved to go to that room to play for the patients after distributing her flowers throughout the facility. She majored in music in college and had hoped then to someday use those skills in ministry.

On Tuesdays, Sara would lead a Bible study in the community room for all those who were able to attend. A number of the residents were spending a great deal of time studying the Scriptures on their own and often shared wonderful insights during group study discussions. Afterward, Sara would spend time with some of the residents who did not receive a lot of visitors. She had made many cherished friends at the nursing home during their time in Middleburg, and would greatly miss spending those special moments with them.

"It's been a good five years, Sara," Steve mused. He was enjoying the break from the packing frenzy and the sudden breeze that swiftly moved across the front yard, giving them a brief relief from the climbing temperature.

"Yes, it has been," Sara agreed. She knew Steve was struggling with this change, even though God had unmistakably confirmed their calling to lead a new congregation. She was struggling inside as well but did not want to show it. This was a happy day, and she needed to be an encourager to both him and her family.

Just then, Peter, a tall slender teen resembling his father, emerged from the empty house. He was wearing jeans and a T-shirt and had a large military-green backpack hanging over his right shoulder. In his left arm, he was carrying his well-used sleeping bag. Peter had just had his seventeenth birthday and would be starting his junior year in high school that fall. He loved sports and enjoyed spending time with his close friends from both church and school. While he wasn't as outgoing as his sister, Mary, he still had several close friends and was well-liked by his peers. He was also a good student at school and dreamed of someday becoming a social worker for troubled kids and families in need.

Mary, fifteen and also in jeans and a T-shirt, followed close behind her brother carrying a broom and a dust pan. She resembled her father as well, only she had dark hair and eyes like her mother and her mother's welcoming smile. She was going to be a freshman that fall and was anxious to become a part of the high school crowd. Mary was a definite extrovert and made friends easily with just about everyone she met. She loved to read and write and excelled in school. It was her goal to one day become a college literature professor.

The teens also found it hard to leave the home they had known for so long, but they knew change had been inevitable because of the condition of the local economy. When Steve announced that he felt moved to accept a new pastorate in another state, they quickly recognized their father's call as a commission from God and wholeheartedly supported his decision to leave the town of Middleburg.

"All clear," Peter announced as he walked down the porch steps.

"Yep, all clear," Mary confirmed with a grin. "All the windows are shut and locked too."

"Great!" Steve returned. "Let's pile in the Jeep. I'll lock the front door."

"Don't forget Samson," Sara called over her shoulder as she headed for the front seat of the SUV.

Peter headed for the Jeep behind Sara and got in the backseat. Mary put the broom and dustpan in a corner of the porch for the next family to use and went over to untie Samson's extra-long leash from one of the porch's wooden pillars. He had been sleeping quietly in the shade under a nearby tree, waiting for the family to finish loading up. Mary led Samson over to the Jeep and helped him in next to Peter, climbing in after him. She got him settled by the passenger's side window so he could look out when they pulled out of the drive, then sat back and buckled her seatbelt. Samson's tail was wagging happily. He enjoyed traveling with the family and was eager to get started. Mary reached over to adjust Samson's bandana. As she did, he playfully licked her face. Mary giggled. Samson loved wearing a scarf around his neck every day. In fact, part of his daily morning ritual was to choose a new one from a drawer filled with neckerchiefs in various colors and designs just for him in a cabinet in the living room.

Samson had been with the Hanson family since he was little more than a puppy. Steve found him one day, cowering behind his old motorcycle in the garage. The family tried to find out who he belonged to, but when their efforts to locate an owner produced no results, Samson became part of the family. He just seemed to fit.

After locking the main door of the house and closing the screen door, Steve said a quick prayer for the new residents, placed the house keys under the mat on the front porch, and headed for the Jeep. Deacon Daniels would be by later to pick them up. He was good at following up on things like that. Steve felt a release as he placed the keys on the porch floor. His work there as the pastor of Middleburg Family Fellowship was finished.

With all the goodbyes already said at the church reception on Sunday, the Hansons said a brief prayer together for safe travel and pulled out of the driveway with Steve at the wheel and Samson's head hanging out the window. Samson barked several times as the car moved onto the street as if to say his own farewell. The family headed down the road, waving at their church as they passed by. They continued, maneuvering through the maze of city streets they had traveled so many times in the past and headed towards the highway a few miles away. It was close to 10 a.m., and Steve wanted to drive a little while before they stopped for lunch.

Everyone was now quiet in the car, deep in their thoughts, watching the familiar sights of their hometown pass by for the last time. Even Samson was silent, sensing the mood of the family. Mary tried to think of the boys she would meet in the new youth group. Peter turned his thoughts to the tryouts for the football team at his new high school. Sara thought of the elderly women she was leaving behind at the Westgate Nursing Home. She knew others from the church would check on them, but it troubled her to leave them at this time in their lives. She had said her goodbyes and promised to write, but somehow, that just didn't seem enough. Their friendships were so important to her. As they drove, she was able to convince herself her ministry at the nursing home in Middleburg was done, and God would continue to touch the residents' lives through other people.

Steve's thoughts were focused on the words of an evangelist he met briefly several months earlier at a denominational convention. The man, whom Steve had never met before, had walked up to him unexpectedly during a break and shared some disturbing prophetic words concerning the new pastorate he and his family would soon be undertaking. He told Steve to be prepared. *It would not be easy, but he and his family would not be alone. God would be with them through all of the spiritual challenges that were to come.* Steve was also warned by the district office that the church in Nordstown, Pennsylvania had experienced problems, but they were not specific. He understood what those warnings could mean. However, his faith was strong, and he knew in his heart that he, Sara, and his children had been called to Nordstown. He had to answer that call and not because of the obvious financial benefits. He quickly dismissed the notion that a higher salary was the primary motivator for going to this new church. Leading this new congregation was God's will. Steve's life had been dedicated to pastoral ministry a long time ago, and he was not about to back down now from any divine assignment, despite the spiritual difficulties that most certainly lay ahead. Undaunted, he had readily accepted the position to become the senior pastor of Nordstown Community Church, and that decision was not about to change. Steve was thankful that he and Sara had both taken the time over the years to be trained in spiritual warfare. That training, he now realized, would prove invaluable in their new ministry assignment.

Sara broke away from her thoughts when they reached the highway, and, looking at Steve, reached over to hold his hand. She knew what he was thinking about. He turned briefly to look at her as she gave him an affirming smile. He returned the smile, then resumed his focus on the road. It would be a five-hour drive to their new home, and he was determined to get there before dark. The new parsonage was ready and waiting for them. Their larger household items had been loaded on a full-size moving van on Monday and were already in Pennsylvania, scheduled to be delivered the next morning.

This was the perfect time to move. It was mid-August, and school had not started yet in Nordstown, where the family would be living. Peter and Mary would have plenty of time to get settled before entering a new educational setting. This high school, being much larger than their previous one, made both teens a little apprehensive, but they were still excited and looking forward to making new friends.

Though Steve was beginning to feel at peace with his decision to go to Nordstown, the evangelist's warning continued to reenter his mind as he drove, so he began focusing on some of the obvious positives of the move. Steve would have a full-time assistant pastor, a youth leader, and a music ministry director. The salary would be more than he had ever made, and the four-bedroom two-story Victorian parsonage with a finished attic was huge. There would be plenty of room to have Bible studies and other church meetings and gatherings there. The backyard would give Samson more than ample room to run around in. The congregation of 585 members, many of them professionals with stable salaries, would certainly be large enough to keep the church budget going strong. In addition, the local schools had a good reputation, and Sara and the kids would have more opportunities to be involved in activities in both their church and their community.

The hours on the road passed by uneventfully. Stopping now and then at parks and restaurants, walking Samson, and changing drivers, the Hansons pressed on. Sara had taken the wheel when the family entered Richland County in southwestern Pennsylvania. They were getting close to their destination. The family marveled at the beautiful hills, trees, and parks as they worked their way through a very different terrain than they were used to in Ohio. The view at points was breathtaking. Some of the leaves were just beginning to change, which made the view even more spectacular. Sara was still behind the wheel when they reached the city limits of Nordstown shortly after 5:25 p.m.

"Do you remember where the church is?" Sara asked Steve as they entered the town.

"Uh, yes, just turn down this road here," pointing to Adams Street, "and it should be just a few blocks on the right."

"Okay," Sara replied. "Almost there!" She was beginning to feel the fatigue of the long ride in her back. She shifted in her seat to ease the discomfort.

Everyone, tired from the drive, was eager to get out of the car again. They all looked anxiously out the window to catch the first glimpse of their new home. Sensing they were close to their destination, Samson became restless.

"There it is!" Mary suddenly shouted. "We're here! We're here!" pointing at a large white Victorian home with an enormous oak tree in the front yard. A long rope swing was suspended from it. Samson started barking and jumping around inside the car, annoying everyone in both the front and back seats of the vehicle. He had had enough of riding too.

"So we are," Sara said, rolling her eyes and smiling, as she put on her right turn signal and pulled into the driveway of the parsonage. Just to the right of the drive was their new church, a large red brick building with beautiful stained-glass windows, many depicting scenes from the Bible. A huge white steeple towered above the roof. The church parking lot was full of cars, and to their surprise, a small crowd of people had assembled and were waiting for the new pastor and his family to arrive. Some of them began waving as they spotted the Hansons' Jeep pulling in.

"Looks like the welcome committee," Peter said, amazed at the turnout.

"Sure does," Mary chimed in, unbuckling her seat belt to get a better look at the group, searching for faces of other teens.

"Steve, did you tell them what time we would be arriving?" Sara asked.

"I gave them a ball park time. I guess they took it seriously."

When the vehicle came to a stop in the driveway of the parsonage, the Hansons all climbed out and quickly crossed over to the church parking lot just a few feet from their driveway. There they were greeted with cheers, smiles, hugs, and lots of "Praise the Lords!" Just above them, the church bell began to ring out loudly. Several "Welcome to Nordstown Community Church" signs waved through the air. Samson was beside himself as he jumped from the car and ran free to check out his new yard next door. One of the teens in the crowd, seeing him escape from his owners, offered to round him up and put him on the back porch of the parsonage. Peter smiled.

"I'll go with ya!" he replied, quickly grabbing Samson's leash from the Jeep. The two took off to chase Samson down, laughing as they tried to corral him while the dog zigzagged across the lawn. Realizing that the teens were in hot pursuit, Samson slowed down just before reaching the creek at the end of the property and stopped short of it, allowing the two to catch up with him. He willingly allowed himself to be leashed and led to his new home. Samson happily entered the screened-in porch when he saw his supper bowl and fresh water waiting for him. There was even a chew bone for dessert.

Curious as to what was happening, a number of the town residents came out of their houses to see what all the commotion was about. Some of them, realizing that Community's new senior pastor and his family had just arrived, came over to join the celebration as well. After greeting everyone, including the entire ministry staff, the Hansons were soon ushered into the fellowship hall in the church basement for a covered dish meal. There they were seated together in a place of honor. Pastor Randy Nelson, the associate pastor, called for everyone's attention, gave a brief welcome, and then asked everyone to stand for the blessing.

"Father in Heaven," Pastor Randy began, "we thank you for hearing our prayers by bringing Pastor Steve Hanson, his wife Sara and their family to Community Church. We're excited they're finally here and look forward to many years of their leadership and ministry among us. May Your hand of protection always be upon them. We also thank you for this incredible meal now set before us and ask Your blessing on it. May we always be truly grateful for everything You provide. In Jesus' name. Amen."

"Amen," everyone responded in unison.

The Hanson family was then invited to be first in line for food while the others filed in behind them, talking with each other as they went through the line. Every possible meat, vegetable, and pasta dish was there, plus scores of desserts. It was a spread fit for a royal family. The celebratory event went on for over two hours and then, sensing that their new pastor and his family were tired, the church group decided to adjourn and led the Hansons over to the parsonage where they could relax for the evening.

After saying good night to some of their new parishioners and neighbors, the Hansons were soon left alone in their new home. Going through the house, they noticed it had just been cleaned. The smell of cleaning supplies was still in the air. Fresh flowers stood in a vase on the kitchen counter, and the refrigerator and some of the cupboards were stuffed full of all kinds of food. When they went upstairs, the family members were surprised to find temporary beds already set up for them to sleep on. They had come prepared to sleep on their bedrolls. There were also clean towels in the bathrooms. No detail was missed. It was an incredible welcome that they would reflect on for months to come.

Before going to bed, Steve felt they should do a house blessing. Taking out his anointing oil from its carrying case he kept in his briefcase, Steve began walking through the house. His family followed, taking turns anointing the doors and entrances in the name of the "Father, Son, and Holy Spirit," as they went. Samson trailed close behind as they entered each room, sniffing the scented oil as it was being applied. When they were finished, the family met in the living room, and held hands as they prayed a blessing over the house and over all those who would enter it. They also asked for God's hand of protection to be on them while they lived there and for God's blessings over their new church, the members of the congregation, and the people of the Nordstown community. When they finished, they hugged each other, said goodnight, and headed for bed, glad for the chance to rest.

The furniture arrived the next day in a large moving van, and many people from the congregation showed up again to help unpack the myriad of boxes stacked everywhere. Women from the church were busy in the kitchen washing dishes and putting them in the cabinets. The teens of the congregation helped Steve unload his reference books and place them on the shelves of the parsonage study, under his direction. Some of the men worked in the garage to unload tools and exercise equipment. Food and cold drinks continued to show up for the workers and the new senior pastor and his family. Despite the hot day, it was a wonderful picture of a church family working together in unity. Laughter filled the house. This truly was a bit of Heaven to the Hansons. Steve began to let go of his concerns and enjoyed the fellowship of other brothers and sisters in Christ.

As Sara was directing the movers in the living room, a woman about her age, with shoulder-length blonde hair and wearing jeans and a green T-shirt, entered the front hallway of the house. She was accompanied by two young boys, who were in shorts and T-shirts, one of whom was carrying a large white casserole dish. Sara went over to greet them.

"Hi, I'm Carol Nelson," the woman introduced herself with a smile. "Pastor Randy's wife. You met him yesterday at the dinner. Sorry, we weren't there to meet you then. The kids and I were out of town visiting my parents." She reached over to give Sara a big hug. "So glad you are all here. We have really been looking forward to this day."

"Thank you," Sara replied, as she hugged Carol back. "It's so nice to meet you. And who are these two good-looking gentlemen?" she asked, looking at the boys.

"These are our sons–Johnny, our nine-year-old and Adam, who just turned twelve."

"So nice to meet you boys," Sara smiled and shook their hands.

"Our dad's the assistant pastor," Johnny said proudly, as he smiled broadly exposing a missing top front tooth.

"Yes, I know," Sara replied with a grin.

"We brought you something for supper," Johnny said, as he offered the covered casserole dish to Sara.

"Well thank you guys," Sara said, reaching for the warm dish. "I'm sure we'll enjoy it very much."

"It's a chicken casserole," Adam added. "Mom made it."

"Well, that makes it extra special," Sara replied.

"Thank you, Carol," Sara said, turning to her new friend.

"You're welcome, Sara. Is there anything we can help you with?"

"I could sure use some help unloading my books in the family room."

"We can do that," Carol replied quickly.

"Great!" Sara responded. "I'll just take this casserole to the kitchen, and we'll get started."

Carol motioned for her two sons to follow her to the family room, and soon the foursome was unloading Sara's books and placing them on the shelves of the bookcases that were already set up. Sara was thankful for their help. It would have taken her hours to unload and organize her books herself. As the afternoon went on, Sara and her new friends had empty cartons laying everywhere. At one point, a couple of the teens from the church came into the room and offered to break the boxes down for easy storage. Sara readily permitted them to take them away and put them in the garage.

While the Nelson boys continued to unload the book boxes, Johnny suddenly exclaimed, "What's this?"

His brother Adam, who was working beside him, leaned over and looked into the large brown box his brother just opened, and said, "Looks like a bunch of hats and purses and stuff."

"Oh my goodness," Sara said, hurrying over to where the boys were working. "That's my dress-up clothes from when I was a little girl. I didn't realize I still had them. They must have been in the attic."

"Really?" Carol said, going over to take a look as well. "I had a box like that too when I was a little girl. My grandmother gave me a whole trunk full of things."

Soon, the two women were going through the box to see what treasures they could find, trying on hats and shawls and laughing while the boys went back to work filling the bookcases. The two women were enjoying the break and the opportunity to get to know each other, along with the chance to recapture the same childhood memory. Others passing by the room laughed when they saw the two mothers acting like school girls. The Nelsons stayed to help until after supper and then headed home, promising to have the Hansons over for a cookout sometime soon.

By late that evening, all of the workers had left and almost everything was in place in the church parsonage. Steve and Sara began to feel at home with their furniture and personal belongings around them. Peter and Mary had already made friends with some of the other teens. They were looking forward to starting the new school year and being a part of the church youth group.

"What great folks," Sara said, as she dropped wearily onto the living room sofa when they were finally alone. Peter and Mary had already headed for bed. "So nice."

"Yeah," Steve agreed. "I think we are really going to like it here."

Samson came over to lick Sara's hand. He had been hiding away in the laundry room most of the day, as the movers and unpackers got the house in order. He was enjoying his new home and was glad he could come out to be with his family again. As Steve relaxed in a well-worn brown imitation leather recliner, his thoughts returned once again to the prophet and his prophetic words about encountering trouble in his new calling. *Perhaps*, Steve thought to himself, this *could be something the ministry staff and I will deal with together . . . a test of character . . . a challenge to the cohesiveness of a new group of ministry leaders . . . Yes, with God's help, we can overcome anything!* Somehow, the danger of any serious spiritual battles seemed so far away at that moment.

In the next couple of days, Steve spent time with members of his ministry staff in his home office and at the church, listening to their hearts and working out in more detail each one's role in the church ministry. He was encouraged by their friendliness and felt the group was responding well to him being in the lead. The staff included the associate pastor, Randy Nelson; the youth leader, Oscar Burton; the education director, Polly Teagarden; the music director, Frank Perkins; the church's administrative assistant, Terri Campbell; the maintenance directors, Mike and Geraldine Bruster; and his office manager, Margaret Hellinger. To Steve, they were his dream team.

Steve spent more time than usual on his upcoming Sunday sermon. He wanted it to be pertinent to the congregation and also encouraging and uplifting. Choosing to preach on the tenth chapter of the Gospel of Luke, where Jesus sent out a special group of seventy disciples for some hands-on experience,[1] he prayed it would inspire the members to reach out to the community in greater ways.

When Sunday arrived, the sanctuary was packed, even in the balcony, with regular attenders and visitors from the local community. Steve's sermon, a combination of teaching, preaching, and humor, was well received at both morning services. Smiling faces and nods showed their approval. Steve was off to a good start. To top things off, his family was well-received during their part of the service. Peter, Mary, and Sara sang together the praise song, "Days of Elijah."[2] Mary and Peter strummed and picked their guitars with enthusiasm, while Sara played the keyboard as they led the congregation in the popular music selection that morning. The combination of their voices sounded heavenly to Steve as they flowed throughout the large sanctuary. The congregation eagerly stood, singing and clapping along with the trio. How proud Steve was of his family at that moment. Like their mother, Peter and Mary both loved music and had often helped lead worship during services at the church in Ohio. Steve felt blessed to have his family up front with him that day. When the services were over that morning, many gathered at the main sanctuary doors to greet the new pastor and his wife and children. A luncheon followed the last service, and the Hansons enjoyed another round of home-cooked food and good fellowship.

The following weeks were filled with hospital calls, planning sessions, church meals, Bible studies, and congregational and community events. Steve even performed a couple of small weddings. In addition, Steve met several other pastors in Nordstown and the surrounding area and talked with them about how Community Church could network with their congregations. He was making some good friends and was soon invited to attend the local ministerial association meetings.

Steve's family was also finding their place within the church and Nordstown communities. Sara was getting to know Pastor Randy's wife, Carol, who served on an Outreach Committee with her. They quickly became good friends and often did things together outside of church ministry. The women had similar interests and were often seen at each other's homes during the week. At times, the two families had meals together. Sara and Carol soon found themselves telling each other things they rarely shared with others. It was a growing relationship built on mutual respect and trust. Sara also started a nursing home ministry like the one she had in Ohio. She found a couple of nursing facilities that were very open to her coming in with her flowers, music, and Bible studies. Sara thanked God for the opportunity to be working with older people again. Careful to keep her promises to her elderly friends in the nursing home in Ohio, Sara made time to write to them every two or three weeks, just to stay connected. Peter and Mary were getting involved with the church youth ministry and in a number of activities at their new high school. They were becoming popular among the teens at both places and were making many friends. The two were also doing well in school.

Knowing things were going well on all fronts, at least for the present, Steve allowed himself to feel more at ease in his new pastorate. His heart was filled with joy as he drew closer to the members of the congregation and his ministry staff. However, Steve knew he could not forget the warnings from the evangelist and the district office, so he kept them in the back of his mind, praying he and his family would be ready for whatever was to come. Life was good at Community Church, and he would make the most of it for as long as it lasted.

Chapter 2

Trouble

*O*ne Tuesday afternoon, when Steve was working in his home office on the agenda for an upcoming ministry heads meeting, he heard a knock at the door. The parsonage study resembled in many ways something one would see in an old Sherlock Holmes movie. The heavy cherry desk and rows of books on shelves lining the walls gave anyone entering the sense they were about to meet the great British detective himself. This was Steve's favorite room in the house, not just because of the esthetics, but because he felt close to God when he worked there.

"Come in, Sara," Steve called out, without looking up. The door opened slowly, and Steve heard someone enter the room. When he looked up from the notes he was writing, ready to greet his wife, standing by the open door was not Sara, but a younger woman in her late twenties.

"Sorry to bother you, Pastor Steve," she said quietly. "But I must talk with you. Mrs. Hanson told me just to knock on your door."

Steve closed the notebook he was writing in and got up from his chair to greet an attractive woman with long auburn hair wearing a dark blue professional pants suit. She was visibly distraught. He extended his hand to welcome her. "Good morning," Steve said cheerfully. "And you are?"

"Oh, I'm sorry," the woman responded awkwardly, moving forward to grasp his hand to return the greeting. "I'm Cheryl Petrie. We haven't met yet. I used to be a member of Community Church but have been attending a church in another town. It's been a while since I've been here."

"Well, I hope we can entice you to come back again," Steve said with a smile.

"That's not likely," she responded, as she headed toward the chair in front of Steve's desk. "Could we close the door? This is kind of personal."

"Of course," he said, as she took her seat. Before closing the door, he asked her, "Would you like a cup of coffee?"

"Tea, if you have it," she responded politely.

"We can do that. I will just ask Sara to bring in some hot water." Steve stepped out of the office to check on getting the hot water. When he returned and closed the door, he noticed tears beginning to well up in Cheryl's eyes. This was a serious matter. He offered her a box of Kleenex. Just then, Sara walked in with the hot water kettle.

"It was already boiling when Steve came in the kitchen," she said smiling at Cheryl. She placed a ceramic tray with a teapot, cups and saucers, and a sugar bowl on the end of Steve's desk. "Is there anything else I can get you? Honey? Maybe a cookie?"

"No, no I'm fine. Thank you."

"I think we're good," Steve told Sara. "Thanks, Hon."

"You're welcome," Sara returned. She immediately sensed that something was wrong, almost ominous, but graciously exited the room, knowing that her husband was well-equipped to handle the situation. She began to pray over Steve's conversation with this woman. Sara closed the door of the office and headed back to the kitchen. The parsonage office door had a glass pane in it, so others could see in his workspace. His office at the church had the same glass panel. Steve liked this feature because people often came alone to counsel with him. Appearances in these kinds of situations were important to Steve. He would not allow any misunderstandings concerning what took place in his pastoral sessions, especially in his own home.

Steve handed Cheryl a cup with hot water, a teabag, and a spoon.

"Thank you," she said, taking them from him. She dropped the teabag in the cup and began to move it through the water.

"Sugar?" he asked.

"No, this is fine," she replied.

"Why don't we pray before we start?" Steve offered, as he sat down at his desk.

"That would be good," Cheryl sniffed and wiped her eyes with a Kleenex.

Steve began, "Father, I thank you for Cheryl and that she belongs to you. Thank you for bringing her to this office today. Please give me discernment on how I can help her. I can see she is deeply troubled about something. Remind her of Your love for her, that You already know why she is here, and that she is never alone. May she leave here today with a load lifted from her shoulders and experience that wonderful inner peace only You can give. Thank you, Lord. In the name of Jesus. Amen."

"Amen," Cheryl said in agreement. The room was silent for a moment.

"Now, how can I be of help to you today?" Steve asked.

"I really need to talk with someone," she blurted out awkwardly. "This will stay confidential, right?"

"Of course," Steve assured her. "Unless it is a legal matter or a church issue that requires disciplinary action. Then I would be obligated to report it to certain individuals."

"I understand. Actually, it is a church issue. A serious one."

Steve became concerned.

"It . . . ," she hesitated. "It has to do with someone on the ministry staff here at Community."

"I see," Steve responded, bracing himself for what she was about to disclose to him.

"It's about inappropriate behavior."

"What kind of inappropriate behavior?" Steve wanted to know.

"Touching. Inappropriate touching," Cheryl choked.

"I see. Please try to relax and tell me what happened." Steve couldn't imagine anyone on staff who would do such a thing.

"Well, a year and a half ago, before you came, I was hired to be the administrative assistant for Pastor Randy."

Randy? Steve thought. He swallowed hard as he heard his associate pastor's name, trying not to look alarmed or jump to any conclusions. Yet, he was shaken inside. Pastor Randy Nelson was well-liked and respected by everyone in the church and local communities. He and his family were also frequent visitors to his home. *She's just getting started,* he told himself. *The alleged perpetrator could be someone else.*

"I better take some notes," Steve said, as he opened the notebook he had just closed on his desk. "I'll need to document this conversation."

"That's fine," Cheryl said. Taking a sip of her tea, she continued, "I was so excited when I was told I was hired. It was the perfect job for me at the time. I was still going to school, finishing up my bachelor's degree in business administration. I thought that would be a great way to help in ministry and use my business skills at the same time."

"Sounds like it was a good fit for you."

"Yes, well, anyway. Things went well the first several weeks. Nothing out of the ordinary, I guess. I did catch Pastor Randy staring at me from time to time, but I never thought much about it."

Steve's fear was confirmed.

"He was always complementing me too. My hair, how I dressed, the perfume I wore, how I spoke with others." Cheryl set her cup down on a coaster Steve had placed for her on his desk and began to nervously play with her napkin. "He also seemed to like to stand close to me when we talked in the office or the hallway," she went on. "Sometimes he patted me on the shoulder when he thought I had done something particularly well. I took it all in stride, thinking it was just his way with people. But then late one Friday afternoon, I found myself alone in the church fellowship hall with Pastor Randy. I didn't think anything about it at first because, well, I felt safe. You know, I felt safe because he was a pastor."

Steve nodded. He was trying hard not to pass judgment on Pastor Randy. He prayed for clear discernment.

"Well, I was almost finished placing the silverware on the tables for the men's breakfast the next morning, when I turned to see Pastor Randy standing right behind me. At first, I laughed, but then I looked at the expression on his face and began to feel like something wasn't quite right. Instinctively, I moved aside, but then he moved there with me. He reached for my hair and brushed it away from my face. Then he said, as he stared at me, 'There, that's much better.' I felt strange. Something inside told me to head back to the office right then, but as I started to go, he caught my arm. I was stunned. This wasn't the Pastor Randy I knew. Then he pulled me closer to him. I was shocked and instinctively said 'no!' to him, pulling myself out of his hold. I told him I needed to go home, but he grabbed my arm again and insisted he wanted me to stay and talk with him."

"Just at the moment, Mrs. Hellinger, the office manager came flying down the basement stairs and into the room. She was intent on finding something she was having trouble locating. I can't tell you, Pastor Hanson, how awkward I felt at that moment, but she didn't seem to notice that anything was wrong. Randy let loose of me once he realized she had entered the room and nervously cleared his throat, trying to act as nothing had happened. He brushed his hair back with his hands and asked if we could help her find something. His face was starting to turn red with embarrassment. Mrs. Hellinger told him 'no' and said she was just looking for the keys to the church storage shed. She thought she had left them in the kitchen. Then she turned and headed for the kitchen door, which was open. I just stood there paralyzed with shock, not knowing what to do next."

"Randy called after Mrs. Hellinger and said he hoped she would find her keys. If she didn't, he had some extra ones in his office. A couple of minutes later, Mrs. Hellinger came out of the kitchen and announced she had found the keys. She looked relieved she had located them. Pastor Randy just said, 'how fortunate,' and stood there waiting for Mrs. Hellinger to leave. At this point, I was able to pull myself back together. Suddenly, I saw my excuse to leave the room and asked Mrs.

Hellinger if I could accompany her to the shed to help her out. I had almost finished in the fellowship hall anyway."

"Mrs. Hellinger seemed grateful for my help and told me that she needed to get some items out for next week's women's sewing day. It would save her some time if I did assist her. So Mrs. Hellinger and I left the room and went to the shed, and Pastor Randy went back to his office. I stayed with Mrs. Hellinger until I thought Randy had left for home. She even helped me finish setting up a couple of things I had forgotten to do, once we brought in what she was looking for in the storage shed. When I felt it was safe to leave the building, I quickly gathered my things from the office and ran to my car. Needless to say, I relived the whole encounter over and over again in my mind while driving home that night. Did I do something to give Randy the wrong idea about me? Did I misunderstand something? No, I couldn't have. And yet, he was a beloved minister in the Nordstown community. Why did he do that? Had he done this before to another woman? Did his wife know? What would his children think?" Cheryl's voice began to grow tense as she relived those moments.

Steve, trying to remain objective, sat quietly as he listened and jotted down his notes. He did not want to interrupt Cheryl with any questions at this point in her story. Instead, he nodded in understanding now and then, letting her know he was paying attention to what she was saying.

"When I got home, I ran inside and locked the door behind me. I turned on the TV to watch the news for a while and then tried to fix some supper. After I had eaten and went back to the living room, I finally, out of sheer mental exhaustion, fell asleep on the living room couch and stayed there for the rest of the night. I was hoping I would wake up in the morning knowing it had all been a bad dream, but the memory of what took place in the church basement the afternoon before was still alive in my head when I got up the next day. Fortunately, it was Saturday, so I didn't have to go back to the office until Monday. I questioned if I should. It all seemed so surreal."

"I decided to skip church on Sunday morning. I felt so awkward. Later that afternoon, as I was doing laundry, there was a knock on my back door, off the kitchen. I thought that was odd because I lived out in the country and didn't often have visitors come to the house unannounced, especially at the back door. I went to see who it was and saw Pastor Randy through the glass pane, standing there on the porch. I hesitated, but decided to open the door."

"Pastor Randy greeted me as if nothing had happened two days before. He told me he hoped I wasn't ill. I told him I just decided to play hooky and tried to force myself to laugh. He chuckled as well and then asked to come in to talk for a moment. My first instinct was to refuse his request, but then I decided that I should confront him about what happened in the church basement. Thankfully, he beat me to it."

"He apologized right away for what happened that Friday and told me he didn't know what had come over him because it was so out of character for him. He said he hoped I wouldn't hold that against him. Pastor Randy went on to say he had a lot on his mind that day. He and his wife had foolishly taken on a little too much lately, and it was taking a toll on both of them. They also just found out a close friend of the family had passed away very suddenly. What he was looking for, was someone to console him, and since I reminded him of his older sister, Jeannie, who had always been the one he went to for encouragement or to unload, he reached out to me. He said he hoped I didn't misunderstand anything."

"I thought his explanation was a little strange and didn't truly explain his actions that Friday but was somehow taken in by his forthrightness, and started to let my guard down. Was it possible I misunderstood what happened? His eyes looked so sincere, and I wasn't able to find the words I wanted to say. He told me he hoped we could put the incident behind us, and promised it would never happen again."

"I told him, 'all is forgotten,' even though I wasn't completely convinced of what he told me. He then asked if I was planning on coming to work the next day. I told him, 'yes,' I would be there as usual. He seemed pleased and held out his hand to me and asked, 'Still friends?' I confirmed that we were indeed still friends and shook his hand. He said, 'good,' and smiled. Then he told me he would see me on Monday, and turned and left the house, closing the back door behind him."

"Though something inside of me told me to cut my losses and run, I did return to work the next day, choosing to ignore the red flags. And for another month, nothing like that happened again. I began to feel safe around Randy once more. Although, he was being overly nice to me, doing special favors all the time. He even bought me flowers and donuts on my birthday. I love donuts. He said his wife, Carol, picked them out for me, and that they were from her as well. I decided he was just feeling guilty. I kept telling myself that one slip like that Friday afternoon in the church basement shouldn't ruin a man's life, marriage, or career, so I remained silent about the incident."

Cheryl paused for a few seconds, trying to choke back the tears that were once more forming in her eyes. Steve saw the change in her composure but continued writing his notes. It was critical to have an accurate record of her testimony. Fortunately, he had developed his own shorthand, so he was able to listen and write at the same time without missing what she was telling him. Cheryl quickly brushed away the tears that were now running down her cheeks and took a deep breath.

"Then, it happened again," she continued. "I don't know what pre-cipitated it, but this time it was worse." Cheryl stopped for another moment to compose herself. She wiped her eyes, then went on, forcing the words out. "One evening, after I had gone home from work, I heard a knock at the back kitchen door. It was Pastor Randy again. He claimed he had forgotten to give me some instructions from Mrs. Hellinger on an upcoming event. Not thinking, I opened the door and let him in. I excused myself for a few seconds and went over to the stove to turn something off that was boiling over. As I did, I could hear the back door closing. I started to feel uneasy inside as I stirred the vegetables in another pot. Suddenly, Randy came up behind me. His cologne was stronger than usual. He grabbed me by the shoulders, spun me around, and started to kiss me. I couldn't believe what was happening! And in my own home! I was shocked."

"Somehow, I was able to pull away and shout, 'NO!' and pushed him backward, into the refrigerator. Then I screamed, 'What are you doing? This is wrong!' For a moment, he just looked at me surprised, and then he shook his head and started back over to me, taking hold of my arms. I screamed, 'NO!' again. This time more forcefully. Pulling free once more, I ran and grabbed an empty pot from off the kitchen counter. I yelled for him to get out, and threatened him with bodily harm if he tried to touch me again. But he only started to laugh."

Then he looked at me and said, 'Come on Cheryl, I know you want me here. I have been watching your signals for weeks.' I froze. How could he say that? . . . How could he even think that?"

"At that moment, I thought of Randy's wife, Carol. I knew she was out of town at a women's church conference, and that their two boys were visiting their grandparents in another city. That made me feel more vulnerable. I told him he was crazy and demanded that he get out of my house. Then I swung the pot at him, but he knocked it out of my hand, sending it flying across the room, and breaking some of my dishes. Randy grabbed me again, and I resisted the best I could, even kicking him. He was so strong. By that point, I was crying uncontrollably. I did not want his advances and kept telling him so. Frantically, I cried out, 'Lord help me!' looking for a way to escape. Even my cry to God didn't seem to faze him."

"Then miraculously, there was a loud noise outside and we heard some shouting. Randy immediately let go of me and ran to the window in the dining room. I leaned against the kitchen counter shaking. It was my neighbor Luke Crider and his cousin Bill. They had come over to fix the riding lawn mower that was stored in the large shed near the woods behind my house. While starting it up, there had been a loud backfire. When Randy spotted them in the backyard, he began to panic. He looked wild-eyed as if he was about to be exposed. He hadn't counted on someone else being on the property. He knew he had to leave right away or the reason for his presence there would be made known."

"I'll never forget what he did next. He turned and glared at me, pointing his finger, and snarled through gritted teeth, 'Don't you ever tell anyone about this! Ever! I will ruin you in this town if you do! This county! You were the one who started this!' "

Steve shifted in his chair, trying to suppress the anger he was now feeling towards Pastor Randy. His face was getting hot. He wasn't sure he wanted to hear any more.

Cheryl saw that her words were having an emotional effect on Steve, but she knew she had to finish her story, and continued to talk.

"Pastor Randy looked outside again, and when he thought no one was watching, he ran out the back door. I stood there completely shaken, almost paralyzed, and sick to my stomach as he left my house. I whispered a thank you to God. Then, still crying, I asked myself what I had done to bring this on. I had trusted and respected Pastor Randy. I was scared and confused. I thought about running out to Luke and Bill and telling them what had just happened, but I stopped myself, not sure how they would respond. Would they believe me? Could they be trusted? They were probably still working on the tractor and likely didn't hear me scream or see Pastor Randy leave. They didn't stop by the house after they were finished with the yard, so I decided it best not to say anything to them. They would have come running if they thought I needed help."

"I went through the next few days thinking about what had happened while nursing the bruises on my arms. The first couple of days afterward, I called in sick to the church office, but then I knew I had to go back to work until I figured out what to do. I wanted to quit, though I didn't know how to leave the church without people asking questions. I also wanted to call the police but thought no one would believe what I had to say about Pastor Randy.

It was so hard going back to work and facing him, or even making eye contact with him, being in the same room with him, and watching him with his wife and children, knowing what he truly was. I even wore long sleeves to work for a while, to cover the slowly fading marks he left on me. I didn't want people to see them. I was ashamed, even though I knew I had done nothing wrong."

"Finally, a few days later, I decided I needed to confide in someone, so I told my best friend Holly Allen. She goes to that Baptist church on the edge of town."

Steve nodded in acknowledgment.

"But instead of being shocked by what I said, she told me she had heard almost the same story from someone else. It was about another woman who had worked for Pastor Randy. She wanted to tell me but wasn't sure if it was true, or if she should even repeat the story until she was sure. And now she was convinced it was. That woman had been his administrative assistant a couple of years before me. Holly warned me not to say anything to anyone connected with my church, because the other woman did, and she ended up having to leave town, her reputation utterly ruined. The whole church congregation turned against her. Holly said she heard it was awful. Holly also advised me to leave Community Church and Nordstown as soon as I could find another job."

"So, you never went to anyone at the church or the district office to tell them about what took place?" Steve asked.

"No, Pastor, I didn't. Well, not at that time. I was too afraid. I resigned from my position at the church at the end of the month and just told everyone that I had another job opportunity more related to my field of study. Fortunately, a position did come open for me soon afterward, and I was able to go to the new job without any questions. I was even able to get out of my lease and move to where I am now."

Then Cheryl stopped and looked at Steve, "I suppose you're wondering why I am coming to you with all this now?"

"Yes," Steve responded.

"Last week, I heard that two other women have had encounters with Pastor Randy over the last five years, one of them a parishioner who was being counseled by him. After praying about it, I felt very strongly that I needed to stand up for all of us and say something. This man should not be in the position he's in. He's not healthy. Will you help us, Pastor Steve?"

Steve dropped his pen and pushed back in his chair, trying to process what he just heard. Everything inside of him was telling him that Cheryl was not lying. After a few seconds, and choosing his words carefully, he said, "As a minister of the faith, I am scripturally and legally obligated to act on what you have told me. I will confront Pastor Randy and listen to what he has to say about this. Then I will take the matter to the board and proceed from there. At some point, I will need a signed statement from you to give to the board and the district office." Then Steve became more serious, "You realize, Pastor Randy could lose his license and have his ordination papers rescinded by the denomination over this. He could even go to prison."

"I know that," Cheryl replied softly. She thought for a minute and then responded, "Do what you have to do. And I will give you what you need. I don't want any more women to go through what I did. Especially with someone who is supposed to be a pastor in a church."

Steve shook his head, wondering to himself why no one had told him anything about the two women before or after moving to Nordstown.

"Thank you for coming to see me today. This is very disturbing. If you would leave me your contact information, I will give you a call when I need to touch base with you again."

"Yes, of course. I have it already written down for you," Cheryl said, pulling a piece of paper out of her jacket pocket. "As you will see, I no longer live in Nordstown. I am about an hour and a half away from here now." Handing Steve her information, she said, "One more thing, Pastor Hanson. There is another woman who wants to talk with you. She is going to call you this evening. She too has had encounters with Pastor Randy. She did not come with me today because she didn't want to be seen, but she will talk with you on the phone. Her name is Nancy Clemens."

Steve thanked Cheryl for the information, and she got up to leave wiping her eyes. He left his desk chair to open the door for her.

As she entered the hallway, Cheryl stopped and turned for a moment, and said, "May God protect you, Pastor Steve. This is not going to be easy. There are others you know. A real hornets' nest. And not just at Community." She turned quickly and left, almost as if to avoid any questions regarding her departing comment.

"Others?" Steve started to say out loud. *Other predators in the church?* he thought in disbelief. But before he could say anything else, Cheryl was already at the front door saying goodbye to Sara. At that moment, Steve remembered again the prophetic message from the evangelist. Was this what he was talking about? If so, what was about to happen? Was he prepared?

Shortly after Cheryl left, Sara closed the front door and came into Steve's study to see what he was able to tell her. She knew by the look on his face that his meeting with Cheryl was about a serious matter, something her husband would have to deal with right away.

Steve put his arm around his wife.

"Things may get a little rough around here, Sara. I can't tell you all the details, but I am going to have to confront our associate pastor on some very serious sexual misconduct allegations. I will need to be talking with the district office as well."

"Oh no. Are you sure Steve?" Sara asked both stunned and alarmed. *Not Randy,* she thought to herself.

"Yes," he replied. "And it looks like the situation could become even more serious after tonight."

"What's tonight?" Sara fought back the multitude of questions that were now forming in her mind. Knowing there would be serious consequences for Randy if the woman's accusations proved to be true, her heart began to ache for Carol Nelson. Carol's marriage could be ruined over this. Sara did not want to see her friend hurt. She also didn't want to see Carol and Randy's boys hurt.

"A phone call on the same type of issue," Steve replied. "If a Nancy Clemens calls on the parsonage line, please page me right away, okay, Hon?"

"Yes, of course, I will," she replied. Sara looked up at her husband and tried to smile. "I know you will do what's right, Steve. God will show you the way."

"I know He will, Sara. I think I will go over to the church now and pray for a while. Please start praying over this too."

I already am," Sara replied, kissing her husband on the cheek, knowing that he needed to be alone with God right then. Tears began to form in Sara's eyes as she turned and headed for their bedroom upstairs to pray. So much was at stake. So many could be hurt over this. The possible repercussions began to run through her mind. Reputations could be ruined, a church family could be devastated, a marriage could be destroyed, legal charges could be made, a celebrated minister could lose his ordination papers, and some precious young boys could lose access to their father for a very long time. The media would have a field day with the story, and the growing friendship the Hansons had with the Nelsons could be lost forever.

Steve pulled his church keys out of his coat pocket and headed for the church. Fortunately, only Mrs. Hellinger was in the office. The rest of the staff had gone home for the day. He stuck his head into the office long enough to let her know he was going to be praying in the sanctuary. Mrs. Hellinger nodded in understanding. She never disturbed or allowed anyone to disturb Pastor Steve when she knew he was in prayer. When he got to the sanctuary, Steve went to the front of the church and dropped down in a pew. He sat quietly, reflecting on his conversation with Cheryl Petrie. She and the others she mentioned were counting on him to help them. *What will Randy say about all this?* he thought. Steve then reached for a pew Bible. He opened it to the first chapter of Titus where it speaks of the qualities of a godly church leader and began to read out loud. "An elder must be blameless, faithful to his wife, a man whose . . ."[1] Leaning back in the pew, Steve stared up at the large white wooden cross suspended from the ceiling.

"Well, You warned me, didn't you, Lord? And yet, I still said 'yes.' So here I am, ready to take up sword and shield. Give me the strength and wisdom I need now to handle this. It's too big for me." Looking back down at the Bible, Steve began to feel peace and warmth come over him. Then a still small voice spoke saying, "You chose well. You and Sara are my pioneers and I have something for you to accomplish here. I will be with you and your family. Trust me."

"Thank you, Lord," Steve whispered, and continued leaning back in the pew, his eyes closed in silent prayer for a long time. A fierce spiritual battle was on the horizon, and he could feel it. Steve prayed until he felt at peace. Then he went back to the parsonage to be with Sara.

That evening, Steve spoke with Nancy on the phone from his study for almost an hour. She had attended Community Church right after Cheryl left and had been Randy's administrative assistant for a while as well. Her encounter with Pastor Randy, though, was worse. Not wanting to cause any trouble, she left the church and the area too. She had contacted Cheryl when she found out Cheryl had gone through some of the same things she had. She wasn't sure she wanted to sign a statement yet but would pray about it. When he finished his call with Nancy, Steve knew he had to talk with Randy as soon as possible. Sitting silently behind his desk, Steve wondered if there were still others yet to come forward.

Chapter 3

The Confrontation

*S*teve and Sara prayed and fasted over the situation with Pastor
Randy until Steve felt he was ready to confront his assistant pastor
with Cheryl and Nancy's allegations. He shared what he could with Sara,
so she knew how to pray. The exposure of alleged sexual sin could be
devastating to Pastor Randy's wife and two sons and the church congregation, should the story get out. Steve also understood Sara's friendship
with Carol and knew this situation could destroy their relationship. Sara
had to know what was going on. The two prayed for Pastor Randy, his
family, and all of the women involved. They also prayed for wisdom for
Steve in handling the situation and for protection over their household.
Knowing the power of prayer, the Hansons continued to look to God
for His help and intervention.

Early Wednesday evening, just before dark, Steve and Sara decided
to go over to the church for a prayer walk around the building. As they
began, they prayed against any spiritual attacks and strongholds of the
enemy and declared the blood of Jesus over their place of worship and
the members of the congregation. They asked that evil be exposed and
expelled from Community Church. As the couple was completing their
second round, they noticed three people, somewhere in their twenties,
standing on the sidewalk directly across the street from them. They
were all dressed in dark clothes and were staring intently at the church.
There was a coldness about the woman and two men, and chills went

down Steve and Sara's spines as they looked over at them. The couple immediately sensed this small group was not out for an evening stroll, yet despite the evil they were sensing, they felt protected. The two smiled politely and waved at the threesome, but when they received no response in return, they continued on their walk. As Steve and Sara rounded the church once more, they noticed the group had gone, and there was no sign of them anywhere up or down the street. Not sure what to think, Steve and Sara took time to pray for the strange trio and then headed home.

Steve and Sara felt they should ask Peter and Mary to be in prayer as well about the situation with the former church employee, but did not tell them exactly what they were praying for. Just indicating it was a serious church matter sufficed for the moment. The Hanson teens took that as the familiar cue to pray about something important without asking questions and to keep that request to themselves for the time being. They knew they would be told more details when and if it became necessary for them to know. This meeting was the hardest thing Steve had ever had to do, and he needed to be covered in prayer. To add to that spiritual covering, he asked some trusted minister friends and family members in other towns and states to intercede on his behalf before, during, and after the meeting with Pastor Randy, being careful again about how much he shared with them.

Feeling a sense of peace about confronting Randy, Steve texted him on Thursday morning and asked him if he would be available to stop by his home office on Friday afternoon around 2:00 p.m. to discuss some ministry issues. He worded it in such a way that Randy would take it as just normal church business. Steve felt that a meeting at his house would draw less attention from the other staff members and the listening ears of Mrs. Hellinger, who seemed to know everything that was going on in the church no matter how confidential some information was being kept. When Randy texted back confirming he was available for a conference at that time, Steve began to rehearse in his mind what he was going to say to him.

Friday afternoon came around sooner than Steve wanted, but he knew he was obligated to proceed with his meeting with Pastor Randy. No reason to wait. Perhaps there was more to the story than he was hearing. He wanted to be absolutely sure he was clear on what had taken place with the women who had brought such serious charges against his assistant pastor. His conversation with his colleague and friend was therefore crucial. Steve did not want to judge or act on the situation too hastily, even though the testimony against Pastor Randy was very strong and convincing. He had to continue to keep an open mind and prayed for clear discernment in the matter.

At 2:00 p.m. on the dot, Pastor Randy knocked on the front door of the parsonage. Sara, who was just around the corner in the kitchen, let him in and told him to go on back to Steve's office. Steve was sitting at his desk with his Bible open to some of his favorite verses in Psalm 91. He stood and went over to greet Pastor Randy when he entered the room. Pastor Randy was a nice-looking man in his late thirties. He was dressed in his dark gray suit that afternoon because he was going to do hospital visits with Steve after the meeting. Randy greeted Steve warmly with a firm handshake and a pat on the shoulder. The two men had spent a lot of time together ever since the Hansons had come to Nordstown, so meetings at the parsonage were not unusual. Pastor Randy looked around the room after noticing there were no sweets on the corner table like there usually were, just coffee.

"I must have done something wrong to miss out on some of Sara's wonderful baked goods," he joked.

It looks like you have, Steve thought to himself. "Oh, uh. I thought we could stop in the hospital coffee shop for some goodies there," he finally managed to say, knowing it wasn't the reason for the omission. Baked goods just didn't seem appropriate for this kind of meeting. "I know you like to stop in there. No sense in eating too much now."

"Makes sense," Randy said with a smile. "This must be important."

"It is," Steve responded, feeling a little nervous inside.

As the men helped themselves to the hot coffee and took their seats for the meeting, Sara was upstairs face down on her bedroom floor right above them, praying for the two men. Samson came in with his tail wagging and laid down quietly next to her. Sara reached over and rubbed the top of his head, thankful for his company. Fortunately, Mary and Peter were in school at that time. Anything could happen during this meeting, and their teens didn't need to be there if things became hostile. Moved by the Spirit, Sara began to softly sing some of her favorite praise and worship songs. As she did, the presence of God filled the room.

"So," Randy said as he casually pushed back in his chair in front of Steve's desk. "What did you want to talk about?"

"Well," Steve started slowly, deciding to get to the point of the meeting right away. "I have to be honest with you first and let you know that I kind of got you over here under false pretenses."

"You did?" Randy looked confused. "Everything ok?"

Steve took a deep breath and went on to explain. "Randy, I had a visit a few days ago from a former employee of the church."

"Oh?" Randy responded. His eyes were full of interest, not realizing yet what was about to happen.

"Uh, yes. She said she used to work for you."

"Ok," Pastor Randy adjusted uneasily in his seat, looking a little worried.

"Randy, she has accused you of inappropriate behavior towards her. She said it happened more than once."

Randy looked like he had just been slapped in the face. "Alicyn," he said suddenly under his breath.

"Who?" Steve asked.

"Alicyn Taylor," Pastor Randy repeated out loud. "She was my administrative assistant a few years ago."

"Oh," Steve remembered Cheryl mentioning an earlier assistant at the church.

"She tried to accuse me of sexual harassment then and the church threw her out. Alicyn had some emotional problems, Steve . . . some serious emotional problems. She also tried to tell people I made advances at her. I guess she thought by accusing me of something inappropriate, she would get some attention. She really put my family through it. . .

So, she's back in town, huh? Trying to start trouble again?"

"Actually, no, Randy. I did not speak with Alicyn."

Randy looked confused and concerned, then began to wring his hands. "Then who then? Who would accuse me, a respected and dedicated pastor, of improper behavior?

"She said her name was Cheryl Petrie."

Randy's face went white. He swallowed hard before he spoke again. His voice began to shake.

"Cheryl? Why in the world would Cheryl Petrie say such a thing about me, especially now? She's been gone nearly two years. I don't understand this." Then looking straight at Steve, almost ready to cry, he said, "It's a lie Steve — a lie straight from the pit of hell!"

Steve, realizing he had hit a nerve, pressed on. There was more he had to say. "Randy, I also received a call from a woman by the name of Nancy Clemens."

At that, Randy leaped from his seat. "I don't believe this!" he said loudly and clenching his fists. "Surely, you are not taking these claims seriously?"

"I haven't told you what Nancy said to me, Randy," Steve said calmly.

Randy ignored Steve's response.

"Who else? Who else, Steve?" Randy asked as he paced the floor nervously. His brow was beginning to perspire. He loosened his tie, unbuttoned the top button of his dress shirt, then brushed his hair back with both hands.

"No one else. Why would you assume that there were more?" Steve was watching Randy's reactions closely.

The room was suddenly silent, and Randy stood motionless, trying to collect himself. He looked panicked, not knowing what to say or do next in defense. His past had caught up with him again, and he didn't want to admit to it, especially to Steve Hanson. At that moment, Steve noticed the sun shining brightly through the office window and crossing his desk. Up until that moment, the day had been somewhat overcast and the sun's strong rays had been blocked from entering the room. To Steve, it was as if the light of truth[1] was trying to break through the spiritual darkness Pastor Randy had allowed himself to become a part of . . . a darkness that had also made its home in Community Church.

Looking directly into Randy's eyes, Steve finally asked, "Is it true Randy?"

"No!" Randy unexpectedly burst into anger, slamming his fist on Steve's desk, then yanking it away quickly, sending a stack of papers flying around the room. He was livid, greatly agitated by the accusations with which he was being confronted.

Though stunned by the display of emotion, Steve managed to maintain his composure. He would not respond in anger. Steve prayed silently. He knew Sara was upstairs praying for him as well. This was more than an encounter with an angry man. It was a spiritual battle, one that was exposing a secret sin in another believer's life, perhaps deep-seated bondage. Randy's actions so far had not suggested his innocence, and that was very apparent to Steve.

When he felt free to talk again, Steve said, "You realize, Randy, there are things I am obligated to do here. You need to talk to me about this. You must know Sara and I care about you and Carol and the boys. I want to hear your side of the story. I am willing to listen to what you have to say."

Randy was breathing heavily now.

"I haven't done anything wrong, Steve," he choked. "Don't you see that? There are so many people here who can attest to my character. You have been around me for a while now too. I've been in your home, and you've been in mine. We've broken bread together on numerous occasions. Our wives are good friends. Do I seem to be the kind of guy who would do reprehensible things like that? What kind of father would I be to my sons? Carol and I have diligently taught them to be respectful of women."

Then finally realizing how he had been sounding, Pastor Randy suddenly calmed himself and softened his approach. He went over to Steve's desk and began to reorganize some of the scattered papers.

"Please, please don't put me and my family through that again," Randy almost begged. "Alicyn almost destroyed my marriage and my career. I can't lose what I've worked so hard for. All those years of training in Bible college and seminary would be thrown away over a terrible lie."

"Then why these accusations, Randy? By other women?" Steve questioned. "Are you telling me they are all lying? That there is no problem?" Steve looked intently at his associate pastor.

"Yes!" Pastor Randy yelled emphatically, losing control again. He angrily turned and started pacing the floor again, clenching his fists as he did. "Alicyn said she would get back at me after she was asked to leave the church. She said she would find a way. And now with a new senior pastor in place, she sees her opportunity. She must have gotten those other women to help her out. Don't you see, Steve? It's a setup!"

Randy was frantic, but Steve wasn't convinced he was telling the truth. If anything, he saw a side of Randy he had never seen before, and he didn't like it. Randy knew by the look on Steve's face that he did not believe him, and that made him even angrier. He nervously pushed his hair back again with both hands.

"Randy, I would like you to calm yourself and sit down," Steve told him, trying to keep himself composed. Randy stood rigid in defiance for a short while, then relented and sat back down in his chair. Steve waited patiently until he did.

Looking straight at Randy again, Steve said, "You know I can't let this go. The accusations are far too serious, especially when I have heard more than one complaint. I would be negligent and in huge legal trouble if I did. I could also face serious disciplinary action from the denomination. Please, my friend, talk to me."

Steve waited for Randy to respond, but when his friend continued to sit in silence, Steve finally said, "Just so you know, I have called a special meeting of the elders for tomorrow night. I would like you to be there. They do not know what this is about yet. I will talk with them first, and then you will be asked to come in and speak. Perhaps you will feel more like discussing the accusations then. I will also be talking with the district office today. They need to know about the situation now, especially since you won't talk with me."

"You fool!" Randy suddenly blurted out jumping to his feet again, his chair forced backward almost tipping over. "I thought you were my friend! Yes, I will be there, and so will my lawyer!" he said irately. Then he shoved the chair out of his way, knocking it over on its side on the floor. Steve watched in alarm but continued to pray inside.

"I'm sorry, Randy," Steve attempted to calm him again. "I know you are upset, but I have no choice. Put yourself in my position. I know you would handle things the same way. If you could just sit down and talk with me about this. Tell me your side-"

"There's nothing to talk about, Steve Hanson!" Randy yelled. "Those women are lying! If you're too blind to see that, then maybe Community Church made a mistake bringing you here!"

With that, Pastor Randy turned and swiftly left the room, slamming the office door behind him, cracking and almost shattering the glass in it. He raced to the front door of the house and slammed it as well as he left to go over to the church.

Hearing Randy shout and the office door slam below, Sara sat up quickly in her room, pushing her hair back from her face. After she heard the front door slam as well, she got up from the floor and headed downstairs to be with Steve, her heart pounding in her chest as she went. Samson got up too and followed close behind her as she hurriedly descended the long, carpeted staircase to the front hallway.

When Sara reached Steve's office, she found him with his head down on his desk. Sensing that Sara and Samson were at the office door, Steve looked up and just shook his head.

"He's in spiritual bondage, Sara, and he just can't see it. . . and so angry. . . . He wouldn't even talk with me." Steve shook his head, leaned back in his chair, and exhaled loudly. "He's calling his lawyer."

"Oh no," Sara said, overcome with emotion. She was quiet for a moment, unsure of what to say. "Well, it's going to be in the board's hands now. They'll know what needs to be done. He'll just have to accept that. Why don't we pray again? I'm worried about how Carol is going to take all this. I can't imagine how it was for her and the kids before."

"Yes, we definitely need to pray again," Steve responded, trying to come to grips with what just happened, so he could pray more effectively.

Sara picked up the chair Pastor Randy had just knocked over and sat down in front of Steve's desk. Holding hands, the couple began to pray for Randy and his family. Samson laid down next to Sara. He liked being close to Steve and Sara when they prayed. Instinctively, he lay quietly until they had finished. He seemed to sense that they were talking to someone greater than all of them.

Inside, Sara desperately wanted to talk with Carol. She wanted to be there for her friend, but she knew she couldn't. Randy would be the one to talk with her about the allegations. *But what will he tell her? Will he admit any guilt? Will he lie?* Sara knew the situation was in God's hands. She had to trust Him to work things out. He would show Steve and her what to do next.

Chapter 4

Where Evil Lies

$\int$teve and Sara had just finished praying together when there was a loud knock at the front door.

"Who now?" Steve moaned. "I'm not in the mood to talk with anyone right now. If it's for me Sara, please make my excuses."

"I will." Sara got up from her chair and went to the front door. Samson stood and followed close behind her. Sara moved the white lace curtains back and peeked through the glass in the front door to see a middle-aged woman with slightly graying black hair standing impatiently on the front porch. It was Mrs. Hellinger, the church office manager. "*Oh boy*," she thought. Sara slowly opened the door.

"Well, hello, Mrs. Hellinger!" Sara said, forcing a smile. How nice to see you today. Can I help you with something?"

"I need to talk with Pastor right away," Mrs. Hellinger responded, determined to talk with Steve.

"I'm afraid, he can't talk at the moment. He-"

"I know what's going on, Sara. I saw Pastor Randy leave the parsonage about 20 minutes ago. He came over to the church, made a phone call, and then left the building in a hurry. When he took off in his car, you could hear his tires screech as he left the parking lot and raced down the road. Please, I need to talk to Pastor Steve now. I know what I'm doing."

Sara looked into Mrs. Hellinger's determined pleading eyes. *Yes,* she felt God telling her, Mrs. Hellinger had an important message for Steve.

"Ok," Sara finally gave in. "He's in the office."

"Thank you, Sara. You'll be glad I was here." Mrs. Hellinger rushed past Sara and Samson and headed down the hall toward the pastor's office. Sara grabbed onto Samson's collar, so he wouldn't follow Mrs. Hellinger to the study. When Margaret Hellinger came to the open office door, she found Steve sitting behind his desk staring out of the window, deep in thought.

"I know what you're going to say, Pastor Steve," Mrs. Hellinger said as she entered the room unexpectedly. "But I have something important to tell you."

Steve looked up surprised. He knew he couldn't tell Mrs. Hellinger he was busy; she had already made it past Sara. Seeing she was determined to say whatever she came to say, he motioned for her to come and sit down. Closing the door behind her, Mrs. Hellinger took her seat in front of the large cherry desk. Some of his papers were still in disarray on top of it and others were strewn all over the floor.

"Steve, I know why you were talking with Randy today."

Steve looked at her cautiously.

"To be truthful, I know why Cheryl and Nancy talked with you."

Steve blinked, realizing that Mrs. Hellinger knew more than he realized. He told her to continue.

"Those stories. Those awful stories you have been hearing about Pastor Randy, well, they're true. I was the one who encouraged the girls to come to you."

Steve looked stunned. "You knew, then why? ...

"Then why have I been silent? It's complicated, Pastor Steve. Very complicated. You heard what happened to that poor girl a few years ago. She ended up leaving town because of the terrible lies that were told about her. Vicious lies. Mostly from Pastor Randy and Deacon Tom Black. And sadly, his wife, Carol, and much of the congregation believed them and stood behind Pastor Randy. They just didn't want to accept the truth."

Mrs. Hellinger went on. "I also had to protect my family. My husband Frank, as you know, is on disability for a back injury and our youngest son is still at home until he graduates from high school this spring. We have two others in college. I'm the only one working right now. I just can't afford to lose my job and the benefits the church has been giving me these past ten years."

"I understand your dilemma," Steve replied.

"And to make it worse, I know there are at least four other leaders in this church who are just as bad. I also know of a few in another church on the other side of town who sexually harass women, along with several leaders within the Nordstown community. They're all connected in some way. But they get away with it because of who they are, who they know, and who they are related to. Money people, Steve, people with power and influence! They hang together no matter what the others do. It's a hornets' nest! A very sick hornets' nest!"

Steve was beginning to realize what Cheryl was referring to when she left his office that day. There was a strong spiritual hold within his congregation that involved more than one individual. It was something that could no longer be tolerated and had to be removed. This, he thought, was why he was sent to Community Church, to expose the demonic influence and help set the congregation free from its lies and destruction.

Mrs. Hellinger went on, "You need to know that the real reason the last pastor left was because of the situation with Alicyn and then later, Cheryl. He knew the truth and tried to expose it, but he was just outnumbered. One day, he even found porn magazines hidden on one of the top shelves in the church library. Even though he knew Pastor Randy spent a lot of time during the week studying in that room, he couldn't prove the magazines were his. He did talk with the district office on numerous occasions about what he knew, but he couldn't convince the victims to go and talk with them. They were too afraid. Some of Pastor Randy's supporters soon found out about the accusations and did their best to protect him. The pressure on Pastor Harold to resign was so overwhelming, he decided to move on. It was beginning to affect his health. After he did, the district had to let the whole matter drop because of a lack of corroborating evidence. Even Alicyn decided it was better to leave town than stay and fight or to involve the district office anymore in the situation. Randy says the church made her leave, but she decided to go before things got worse. She had had enough."

"How did Pastor Harold know about Cheryl?" Steve asked.

"I told him. I had been watching Randy around Cheryl and figured he was about to strike again. One day, in particular, I just about caught him in the act in the church basement. I could tell by the look on Cheryl's face as I started coming down the basement stairs that something wasn't right. That's when I hurried down the rest of the steps and made up the story about losing my keys. What I really was doing was helping Cheryl get out of the room. Weeks later, when Cheryl resigned from her position at the church, I went to see her after she moved. We talked for a long time."

"But why come to me now?" Steve wondered aloud.

"Because things are happening again. Bad things. Actually, to another woman in the congregation who is new to the community. The previous victims know, and they are livid. They desperately want to expose this evil now, so no one else gets hurt. They just aren't sure what to do. They want the church to handle it. I know you called a board meeting for tomorrow evening. You better let the district know what is happening first before you enter that room. I guarantee you it's not going to be pretty."

"That's what I plan to do," Steve told her.

"I'll do what I can to help, but I don't want people to know that …"

"Don't worry, Mrs. Hellinger, you have taken a big risk already just by coming to me. For that, I am truly grateful."

Steve paused for a moment.

"You know, I can't help but wonder what set Randy on such a path of destruction. He graduated from some very impressive schools and is admired by many in the Nordstown community. How did he go from that to sexual predator?"

"From what I understand, he grew up with it."

"How do you know that?"

"Pastor Harold had an opportunity to talk with one of Randy's younger cousins about him. She had been praying for her family for a long time and told Harold that Randy's father and some of his uncles had been hitting on women and looking at pornography for decades. Randy had struggled with pornography himself from the time he was twelve. He had found some of his father's old issues up in the attic of his home. Randy recognized the problem to some degree in his late teens when he gave his life to Christ, and even tried to escape the perverted behavior by going away to Bible college and then seminary. He also thought marrying Carol, whom he met his first year of college, and having children would make things different. But unfortunately, when he returned to Nordstown to take a position at Community Church, he found himself pulled back even deeper into the same spiritual trap some of his other family members were caught in. It was still inside of him, even after going to schools with high moral standards. Bottom line, though, Randy made a choice when he came back, and it's been a tragic one for him and his family and the church. He chose the lusts of the flesh over his love for God. And to add to the heartbreak, Carol can't see the truth about her husband. She only sees the man she fell in love with at Bible college."

Steve shook his head. "Thank you for sharing that with me, Mrs. Hellinger. It helps me know how to pray for Pastor Randy." . . . "And his family," he added.

"There's one more thing I feel I should tell you before I go."

"About Pastor Randy?"

"No, not exactly. It's something that the pastors in this area are aware of, but maybe haven't shared with you yet."

"Oh, what's that?"

"Well . . . This part of the county is well known for its occult activity. The police have found evidence of a number of covens in and around the city in the last ten or so years. . . Those people move around a lot."

Steve lifted his brows. "Are Randy and his family involved . . ?"

"No, I don't think so," Mrs. Hellinger cut in. "But that kind of activity can certainly influence the spiritual climate of an area."

"No doubt," Steve replied. "Thank you for telling me. I will talk with some of the local pastors about what you just told me."

At that moment, Steve remembered the strange threesome he and Sara encountered, standing across the street from the church earlier that week. He would continue to pray for them, and others like them, who had tragically allowed themselves to become children of the darkness[1] and slaves to the deceiver of the world.[2]

"Good idea. They can fill you in on a lot of things," Mrs. Hellinger returned, as she stood up from her chair. "And, you're welcome. I'm glad I was able to talk with you this afternoon." Then, looking at the clock on the wall, she said, "I'd better get back to the office."

Mrs. Hellinger's mission was accomplished, and she knew she had better leave before Pastor Randy came back to the church from wherever he had gone. Their administrative assistant, Terri Campbell, was off that day, so she was the one in charge of answering the phones in the main office.

"I will be praying, Pastor Steve."

"Thank you, Mrs. Hellinger."

As she was leaving, Mrs. Hellinger stopped and looked at the glass in the office door. Seeing the large crack, she shook her head, glanced back at Steve and said, "I'll order you a new glass pane when I get over there."

"Thank you for that too, Margaret."

"No problem, Pastor Steve," she replied, reaching for the doorknob.

As his office door closed, Steve picked up the phone and began to dial the district office. To his relief, he was able to talk with the district superintendent, Dr. Michael Schaffner, right away. Dr. Schaffner was very open to Steve's call and filled him in on the last time the district had been involved in the situation at Community Church.

"It sounds like you have a strong case there, Steve. What you're going to need is a lot of backing from those women, and the congregation in general. We can't remove someone from a pastorate or revoke a license until we have clear evidence of ungodly and illegal behavior."

"I understand, Dr. Schaffner," Steve responded.

"Would you like me to send someone from the district office to the board meeting? Normally, that is not standard procedure, but since this meeting is on the same issue we dealt with before, I feel it is appropriate."

Steve thought for a minute. "You know, that may not be a bad idea. Randy threatened to bring a lawyer with him."

"All the more reason to have someone there with you. I will see if Paul Samples is available to come on Saturday. He's been our attorney for years. He's not a pastor, but he is usually the one involved when the district has to deal with a legal issue. I will let you know for sure in the morning."

"Thank you, Dr. Schaffner. That would be a real help tomorrow evening."

"No problem, Steve. You're going to need all the help you can get with that bunch. I'm sorry we didn't tell you about Pastor Randy before you took on that church, but since we had no evidence, we had to watch what we said to you. We did let you know that the church had its challenges before you said 'yes' to going there. You seemed determined, though, to take on anything the Lord was calling you to."

"I remember Dr. Schaffner, and I appreciated what you were able to tell me. And just so you know, I am still willing to do what I was sent here to do."

"And I believe you will be faithful to your calling, Steve. Hang in there. You're not going this alone."

"I know that, sir. Thank you again! Goodbye now."

"Goodbye."

When Steve hung up the phone, he felt both relief and anxiety. Just then he heard the kids coming in the front door. Peter and Mary had just gotten home from school. They were later than usual because of after-school activities. Both were excited. Sara and Samson went to meet them at the door.

"I'm playing first string this Saturday afternoon!" Peter proudly announced, jumping up and down and tossing his football lightly into the air as he entered the front hall. I will be playing wide receiver. No more bench time. Coach says I'm ready!"

"Congratulations, Son," Steve said coming down the hall from his office. He had heard his son's announcement and patted Peter on the back when he got close to him, showing his approval.

"We're so proud of you," Sara said, as she hugged him.

"And guess what?" Mary eagerly jumped in. "I'm going to be a reporter for the school newspaper!" She screamed and did a quick dance to show her enthusiasm. "How cool is that?"

"Wow!" Steve exclaimed, giving his daughter a big hug. "Maybe in a few years, we'll be watching you on the six o'clock news."

"Oh, Daddy," Mary said, slightly blushing and playfully pushing his arm.

"I knew you would be chosen," Sara chimed in. She went over and gave her daughter a big hug as well. "So proud of both of you," Sara told her teens.

"Yes we are," Steve agreed.

Mary and Peter began filling their parents in on all of the details of the eventful day, each talking nonstop. Their excitement was catching and soon everyone was laughing and joking together. Samson, watching the exuberant emotions displayed by the family members, began running around the room barking and wagging his tail. He was happy too. There was celebration in the air, and, before they knew it, they were all heading for the kitchen. They decided to celebrate with pizza for dinner. Peter was soon on the phone, ordering two extra-large pepperonis with extra cheese and two-liter bottles of soda from a local pizza restaurant. This special moment with the family was exactly what Steve needed.

Later that evening when everyone was asleep and the house was quiet, Steve slipped out of bed, changed into jeans and a sweatshirt, and, taking his telescope with him, went outside to look at the stars. He slowly scanned the sky, marveling at God's creation and soon found himself, once again, talking with the Creator. This gave him deep comfort after a turbulent day. Steve cherished those moments alone with God. It helped him grow in his relationship with Him.

"Lord, I'm really going to need your help tomorrow night. Give me the words. Help the board to see through all the deceptions. Open blind eyes."[3] The fall air was chilly, but Steve soon felt the same warmth and peace he had experienced a few days before in the church sanctuary. He knew that God would be with him no matter what happened the next evening. He understood that what he was about to do was not going to be easy and would require his resolve to stand firm. Thanking God for His love and strength, Steve grabbed his telescope and headed back to bed. Tomorrow, he would do spiritual battle. Tonight, he would sleep.

Chapter 5

The Fallout

Steve woke the next morning to the sound of the home phone ringing. Looking at the clock on the nightstand, he saw that it was after 8:00 a.m. Sitting up quickly, he remembered that Dr. Schaffner would be calling that morning. Throwing back the covers, he swung his feet around and hit the floor running in his pajamas to answer the call. As he reached the extension in the hallway, the phone stopped ringing. Suddenly, Sara called up to him.

"It's for you, Steve. It's the district office."

Relieved, Steve called down to her saying he would take the call upstairs. Sara listened for Steve to pick up the other phone and then, laying the receiver down softly, went back to the kitchen to finish making breakfast for the family. Peter and Mary were already up, dressed, and setting the kitchen table.

"Hello–yes, this is Pastor Hanson. You're who?" Steve asked the caller. Samson came up the stairs and started licking his hand. "Oh yes, Mr. Samples. I didn't realize you were the one who would be calling this morning. Uh, yes, board meeting tonight at 7:00 p.m. at the church. Can you be at the parsonage by 5:00, so we have a chance to talk before-hand?" Paul Samples confirmed that he would.

"Great!" Steve responded. I'll see you then."

After giving Paul some quick directions to the church, Steve hung up the phone feeling reassured. He indeed would not be going into the meeting by himself. Steve was also glad he had called the board, consisting of the church's deacons and elders, together as soon as he did. Remembering Randy's explosive reaction the day before, the sooner he met with them the better. Some of them probably already knew why they had been summoned. Considering this possibility, Steve decided he had to be prepared for anything that evening.

Steve changed into jeans and T-shirt and went downstairs to eat breakfast with the family. Mary and Peter were at the kitchen table and had already started eating, their plates half empty. Samson was sitting next to Mary enjoying a special treat of turkey hotdogs. He couldn't seem to get enough of them.

Peter would be leaving later that morning to report in for the big game at the high school that afternoon. The excitement was alive in his voice.

"Coming to the game, Pop?" Peter asked eagerly as he looked up from his plate.

"Yes, I will be there for the first half. I have a board meeting this evening I need to get ready for, so, unfortunately, I won't be able to stay for the whole game."

"A board meeting?" Mary questioned. I thought you met with them at the end of the month."

"Normally I do, but I called a special one," Steve said as he reached for the orange juice.

"Anything we should know about?" Peter asked as he filled his plate with another helping of pancakes and bacon.

"Not right now," his dad returned. "But I would like you to pray about it. It's connected with the reason why we asked you to pray the other day."

"Sounds serious," Mary responded looking for the grape jelly on the table as she buttered her rye toast.

"Well, we'll just pray for the best. Anyway, Peter's got a big game today. Let's all think about that right now. First things first!" Steve replied.

Peter and Mary smiled at their dad's comment. Sara nodded in agreement from the stove, then filled up a plate with more pancakes and joined the others at the table. Understanding that their father could not tell them everything, Mary and Peter went on to talk about other things.

After breakfast, everyone got ready for the big day. Peter was the first to leave the house. His friend Simon Whitaker, who was a year ahead of him in school, picked him up in his older brother's car. The two were going to work on a couple of strategic moves in the field house before they had to report to the coach for the game. Mary left a half-hour later with two friends from school. They all rode their bikes over to another friend's house to hang out and listen to music until it was time to leave for the game.

Early that afternoon, Sara and Steve sat in the bleachers at the high school stadium anticipating the beginning of the football game. The band was already playing on the field in their brightly colored red and silver uniforms when they arrived, and excitement was in the air. Soon an announcement came over the PA system. As the teams were introduced, cheers went up from both sides of the field. The home team was introduced first.

Peter was among the players leading the way as they burst onto the field with great energy–running, jumping, yelling, and giving each other high fives as they went. He looked tall in his red and white uniform, and his padding and equipment made him look much broader than he was. When the visiting team joined the home players on the turf, everyone was asked to stand for the national anthem. The band began to play the *Star-Spangled Banner* and the guest singer, Veronica Browning, started to sing, motioning for everyone to join her. She was a member of Steve's church and a popular soloist at Sunday services. She often sang at community events in the Nordstown area as well. Her strong lyric soprano voice rang out across the stadium, inspiring many of the people to sing along. When the song ended, everyone cheered.

Peter's parents were full of pride as they watched their son huddle with his teammates just before the referee blew the whistle for the teams to line up. Mary was out in the crowd with her friends, Tracy, Erica, and Susanna, eating popcorn and corndogs, laughing, and having a good time. She was assigned to write about the game for the school newspaper and had her reporter's pad hung around her neck on a lanyard. Moving freely on both sides of the stadium, now and then, Mary would stop and interview interesting looking people about their perspective on the game. She asked which side they were cheering for, which player they predicted would make the most points, which team they thought would win, and anything else she could think of while she had their attention. She wrote their responses down carefully, so she could easily decipher her notes later. Her three friends talked with other spectators when Mary was busy interviewing someone. They didn't mind waiting for her. They were just enjoying being a part of the crowd and the excitement.

Steve stayed with Sara until half-time and then decided he needed to get back to the office to prepare for the meeting that evening. Before getting up, he reached over and kissed Sara on the cheek.

"Let me know how it turns out, ok, Hon?"

"Of course," Sara replied, quickly grabbing his hand and giving him a forced smile. He nodded with a partial smile and then turned to leave for home. Sara watched her husband work his way through the crowd of spectators toward the parking lot, praying for him as he went. When she could no longer see him, she turned her focus back to the half-time show. Sara stayed for the rest of the game. It was important for her to be there in the stadium until the final play was made. Peter would be looking for her in the crowd. He always seemed to know where she was sitting.

Once the game ended, Sara went home alone. Both kids had rides after the game. When she reached the house a little after 5:00 p.m., Sara noticed an unfamiliar car in the driveway. She soon discovered that it belonged to Mr. Samples from the district office. He had decided to come early, so he and Steve had more time to talk. Sara stopped in the study for a moment to greet Paul, an accomplished lawyer in his early fifties, and let Steve know the outcome of the game. Then she headed to the kitchen to make supper for the two men and herself. Mary and Peter would be eating at the after-game dance and then going to the movies with some of their friends. The home team had won, and they would be enjoying the fun for a few hours. Sara was glad the teens weren't home right then. They would know soon enough what was going on.

Steve and Paul continued to talk until they were called for a light supper in the kitchen. Sara warmed up some soup she made the day before and put together some fresh salads and sandwiches for them. Steve and Paul were glad for the break and managed to talk about other things during their meal with Sara. Samson wandered around the room as the three ate. Finally, he found a warm spot on the kitchen floor and laid down. Sara was glad for Samson's presence in the room. He would be a good comfort to her again when the men left for the church.

Watching Steve and Paul cross over to the church parking lot after supper, Sara went into the living room and sat down at the piano. She felt moved to start playing. For Sara, music was one of the most intimate ways to be in prayer to the Father. Lifting her hands and gently touching the keys, she began to play softly. Soon she was singing her favorite song by Petra, "The Battle Belongs to the Lord"[1] . . . As she played and sang, Sara thought of Steve and the spiritual battle he and Paul were about to enter. Samson lay quietly on the floor close to her, his paws crossed in front of him as if he was in prayer as well.

As Steve and Paul came to the front door of the church, Steve sensed that Sara was at the piano at home. He took comfort knowing she would be singing her favorite worship song. One they both took encouragement from on many occasions. Sara was not just his wife and partner in life, but also his best friend. Spiritually, each was able to sense when the other needed prayer, no matter where they were at the time, together or apart. They were each other's greatest intercessors. Steve knew from the first time he met Sara at Bible college that they had a special connection and that someday they would be in ministry together. That connection became even more precious to him on the day, twenty-two years ago, when he placed a wedding ring on her finger and the two became partners for life. How thankful he was for Sara as he reached for the front door of his place of worship.

As Steve and Paul walked down the hall of the church, they spotted Pastor Randy sitting on a sofa in the waiting area just off the conference room where the meeting was being held. He was seated next to someone in a dark blue business suit. The man in his late thirties was rummaging through a leather briefcase and talking to Randy at the same time. Looking at Paul, Steve motioned toward the two seated in the lounge. Paul nodded as they walked past them and entered the conference room, closing the door behind them. Already assembled at the large oak conference table, and unusually silent, were most of the board members, some dressed in business casual and some in work clothes. All of them were either sipping on coffee or eating cookies. They ranged in age from their thirties to their sixties. Deacon Tom Black had not arrived yet. He would complete the group of eight male members of this board. Tom Black was Pastor Randy's paternal uncle. Steve and Paul took some refreshments and joined the others at the table. When Steve greeted the board members, they barely acknowledged his presence. Although many had recognized Paul, Steve decided to wait until everyone was present before introducing him to the group. Steve whispered to Paul what he planned to do about the introduction and then took his seat. Paul nodded and sat down next to him.

Deacon Black, a medium-build, salt and pepper-haired man in his sixties, whom Pastor Randy resembled in some ways, arrived a short time later, acting greatly annoyed and slamming the door to the board room when he entered. Unable to restrain himself, he walked over to Steve, looked straight at him and loudly said, "Are you insane?!"

"Nice to see you again, Tom," Paul Samples quickly jumped in, noticing that everyone's eyes were on Steve. Not wanting the situation to get out of hand before the meeting started, he said to Tom, "Why don't you have a seat, so we can pray."

"Yes, Tom," Steve echoed as he swallowed hard. "Please have a seat," pointing to an empty chair. "We're ready to begin."

Tom, appearing somewhat defused at that point, turned and went to sit in his regular chair at the conference table. Steve took a moment to introduce Paul to the Board and then began to pray. He asked for God's guidance that evening and that the group, with the help of the Holy Spirit, would work together to handle the situation they were about to discuss according to Biblical and district standards.

When Steve said, "Amen," Tom did not hesitate to pick up where he left off. "Why are you starting this all over again, Pastor Steve?" he asked in a snarky tone.

"Excuse me?" Steve looked over at him.

"I said-"

Tom was abruptly cut off by Paul Samples. "Tom, you are out of order here. The board, at least officially, has not heard why Pastor Steve has called them together yet."

"We know," Jon Phelps, one of the older board members, volunteered the information. "Tom has been on the phone with all of us."

Steve glared at Tom. "And why in the world would you do that, Tom? You had no right to . . ."

"I had every right," Tom sneered. "I had to stop you from stirring things up again."

Suddenly, everyone in the room was talking, offering their own opinions about the situation to each other and Steve. Some questioned his decision to bring damaging allegations against Pastor Randy to the board, ones they had dealt with before. They felt they were able to put that madness behind them a long time ago and didn't want to deal with it once more. Tom Black added fuel to the fire by reminding everyone what Randy and his family had gone through because of the false accusations of a, "lying little witch with deep-seated emotional problems."

Recognizing the discussions were being used as a diversion, Paul Samples decided to take over the meeting. "Excuse me, gentlemen. Excuse me!" he said, his voice growing louder the second time.

The room began to quiet.

"As the appointed representative from the district office, I must remind you all that Steve Hanson is your called and contracted senior pastor, and he has certain legal and moral obligations he must fulfill. What he has done follows good and proper church procedure. This meeting of the board was called to discuss a matter that could have serious legal consequences. This is not something you can criticize, regardless of who is involved. Now let's relax and allow Pastor Steve his time to say what he has to say." Then looking at Deacon Black, he said, "Tom, I suggest you change your attitude, or I will have to ask you to leave the room."

Everyone's eyes were now on Tom to see what he would do. Realizing he did not want to be removed from the proceedings, he nodded in agreement. Being a relative of the alleged perpetrator gave him no special rights or privileges in the eyes of the district. He just had to accept that, at least for now.

Steve thanked everyone for coming that evening and proceeded to talk about what had recently transpired, sharing only those details he felt necessary for them to know at that time. He was careful not to indicate Mrs. Hellinger's role in the situation as well. When he finished, the room was once again silent.

"That's hogwash!" Tom suddenly blurted out. "Those women saw a chance to get the new pastor involved in their slanderous plot, and you fell for it."

"I understand you want to protect your nephew, Tom, but the fact of the matter is..." Steve started.

"The fact of the matter, Pastor, is that you're as gullible as the last pastor we had at this church. And obviously, he's not here anymore. Look at all we have done for you and your family since you came. We opened our hearts and homes to you, and this is what we get in return?"

The other board members quickly chimed in with similar comments. Steve was stunned. This couldn't be happening. It was ludicrous. Doing his job was not a personal affront to their kindness when he and his family came to Community Church. These men were clearly out of line in what they were saying to him. Appalled at the irrational response from the group, Paul Samples decided to take over the meeting again. He began banging his ceramic coffee cup on the table and continued to do so until once again he had everyone's attention.

"I think you are all missing the point here. You shouldn't be attacking Steve. There are new accusations now. This is not a rehash of the old ones. In case you forgot, I was involved the last time Pastor Randy was accused of sexual misconduct. Now, let me tell you–if we don't do something about this now and those women go to the police or get a lawyer, you will have a real mess on your hands."

"Those women aren't going to do that," Tom sneered. "Because there's nothing to tell. They want Pastor Steve to do their dirty work for them."

Everyone in the room began talking again. It was obvious who they were siding with, whether or not they were fully convinced of what Tom was saying.

Steve looked at the group and silently asked God to intervene. "I can't believe I am hearing what I am hearing," Steve heard himself say loud enough to be heard over the other voices. Everyone stopped to listen to him.

"It is our moral and sacred obligation as leaders of the church to see that this situation is handled properly and that everyone has had a chance to be heard. Now… I am going to ask Pastor Randy to come into the room at this point, so he can give us his perspective on the situation." Looking at Mike Weaver, the youngest of the board members, he said, "Mike, would you tell Pastor Randy, and I assume his legal counsel, they can come in now?" Mike nodded and left the room to get the two men.

As soon as Pastor Randy and his attorney appeared at the door, Steve felt a dark presence enter the room. It brought a heaviness that was very apparent to him. He knew he and the others at the meeting were encountering pure evil. Steve quickly turned to Paul to see if he was sensing the same thing. He could tell by the look on Paul's face that he was. Steve knew this demonic presence was something that needed to be exposed and rebuked, but the problem was that most of the men sitting around the table had no idea what just happened and probably didn't understand how to deal with it. Both Steve and Paul were now praying internally for God's light and truth to clear the room of this darkness and for blind spiritual eyes to see.

Randy walked into the conference room with a look of meekness. It was almost theatrical but very convincing to those in the room, except Steve and Paul. Paul, who had dealt with Pastor Randy before, was seeing the same deception he had witnessed the last time Randy faced the board and the district. Steve saw Randy's present demeanor as a complete opposite of what he had witnessed in his office just the day before.

Randy sat down at the conference table with his attorney, Sam Keeler, who took a seat to the left of him. Pastor Randy did not hesitate to make his lawyer's presence known to the group and introduced him as his legal counsel. Paul Samples, in turn, made sure the visiting attorney knew that he was also a lawyer and was representing the district office at this special meeting.

When Randy heard the summary of allegations, he began to break down.

"I swear. I swear to you all," he sobbed, tears flowing down his cheeks, "none of that is true. I don't know why this is happening again. I have worked so hard to be a good pastor to this congregation. I thought this was over a few years ago, and now it's come back. I can't do this. I can't let Carol and the boys go through this another time! It's so humiliating! So unfair! Please, you've got to believe me! Those women are sick! Would I risk everything I have and worked for, everything I love, for cheap adulterous affairs?" The tears continued to stream down his face. This was almost too much for Steve to watch, his stomach tightening inside.

It was obvious that Randy's response was having a strong emotional impact on the group. It was also obvious that the presence of his attorney made some of the board very uncomfortable. When Randy finished, his attorney looked at the group and began to speak.

"You know, Gentlemen, at this point, I see no case against this man, lest you have some proof, some written statement. Unless those women are willing to come forward and address this group, I suggest you drop it right now. Because if you don't, my client may be inclined to bring charges against the church and those women for defamation of character. I would also like to add that if you have any direct questions for my client regarding these so-called indiscretions, they need to be given to me first, so I can discuss them with Randy before he answers them with you. And all of his direct responses will, of course, only be made with me present."

At those statements, the board members looked extremely uneasy and began murmuring among themselves again about the situation.

"No, we can't proceed without proof."

"Those women have falsely accused our assistant pastor."

"Pastor Steve needs to put a stop to this insanity, so it doesn't split the church or hurt Pastor Randy's family again."

"We don't need the publicity!" "Not again!"

Paul Samples stood and raised his voice over the noise.

"At this point, I would like to say that the district office has every intention of seeking truth in this matter and will do so until we have it. I would strongly suggest that you each be in prayer over this situation and open-minded to any piece of evidence or testimony that may be presented to you and the district office."

Knowing Pastor Randy wasn't about to answer any direct questions that evening regarding the allegations made against him, Paul turned to Randy and said, "Thank you for coming Pastor Randy and sharing your emotional testimony. As the law states, you are innocent until proven guilty. However, I am concerned that you chose not to directly discuss anything that transpired between you and each of those women. We have lots of questions, which you still need to answer. Bringing in an attorney does not absolve you from talking with us about what we need to know. You may not consider this a legal issue at this point, but it is still a church and district issue. Your ordination papers could be taken from you. I hope you realize that."

Then turning to Randy's attorney, he said, "Thank you counselor for coming as well. I am sure we will be having more conversations regarding this issue as things progress. If you two would kindly leave now, Steve and I would like to finish up our official duties here."

Randy and his attorney stood to leave, thanking everyone for the chance to hear Randy's response to the accusations. Randy, wiping his eyes with his handkerchief, left the room peacefully. Tom Black smiled to himself as he looked on, believing that Steve would soon be forced to drop the whole matter.

When the door of the room closed, the heaviness seemed to lighten in the room. Paul Samples looked at the group. Taking a deep breath, he began to speak once more.

"We trust that what you have heard tonight will stay in this room. Like you, we want to get to the bottom of this situation. And we can't do that with a lot of gossip and accusations going around the congregation. Let's remember Who we serve and that we are all brothers in Christ."

Looking then at Pastor Steve, Paul asked him to lead the group in a closing prayer. When Steve had finished, the board members were dismissed, each promising to keep the meeting confidential. After the room emptied, Steve and Paul lingered in the conference room to talk about what had just transpired.

"This is the same response we got the last time Steve. Hopefully, those women will be willing to talk to the board and the district now. If not, there's not much we can do. A police report or two would be nice, but at this point, that doesn't seem to exist. If we go directly to the police ourselves, and the women won't talk with them, we are still in the same boat. The women need to press charges. Please tell them that their silence ties our hands on what we can do."

"I understand. The ball is in their court. Thanks for coming tonight, Paul."

"No problem, Steve. I will let Dr. Schaffner know about what happened tonight. I suggest you follow up with a phone call to him on Monday afternoon. He has some free time then."

"I certainly will," Steve responded as they locked up and headed back to the parsonage. Walking out in the cool night air, Steve thought about the board and their responsibility to the congregation, especially those new or immature in their faith. Biblically, most of those members should not be in the positions they were in. Instead of providing strong spiritual leadership for Community Church, they were, in effect, the blind leading the blind.[1] Perhaps more mature congregants would take their place in the future. He would be praying for that to happen.

Sara was watching from the living room window for Steve and Paul's return. The other cars were already gone from the church parking lot, so she knew the two would be back soon. When they arrived, Sara gave Steve a big hug, glad the meeting was over. Then Steve and Paul followed Sara to the dining room, where she served the two men some coffee and strawberry cheesecake. The three talked about the meeting for over an hour. Sara sat dumbfound as she listened to what had taken place that evening. She too recognized the spiritual ineptness of their current church board.

Looking at his watch, Paul realized it was time for him to head home. He suggested they pray over the situation for a few minutes before he left. Holding hands, the three lifted their voices to God and asked for direction, discernment, and for the truth to be revealed. When they finished, Paul gathered his things, thanked his new friends for their hospitality, and headed for his car. The Hansons stood at the front door and waved goodbye as Paul pulled out of the driveway.

Steve and Sara were now alone in the house. It was almost 10:00 p.m., but the kids wouldn't be home for at least two more hours. Taking advantage of their children's night out, the couple decided to go over to the church to pray together. Once in the sanctuary, both were soon on their faces before God with only the altar spotlights on at the front of the room. There they laid quietly on the soft maroon carpet until each felt encouraged. Finally, Steve sat up and Sara followed. They stood and took a seat on a nearby pew bench together.

Steve pulled out a pew Bible and began to read from Ephesians 6. "For our struggle is not against flesh and blood…"[2] When he finished the chapter, he looked up to heaven and began to pray a prayer he learned when he was just three years old. Sara joined in when she heard the familiar words. 'Our Father in heaven, hallowed be your name, your kingdom come, your will be done, on earth as it is in heaven. Give us today our daily bread. And forgive us our debts, as we also have forgiven our debtors. And lead us not into temptation, but deliver us from the evil one.'[3] For yours is the Kingdom, the power, and the glory, forever. Amen."[4] The couple prayed quietly in the sanctuary for a few minutes more then headed for home.

Later that evening, when the teens came home, Steve and Sara gave them a brief heads up on the situation at hand. They felt they should only say that one of the ministry leaders was accused of improper behavior, and Peter and Mary might hear something said about it at church. They didn't give names or details but told their son and daughter to keep the situation to themselves, yet bathe it in prayer. Peter and Mary would know more when it became necessary. Steve and Sara prayed the board would also keep the situation confidential, so it did not get out of hand or gain public attention.

The next day was Sunday. Steve got up that morning with a definite sense that something had changed. It was almost a feeling of dread. After breakfast, he grabbed his sermon notes and headed over to the church earlier than usual. To his dismay, his feeling proved quite accurate as the morning progressed. The usual greeting at the beginning of each service was not met with the same enthusiasm as it had before. Heads were not moving in agreement during his sermon like they had, and a number of people were not taking time to talk with him and Sara after the service. Carol Nelson left the sanctuary that morning after service through the back entrance, not wanting to stop and talk with Sara. She wouldn't even look Sara in the eyes when Sara greeted her and the boys that morning. This deeply troubled and saddened Sara, but she knew there was nothing she could do at that time to make things better. Carol was clearly going through a lot of emotions. Betrayal by a close friend was probably the hardest thing to deal with. Keeping her distance was Sara's best response for the time being.

Steve knew without a doubt that the board had not kept their promise to remain silent on the situation. The gossip mill had been going strong throughout the night. And because of that, the fallout had begun.

Chapter 6

Losing Ground

That afternoon, Steve went into his office at the parsonage to think and pray. It was difficult answering his teens' questions at lunch about what was happening. They too had experienced the change in the atmosphere at the church that morning. Picking up the phone on his desk, he began to dial Cheryl Petrie's home phone number. There was an urgency now to let the women know that he needed their help and right away. He had not anticipated things heating up so quickly. After a moment of silence, the phone rang a few times, then Cheryl's voicemail played. Leaving an urgent message for her to contact him, he knew she would return his call as soon as possible. Hanging up the phone, Steve decided to take a walk through the neighborhood. He stopped by the living room, where Sara was reading a book, to let her know he was going out for a while. When Samson saw Steve put on his jacket to leave, he wanted to go with him, but Sara hung on to him as Steve left the house. She knew this was one of those times when her husband needed to be alone with God.

"Come on, Boy," Sara said, tugging on his collar to keep him from heading out the back pet door. "Steve will take you with him another time."

Samson's large brown eyes met Sara's. Wagging his tail and whining softly, he seemed to be pleading with her to let him go with Steve, but Sara knew it was best he stay home. After a few more attempts to free himself, Samson realized that Sara wasn't going to give in, so he relaxed. She guided him to the kitchen, quickly secured the pet door to the back porch, then let Samson run free in the house. He just couldn't be allowed to follow Steve.

As Steve started his walk, he began to feel the anxiety from the day's events slipping away. The fall air was cool and exhilarating. He remembered again the words of the evangelist and knew they had been spoken for good reason. God had sent him and Sara and their family to be a light in a dark place. This place looked good on the surface, but in truth held many unhallowed secrets. The Hansons were pioneers in a church fellowship that needed to learn and understand how to function in both the natural and supernatural, according to the Scriptures and the leading of the Holy Spirit. Only then, could these people be set completely free of the satanic influences and strongholds that were holding their church fellowship captive.

As he pondered the recent goings-on at the church, Steve decided he would begin a series of sermons the following week on the discerning of spirits and engaging in spiritual warfare. He realized the series would have to be presented in such a way so as not to point directly at Pastor Randy. There was still much to uncover in that situation, and the congregation didn't need to know any more than what they already did. Yet, this was decidedly a teachable moment, and he had to seize the opportunity to start preaching on discerning spiritual issues, especially those that were demonically inspired. He would go slow, but be deliberate in what he shared in his messages. Perhaps he would even offer a special follow-up weekly Bible study on the topic. Remembering once again what he had been told about the occult activity in the area, Steve was motivated even more to proceed with his plan. As he walked, an outline for the sermon sequence quickly came together in his mind.

After several minutes, Steve realized he was about to pass the Brown family's home, a large red brick ranch with white shutters. The Browns were long-time members of Community Church and were well respected both there and in the Nordstown community. As he approached the end of their driveway, Steve noticed that Bob Brown was outside raking leaves in the front lawn that had fallen from his now almost bare trees. He was wearing work clothes and his favorite red plaid flannel jacket. Grateful for a chance to talk, Steve decided to engage Bob in light conversation.

"Hello!" Steve greeted Bob warmly, as he approached the Brown's driveway.

"Hello, Pastor," Bob called back without a smile and little emotion, stopping only long enough to acknowledge Steve's presence. Bob and his wife Lucie were both in their mid-sixties but looked years younger. Bob was a retired business owner, and Lucie was a retired elementary school teacher. They were a loving and generous couple with a good sense of humor. They were also big fans of Pastor Randy and obviously knew about what had transpired the night before at the elders' meeting.

Steve was hesitant after receiving Bob's cold greeting but decided to stop and talk anyway for a moment or two. It just did not feel right to keep on walking.

"Great afternoon to be outside," Steve said with a big smile, as he drew close enough to engage in conversation with his friend.

"Yeah, I guess," Bob replied adjusting the black ball cap on his head and brushing his salt and pepper hair from his forehead. Ordinarily, it was hard for Steve to break away from Bob when he met him in the hallway at church or some other place out in the community. Bob's wife, Lucie, often had to physically pull him away from Steve, so he could go on to do other things. Even so, Steve enjoyed talking with Bob. Recognizing he was getting the cold shoulder, Steve tried to pull Bob into a conversation again.

"You think we're in for a cold winter, Bob?"

"Uh, yeah, sure, probably." Bob knelt to scoop some leaves into a large green heavy-duty garbage bag.

At that moment, Lucie came out on the front porch. She was wearing blue jeans and a Steelers T-shirt. Her shoulder-length blonde hair was pulled back in a ponytail. "It's time for the game!" she announced loudly, not even acknowledging Steve's presence.

Bob perked up, realizing that he had an excuse to leave the conversation Steve was trying to start. "I'll be right there, Honey!" he called over his shoulder.

Lucie nodded. Then turned and went back into the house, closing the front door behind her.

Bob looked at Steve for a moment, almost as if he wanted to say something more, but then decided to end the conversation with, "Have a good day, Pastor."

"Uh, yes, you too, Bob," Steve said sorrowfully.

Taking his rake and a half-filled garbage bag with him, Bob headed toward the house. He was now walking quickly, intentionally trying to escape the conversation with his pastor. When he reached the open door of the attached garage, he placed the rake on a hook on the wall and pushed the button for the large white door to close behind him.

Watching the garage door slowly go down, Steve could see Bob enter his house through a side door. He was stunned by Bob's icy attitude toward him. It was so uncharacteristic of him. He thought that Bob, of all people, would have been more open-minded about the situation, or at least be willing to talk about it. An investigation was warranted into a church ministry leader's alleged conduct — surely he understood and supported that. And surely the whole church would realize that as well if they had a better understanding of the situation. It was hard to know what they had been told. Steve realized that the congregation had been down that path before, but weren't they at least somewhat concerned why it was happening again? All Steve wanted to do was get to the truth and see that justice was done, even if it meant proving Randy's accusers wrong. Isn't that what the church should want as well? Why then the pushback?

Shaking his head as he watched his friend turn his back on him, Steve continued down the street. He prayed for Bob and Lucie and tried to push the encounter aside in his mind. He turned his focus instead to the changes in the trees, giving God thanks for the beauty of the season. The leaves were turning red, gold, and orange, and falling softly in great numbers to the ground everywhere. The smell of fall was in the air. It was the beginning of a wonderful festive time of year on the church calendar. Without warning, a flock of geese appeared overhead in their usual V flight pattern, squawking loudly as they passed. They were heading for their winter home. It would not be long before the first snowflakes would fly. Watching the geese disappear in the clouds, Steve almost wished he was flying away with them.

After a few more minutes, Steve came to the community park at the edge of his neighborhood. A couple of people were there walking their dogs, but it was mostly vacant. Steve couldn't help but think of Samson when he saw the other dogs. He felt bad leaving him behind but knew he needed to be alone with God for a while. No time for playing Frisbee. Heading to the walking path, he began to hike through the woods, thankful for the solitude. As he started to follow the trail, a sudden breeze seemed to go right through him sending a chill up his spine. In response, he zipped up his brown flannel-lined fall jacket and continued on eventually coming to a small stream. Steve eagerly sat down next to it to enjoy the peacefulness. He dipped his hand into the cool water and watched the tiny waves and bubbles wash over his skin. The water was clear and running rapidly. At that moment, the presence of God was quietly evident around him. Steve smiled. It was a welcome feeling of warmth and security.

Steve leaned back against a nearby oak tree and thought about all that had transpired in the last several days. Despite what happened, he knew without a doubt he was not alone. Steve lingered at the creek for a while, meditating on the goodness and faithfulness of God. He soon found himself reciting parts of Psalm 91 . . . "He will cover you with his feathers, and under his wings you will find refuge; his faithfulness will be your shield and rampart." . . . [1] Suddenly a drop of water hit him on the head. Steve peered up at the now gray cloudy sky. It looked like rain. Feeling refreshed, Steve stood and decided to head back home. Sara would be worried. He must have been gone for a couple of hours.

When Steve entered the front door of the parsonage, Sara was standing in the kitchen near the hallway talking with someone on the phone. "Yes," she replied. "He just came in the door." Turning to her husband and hugging him, Sara whispered, "It's Cheryl Petrie returning your call."

"Thanks, Hon," Steve said with a smile, giving his wife a quick kiss on the cheek. "I'll take it in the office."

"He'll be right with you, Cheryl," Sara spoke again into the phone.

Steve closed the door of the office after him. He took a deep breath and picked up the phone receiver on his desk. After thanking Cheryl for returning his call, Steve began to recap what had taken place since her visit to his office, briefly describing Pastor Randy's reaction to the allegations. He emphasized the importance of contacting the other women and encouraging them to come forward to talk with the district office. They could not back out now. His hands would be tied if they did not quickly take advantage of this opportunity. Cheryl promised she would contact them right away and would call him in a couple of days.

Beginning to sense the gravity of the situation, the Hansons sat in silence during the evening meal, each with his or her thoughts on what had taken place that day. Samson intuitively began to walk around the kitchen table and tried to nudge the family members to be more animated, licking and prodding each one of them as he made the circle. Recognizing and appreciating his efforts, Sara finally broke the silence. She and her family needed to do something to change their perspective, and fast. They could not allow the church scandal to pull them down. They had to remain strong in the Lord[2] and alert during this spiritual battle.

"Why don't we all go out to Lee's Burger and Dairy for dessert?" She said trying to force a smile. "It will do us good to get out. There's no youth group tonight, so what better time to go?"

Mary and Peter looked at each other and then started to giggle. The silence was broken.

"Okay. I'm having a strawberry sundae," Mary announced.

"I'm having a hot fudge sundae," Peter returned.

Both looked at their father, and he realized that he was outnumbered.

"Sure, why not?" Steve said, giving in and tossing his napkin on the table. Steve got up to get his car keys.

Soon, everyone was talking and laughing together. Samson began running around the kitchen barking loudly. He would be allowed to ride along in the car and most likely be treated to a bowl of vanilla ice cream on the way back home. Within a few minutes, the family members were grabbing their jackets and piling into the Jeep for what would prove to be an uplifting outing for everyone. Steve knew that laughter was some of the best medicine[3] when feeling discouraged and began to lose himself in the moment, leading the family in some old camp songs as they drove down the street.

The family stayed at Lee's for over an hour, then decided to head home and watch a movie together. Samson had fallen asleep on his favorite blue blanket on the back seat of the Jeep as the cool evening breeze entered the vehicle through the partially opened windows. When he woke up and saw the cold treat they brought for him, he jumped up and greedily devoured it. Licking his mouth for any last traces of the ice cream, he barked happily in appreciation. Then Steve started the car and headed to the parsonage. After the Hansons arrived home, they watched their favorite movie together before heading to bed.

The next morning began like any other Monday morning. Mary and Peter were excited to be back in school with their friends. Both were becoming popular at their new high school and were enjoying the attention. They were respected by staff and students alike. Sara prepared for her usual trip to a nursing home community. She loved talking with the residents and leading Bible studies for those interested in joining them. Her newest study was on the book of Acts.

Steve entered the church office with his usual friendly morning greeting to his office staff. Mrs. Hellinger was at her desk as he entered. Most of the ministry staff would not be in that day, because Monday was their day off. His dream team needed their time with family. They gave so much to the church during the rest of the week. Steve, just went to his church office on Monday mornings, then spent the afternoon either studying at home or spending some time with Sara if she wasn't visiting the nursing home.

"Good morning, Pastor Steve. Could I have a moment with you before you get started for the day?" Mrs. Hellinger asked as he entered the main office.

"Yes, of course," Steve responded. "Come right in."

Looking out the window first to make sure no one else's car was in the church parking lot, Mrs. Hellinger headed for Steve's office. Mrs. Hellinger made herself comfortable in the chair across from Steve's desk while Steve closed the door.

"Most of the congregation knows about what happened last week," she began.

"I assumed so," Steve replied, placing his briefcase on the filing cabinet. "Doesn't speak well of our board, does it?" He took his seat behind his desk.

"No, it doesn't. In fact, it's shameful. Unfortunately, they like to take matters into their own hands. They will only let the pastor lead when it suits them. It's been that way ever since I started working here. Oh, don't get me wrong, there are some good guys on the board. They just don't see, Steve. They have spiritual blinders on, and they don't want their happy little worlds turned upside down again."

"Well, maybe it's time their happy little worlds were shaken up. How can they presume to run a church when they can't even see right from wrong? It's the blind leading the blind. They need to have a better handle on spiritual issues."

"I agree. But those women are going to have to help you stop this madness." She paused and then became more serious. "Steve, don't be surprised if they don't."

Steve was taken aback. "What do you mean?"

"I mean there are those in this community who would think nothing of intimidating them into keeping quiet."

"You know something?"

"I know what happened the last time, Steve. And it was ugly."

"I thought you said those women wanted to help."

"They do, Steve. Now. But after some pressure is brought to bear, who knows."

"Pressure? Has it started?"

"Yes."

"I see. How about that girl in the congregation? Will she come to talk with me?"

"Actually, she has decided to go to another church."

"You have spoken to her then."

"Not directly. But someone figured out what was going on, and, after talking with me, warned her about Pastor Randy, so she's leaving."

Steve peered out the window for a moment when he heard a car door slam.

"It's Deacon Black," Steve warned.

"I better get back to my desk," Mrs. Hellinger stood up quickly. "We'll talk more later."

Just as Mrs. Hellinger was settled back in the chair behind her desk, Deacon Black came bursting into the church office.

"Is Pastor in?" he asked gruffly.

"Uh, yes, he just got here," Mrs. Hellinger responded, acting as if Pastor Steve had just walked in the door. "Is something wrong?"

Ignoring Mrs. Hellinger's question, he headed straight to Steve's office door. Without knocking, he opened the door and walked right in. Not surprised at his rudeness, Steve remained seated. Saying a quick prayer, he decided to speak first before Deacon Black had a chance to.

"Well, Deacon Black. You're just the person I was hoping to see this morning. You must have read my mind."

Deacon Black was caught off guard for a moment.

"I bet you've come to apologize to me," Steve said with a smile.

"Apologize? What in the world would I have to apologize to you for?

"Well, for starters, sharing information about the board meeting with the congregation. That was a closed meeting on Saturday. I didn't share anything about it with them. You're a deacon Tom, a leader in the church. You and the others gave your word. You had no right-."

"I had every right." Deacon Black snarled. "That's my nephew you're trying to railroad. He's worked hard to get where he is today."

"Railroad? Tom, there have been some serious allegations made against your nephew by more than one woman. And as we all know, he has had similar allegations made against him before. How can you ignore that? You know what the Scriptures say. You know what church policy says. Why are you interfering with something you know I have to do? What are you trying to cover up, Tom?"

At that, Deacon Black became incensed. "I know my nephew!" he shouted. "And those little witches are not going to ruin his life!"

"Do you?" asked Steve. "There's a lot at stake here. Not just your nephew's ministry career," Steve's voice was starting to get louder. "Tell me, Tom, why has your nephew refused to talk with me or the district office about those allegations? That does not help his situation at all. It implies guilt."

"Why you ungrateful . . . I want your resignation!" Tom suddenly demanded.

"What?" Steve looked at Tom astonished. "Are you crazy? I'm not going to resign for doing my job. You ought to be ashamed of yourself for even thinking about asking me to leave."

At that moment, Mrs. Hellinger suddenly came rushing into the room. "I agree with Pastor Steve, Tom, you're making a fool out of yourself. I can hear you clear down the hall. You pulled the same stunt on the last pastor. You're the one who should resign! And as far as I'm concerned, you're way past due!"

"Me? Stay out of this, Margaret," Tom Black looked at her, indignant toward her statement.

"Yes, you! And no, I won't stay out of it. This is my church too! Now you've caused enough trouble here for one day, it's time for you to leave. Get out of here Tom!" she said almost shouting while sternly pointing at the door.

Steve and Tom were both stunned by Mrs. Hellinger's bold demand. When he could talk again, Deacon Black glared at Steve and said, "You haven't heard the last of this Pastor Steve. I'm calling an emergency meeting of the elders for tomorrow evening!"

"Good, I'll see you there," Steve said looking Tom straight in the eyes.

Mrs. Hellinger waited at the door with her arms folded to make sure Deacon Black was on his way out of Steve's office. When he left the room and main office and was out the front door, Mrs. Hellinger grinned at Steve and said, "Well, we all have our limits."

"I guess so," Steve smiled back, shaking his head.

"Better get ready for tomorrow night. It's going to start getting really nasty around here," Mrs. Hellinger warned. Steve nodded and Mrs. Hellinger closed his door and headed back to her desk.

The rest of the morning was filled with calls from various members of the church wanting to know what was going on. Steve was glad that people were contacting him directly, but he also had to be careful what he said to them. As it approached 12:30, Steve was anxious to get back to the parsonage for lunch. He needed to be near Sara. After lunch Steve made a call to the district office and talked with the district's attorney, Paul Samples. They decided that Steve would handle the meeting on Tuesday evening alone, but he would fill Paul in afterward on what took place. He began working on his notes for the elder's meeting the next day, but in spite of his efforts to work from the privacy of his home, phone calls from concerned and irate members of the church continued to come in throughout the afternoon.

As the day went on, Steve wondered how Cheryl Petrie was doing convincing the rest of the victims to make official statements. He was hoping to talk with her again before the emergency board meeting but knew that was pushing it. Thinking back on his last conversation with

Mrs. Hellinger, Steve began to realize he might be doing this battle without the direct help of the women. If that was the case, he knew the matter would soon be dropped and business as usual would resume at Community Church. There had to be another way to get to the truth.

Steve and Sara prayed over the meeting throughout the next day, sometimes together and sometimes alone. They decided that Mary and Peter needed to have more of a heads up on what was happening, especially since Carol Nelson and her boys would not be coming over for visits anymore. Eventually, someone would talk to them, if they hadn't already, about what was going on. So, they agreed to tell them that Pastor Randy had been accused of sexual misconduct by more than one individual, and the situation was being handled by the board and the district office. They left out as many details as possible but answered their children's questions as best they could, so there was no confusion on the issue. They also instructed Peter and Mary to be *very* careful in what they said to others about what they knew about the situation. Finally, they asked them to be praying when their father went into the next board meeting.

When Pastor Steve entered the conference room at the church that evening, he found the atmosphere somewhat cold. Everyone was there, including Tom Black. The members were talking with each other standing around the table where coffee and a fresh plate of cookies were located. Steve was greeted as he came in, but not as warmly as he had been before the situation with Randy started. He soon became suspicious of what was about to take place. After engaging in some small talk, Steve took his coffee and cookies and sat down with his notes. Sensing a strong opposition rising, he prayed for wisdom and began to recite Ephesians 6: 10-20 to himself. Steve was about to reenter the battle.

When everyone finally took their places at the conference table, Steve opened in a word of prayer and then looked around at the group to see who was going to talk first. The board members, though, were silent. He knew, however, that he had to confront them about their lack of discretion. Why hadn't they kept their promise to remain silent about what had taken place at the last meeting? "You know, Guys," he began slowly, "I am perplexed as to why you took it upon yourselves to tell the whole congregation about the situation with Pastor Randy. I'm sorry, but that was totally irresponsible. I have only discussed the matter with those who needed to know about it. This thing could have been taken care of without letting the parishioners find out a lot of details. Please explain to me why you ignored the Bible, church procedure, and common decency and caused such a stir among the members of the church? I have been on the phone with a number of them the last couple of days."

"Steve, not *all* of us were responsible for those calls," Deacon Dave Mills interrupted, indicating himself and another board member sitting next to him. "It was the rest of the group here that went back on their word."

"I see," Pastor Steve stared at the group. No one said anything.

"However," Deacon Mills went on. "We, as a group, want to let you know that we have met before you came tonight and have unanimously decided that we do not wish to pursue this issue any longer."

"Excuse me?" Steve looked at him dumbfounded. "You can't just dismiss these charges."

"No one has made a formal complaint, Steve. We are going on hearsay. Unless we have some real hard evidence or written statement, the case against Pastor Randy is closed."

"You're not serious."

"We know Pastor Randy, and we know what he and his wife and family went through the last time this happened. This is just more of the same thing." He paused for a moment. "While we have greatly appreciated everything you have done so far since you and your family came here, we also feel it necessary to tell you that pursuing this nonsense could have adverse effects on your tenure here at Community Church, Pastor Steve."

Steve looked at him shocked. "I have a three-year contract," Steve pointed out. "You can't change that. I have done nothing wrong. This is blackmail! I can't believe I am hearing this from you!"

"Call it what you want, Steve, but we are not going to stand by and let a respected pastor go through this again. Those women are lying. So, we are respectfully asking you to back down on this issue, now . . . Let it go Steve. And tell the district office we have no need of them coming back in again."

"We need to be in prayer about this," Steve responded. "You're not seeing the whole picture, Deacon Mills. Don't you want to know the truth? There are spiritual and moral issues that must be addressed here. We're talking about possible serious unrepentant sin!"

"No, you're the one not getting it, Steve. You are barking up the wrong tree . . . The choice is yours, Pastor. Let it go, or we will be forced to take measures against you."

At that, Tom Black spoke up. "Well, I guess we have made ourselves clear here. Unless anyone else has something to say, we'll leave Pastor Steve alone now to think on this. Meeting adjourned everyone." With that, the group got up from their seats and began filing out of the conference room, none of them looking back at Steve as they left.

Steve's head was whirling as the last elder left the room. "Oh Lord, what just happened here? This is wrong! So very wrong!"

Steve picked up his coffee cup and headed for the church office. He quickly called Paul Samples. When Paul answered, Steve, relayed to him what had just taken place at the meeting. Paul had already assumed the worst before Steve even called. He advised Steve to contact Cheryl again to see what the women were planning to do.

When Steve got home, Sara was waiting for him in the living room. Peter and Mary were up in their rooms doing homework.

"We need to pray," he said, as he entered the room. As she went over to greet him, Steve reached out and pulled Sara close to him, kissing her on top of her head. Samson came over to the couple wagging his tail and looking up at them with his big brown eyes. He knew they needed comfort.

After hugging Sara, Steve turned and dropped down in his favorite recliner. "They're threatening to terminate me if I pursue this issue with Randy."

"What?" Sara responded in disbelief. "That's insane! They can't do that!"

"I know," he replied. "They're covering for him, Babe. They don't care about those women."

Sara went over and knelt next to Steve's chair. She took his hand and instinctively they began to pray in the spirit together. Samson lay next to them silently. That night, they went to bed understanding that whatever happened, they still had each other and their kids and that God would be with them every step of the way. Having faced some difficult spiritual battles before, their resolve to stand strong in the Lord would be no different this time. They knew Who they belonged to. They had to trust Him to help them do whatever needed to be done in this situation.

On Wednesday morning, Steve called Cheryl and waited expectantly for her to answer. When Steve heard Cheryl's greeting at the other end, he breathed a sigh of relief.

"Hi Cheryl, this is Pastor Steve."

"Hi, Pastor Steve," Cheryl returned the greeting. "I am so glad you called. As a matter of fact, I was planning to call you later today."

"Is now a good time?" he asked hopefully.

"Yes, as a matter of fact, it is. I am on a long break right now, so this is perfect. I suppose you are wondering about the women. Well, it seems that they have changed their minds about coming forward. Let's just say that they have been "strongly" encouraged to keep their mouths shut."

"Oh no," Steve said quietly.

Yes, we have all been getting anonymous phone calls, warning that it would be healthier for us if we don't get involved with the district office or the police.

Steve was silent.

"Steve, I am rethinking myself what I need to do. I'm sorry I got you into this. These people are not going to let this go. They've got money. They've got lawyers, and lots of friends and family to back them up. And worst of all, they have most of the congregation convinced that Pastor Randy is a saint."

Steve didn't know how to respond. Swallowing hard he finally said, "Please pray about this, Cheryl. Ask for guidance."

"I will," Cheryl replied. "I'll call you back in a couple of days after I have had some more time to think."

"Thank you, Cheryl." When the call ended, Steve knew he was now in a place he didn't want to be . . . a place of few options.

As the days after the board meeting went by, Steve could feel the tension mounting between him and Pastor Randy. Randy barely looked at him anymore and often remained silent during ministry staff meetings. Any attempt to pull him into the discussions was fruitless. This frustrated Steve. In addition, the friendly exchange that once existed among the ministry team had become dry and routine. The energy was gone. Their wonderfully inspired prayers together were now empty sounds, and his relationship with them was becoming cold and detached. Some of them kept their office doors closed during the day so they wouldn't have to talk with Steve as he passed by in the hallway. It was obvious his dream team had also sided with the associate pastor. What could he do to convince them he was doing the right thing?

Randy continued to refuse to talk with Steve about the women who had accused him of sexually assaulting them. He even declined invitations to go over to the parsonage for any staff or personal meetings. This deeply troubled Steve, but there was nothing he could do to force Randy to interact with him. To make things worse, Randy would only communicate with Steve on church business through the office staff, who would relay to Steve what Pastor Randy wanted him to know. Randy only talked directly with Steve when it was absolutely necessary to do so.

As time passed, some of the parishioners Steve had spoken with on the phone were warming up to him again, but most maintained their distance. Someone was still stoking the fire against him, and he knew for the most part who that was. By Friday morning, Cheryl Petrie called and said she wanted to make a statement to the district office. Steve gave her Paul Samples' number, and she promised to contact him right away.

That evening, Paul Samples called Steve. He requested a meeting with the board of Community Church again soon. He would bring a summary of Cheryl's statement with him. The situation was far from over.

Chapter 7

The Decision

Attorney Paul Samples arrived at the parsonage the following Thursday evening a few hours before the board meeting. Steve and Sara prepared for the worst, or at least they hoped they had. Paul and Steve went directly to the home office where Sara had hot coffee and fresh chicken salad sandwiches ready for them. Generous slices of apple pie sat next to them on a tray. As the men talked, Samson anxiously paced outside of the office door. Sara went upstairs with Mary and Peter to pray.

"What do you think is gonna happen, Mom?" Peter asked as the three knelt in Steve and Sara's bedroom.

"I don't know," Sara replied softly.

"Are we going to have to move again?" Mary asked with tears in her eyes. "I really don't want to leave my new school or my new friends."

"We're far from that, Honey." Sara reached over and brushed away the tears that were starting to fall down Mary's cheeks. "It'll all work out. You'll see. The important thing is that we stand strong together for what God wants us to do."

"The kids at church and school have been talking about this thing with Pastor Randy, Mom," Peter shared. "They're confused. Some are starting to act funny around us — like Dad's done something wrong."

"Do you believe he has, Peter?" his mother asked pointedly.

"No, Mom, of course not. We know Dad. The kids have just been listening to all the gossip. A lot of it is coming from a few of the ministry heads at church."

"I know," Sara responded. "Your dad and Mr. Samples are trying to get that under control."

"Jeremy Alston said this thing happened before with Pastor Randy — a few years ago," Mary added. "A lot of people got hurt then." She paused for a moment. "So, if he was accused before, and is being accused now by other women, wouldn't you think that maybe he might be guilty?"

Sara thought for a moment. ". . . I can't say for sure he is guilty, so we need to pray that the whole truth comes out and is dealt with properly. We also need to pray this situation doesn't split the church again." At that moment, Samson came quietly into the room and lay down next to Mary.

"You always know when it's time to pray, don't you, fella?" Mary said smiling, stroking Samson's head and rubbing his floppy ears. "Arf!" Samson barked softly. They all laughed.

Soon, the three were in prayer while Steve and Paul were planning their strategy for the evening in the office below. When they finished praying, Peter and Mary went to their rooms to finish their homework, and Sara went downstairs to the kitchen to make some chocolate fudge with Samson trailing behind her. Making fudge was one of her favorite things to do in the fall, and it would help take her mind off the situation at hand.

At 6:30 p.m., Steve and Paul opened the door of the home office to leave for the church. Smelling the sweet aroma as they passed by the kitchen, Steve stuck his head in to confirm what his nose was telling him. "I hope you're saving some of that for us when we get home tonight," Steve joked.

"You bet, Sweet Darling," Sara smiled. She ran over and gave him a quick kiss on the cheek. "I will be praying for you guys," she said to the men as they left.

"Thanks, Sara," Steve replied.

"Yes, thanks, Sara," Paul echoed his appreciation as he went out the front door just behind Steve. "And thanks for supper. It was great!"

"You're welcome, Paul," Sara replied smiling. "Glad you enjoyed it."

Quickly returning to the kitchen, Sara added some walnuts to the bubbling fudge and poured the mixture into a large buttered pan, leaving it on the counter to cool. Then she wiped her hands and headed to the piano in the living room, praying for Steve and Paul as she went. Sara closed her eyes and began to imagine heavenly music as she sat on the bench. Lifting her fingers to the keys, she started to play a melody she had never heard before. It was something that just seemed to flow from above. As she played, it was as if she was accompanying an orchestra already in concert. Peace filled the room, and Sara became lost in the music. The joy of the Lord began to well up inside of her, and tears flowed from her eyes. As the song progressed, Sara could hear angelic voices singing praises to God reaching octaves no human being could attain. She continued to play until the singing faded. Aware of her surroundings again, Sara prayed once more for Steve and Paul. She then got up to read some of her favorite scriptures, knowing God was working things out. Feeling encouraged, she turned on the television to watch the news until the two men returned to the parsonage.

At 9:04 p.m., Steve and Paul came through the front door. Both looked exhausted. Sara knew right away it had been a challenging evening. The spiritual conflict must have been fierce. Sara got up from the sofa and went to greet them.

"Hi, Hon!" Steve said as he reached out to hug Sara. The two held an embrace for a few seconds, and then Steve stepped back to allow his friend room to put his briefcase down on the floor. "What a night," he said, removing his tie.

"It certainly was," Paul agreed, shaking his head.

Then smelling the sweet odor coming from the kitchen, Steve asked, "Got some of that fudge for us?"

"You bet," Sara responded with a smile and headed for the kitchen. She turned on the light as she entered. The two men came in and sat down at the kitchen table, happy for the break from what they had just endured.

After serving Steve and Paul some fudge and hot coffee, Sara sat down at the table with them, helping herself to a piece of the mouth-watering confection. "So, what happened, or should I ask?"

"Well," Paul began. "Cheryl's statement was strong, but there was still quite a bit of resistance, especially from Deacon Black."

"I figured as much," Sara responded as she took another bite of fudge.

"What we have now is a split board — sixty/forty, if you will. Some of the board was surprised at Cheryl's statements. They had all held her in high regard, so her testimony had quite an impact. They had thought she left town for a new job. The board never imagined that she would be someone accusing Pastor Randy of improper behavior."

"So, what was decided?"

"Well," Steve jumped in, "they said they would cooperate with the district office and keep their silence on this matter until everything is sorted out. The district still wants to hear from the other women before moving forward too fast. They also want to hear more from Pastor Randy. His refusal to answer questions is not helping him, at least from their perspective. On the other hand, many of our board members don't seem to care if he answers them or not. They're still convinced of his innocence."

"I see," Sara said quietly, thinking about the new turn of events.

"I don't trust that Tom Black, though. He is not going to just sit back and let his nephew lose his credentials. He's up to something. I could tell by the way he was acting tonight," Steve told his wife.

Paul agreed.

"Was Randy there tonight?" Sara asked.

"No, not tonight. But he will definitely be at the next meeting when the district starts formal proceedings against him. And I'm sure his attorney will be there as well."

"Oh boy," Sara said concerned, thinking again about her friend Carol.

"At least we had everyone's attention tonight," Paul added. "That's a big change from the last time I was here."

Samson came over to the table for his share of the snack. "No, big guy," Steve told him. "You can't have chocolate." Samson looked disappointed.

"How about a nice, juicy turkey hot dog?" Sara asked, getting the dog excited. He started running and jumping around the room and barking. Sara went to the refrigerator and pulled out a turkey hot dog from the meat drawer. She barely got it in Samson's bowl when he started devouring it. Sara laughed as she rejoined the men at the table.

After finishing their snack, Paul got up to leave. Thanking Steve and Sara for their hospitality, he was soon in his car and on his way home. He smiled as he drove down the double-lane highway. Sara had given him some fudge to share with his family, and he was anxious to enjoy more of it when he reached his destination.

Steve closed the front door, turned to Sara and pulled her close. "I am so glad that's over. Let's head for bed. I could use a good night's sleep."

"Right with ya," Sara smiled. "I'll finish cleaning up the kitchen in the morning."

The two went quietly up the stairs. Noting that the lights were off in each of their kids' rooms, they too retired for the night. Steve fell asleep as soon as his head hit the pillow. There was a sense of relief after the board meeting. He would rest now, at least that night.

After sleeping for a few hours, Steve woke up abruptly to the sound of Samson barking downstairs. He looked at the clock and saw it was 2:31 a.m. It seemed strange to him that the sound didn't wake up Sara or the kids. Peter was the one who usually got up when Samson needed to go outside. Steve forced himself to sit up. Then, rubbing his eyes, he put on his slippers, pulled on his robe that was laying across the chair near the bed, and headed downstairs to let Samson out for a quick walk in the backyard. When he got down to the kitchen, Samson was waiting anxiously for him, wagging his tail.

"What's wrong, Buddy? Need to go outside?"

Samson barked. Steve opened the back door and then the screened-in porch door for Samson to exit. Samson went out quickly, but only went partway into the yard when he turned and barked.

"Go on now, Samson. I'll wait for you."

Samson barked again. He wanted Steve to follow him.

"What?" Steve asked. "Not now, you silly dog. I need to get some sleep. This isn't time to play."

Samson barked again. He began pacing the ground. Not knowing what to think and too tired to argue with his furry friend, Steve went back into the house, grabbed the flashlight from the kitchen floor near the door, and headed outside again. He wanted to see more clearly what Samson was barking about. Perhaps there was a cat up a tree or a rabbit hiding in the bushes. The air was cool outside, but it wasn't cold. As he reentered the yard, Steve realized Samson had disappeared.

"Come on, Samson. I told you this isn't time to play," Steve said wearily.

Just then, there was a stirring in the wooded area at the end of the parsonage property. Feeling a little uneasy, Steve turned to look, and was struck by what he saw. There standing among the trees was a huge man, at least nine feet tall, with shoulder-length brown hair and dark brown eyes. He was dressed in a flowing white robe with a gold belt around his waist. He was broad, muscular, and powerful-looking, yet his eyes were tender and loving. A bright light streaming down from heaven was shining on and through him. Steve was speechless, and he felt like he couldn't move. The man looked down at him and smiled. His smile felt like pure joy, and a gentle peace quickly came over Steve. There was no sense of fear. Unsure of what to say or do, Steve just stood there staring at the man. He was obviously an angel. Steve had never seen an angel before, but he did not doubt that he was encountering one.

The angel lifted his right hand and pointed at something he wanted Steve to see. Steve looked in the direction the angel was indicating and saw a squadron of heavenly beings standing around his house and yard, each holding a lantern with a flame of fire in it. Every direction he turned, there were angels. A verse from the book of Zachariah suddenly came to his mind. " '*And I myself will be a wall of fire around it,*' declares the LORD, '*and I will be its glory within.*' "[1] The angels were there for him to see for just a minute, and then they vanished. Steve turned back to look at the first angel again. He was still there smiling at him. But then, as suddenly as he appeared to Steve, he was gone. Steve found himself standing alone in the backyard stunned, full of wonder and thankfulness for what he had just witnessed. Just then, he felt Samson licking his right hand.

"There you are, Boy." Steve smiled. "Where'd you go? Did you see what I just saw?"

Samson just sat there with his soft brown eyes peering up at him, wagging his tail happily. Looking back over to the trees again, Steve hoped to catch another glimpse of his heavenly visitor. When the angel did not reappear, Steve turned and headed back to the house.

"Come on, Samson. Time to go back to bed."

Samson obediently followed Steve into the house. Closing the kitchen door securely behind him, Steve went over to the kitchen window and pushed back the curtains to look at the trees again. Seeing nothing more of the angel, he turned out the kitchen light, placed the flashlight back on the floor where it had been, and headed upstairs to his bedroom. When Steve made it back to bed, he found Sara still sound asleep. Steve climbed under the covers next to her but lay awake for a while, reliving the angelic encounter. What an incredible experience! Staring up at the ceiling, he thanked God for the glimpse into the supernatural and for the reminder that he and his family were being watched over. Then, rolling on his side, he was soon sound asleep.

The next morning, Steve got up feeling energized and encouraged. The memory of the supernatural visitation the night before was still fresh in his mind. He began to wonder whether the experience had been real or if it had been a dream or a vision. In any case, Steve recognized it as a message from God. He and his family had a myriad of angels looking after them as they worked through a very challenging situation.

As everyone hurried the next morning to get ready for the day, Steve decided to keep his heavenly encounter to himself until later that weekend. He wanted to share it with his family when they had more time to sit and talk about it. Peter had a game that evening and was focused on that, Mary had a deadline to meet for an article she had written for the school newspaper, and Sara was getting ready for a community craft show she signed up to take part in at the Methodist church a few blocks away.

"Well, you're looking chipper this morning, Steve," Sara observed as she sat down at the kitchen table.

"Yes, well, I had a good night's sleep," he responded.

"How'd things go last night, Daddy?" Mary asked cautiously.

"Actually, better than we expected," Steve replied. "But you never know about that group. We'll talk more about that this weekend. Just don't worry about it today, okay?"

"Okay, Daddy."

"Going to make it to the game tonight, Dad?" Peter asked expectantly.

"Your mom and I will both be there to cheer you and your team on."

"Great!" Peter responded as he speared another sausage from the meat plate.

Soon everyone was going their separate ways for the day. Steve spent some of the morning fielding questions again from concerned parishioners, but for the most part, the rumor mill seemed to be dying down. Mrs. Hellinger took the day off to go to the craft show at the Methodist church as well, so Steve was the only one in the main office. Some of the other church staff were in their workplaces in different parts of the building, but they were still keeping to themselves. Steve made it a point to go past their offices to say hello and give them an encouraging word concerning their work at the church before they left to go home that day. The only office he found himself avoiding was Pastor Randy's, which was right off the educational wing of the church and a good distance from the main office.

Oddly enough, the day went by with little problems, so Steve felt good about leaving the office early and joining his wife Sara at the pre-game events at the high school. The game itself that evening was exciting. The home team won with the final touchdown, and everyone from Nordstown left that evening happy and jubilant. Sara and Steve headed for the car as soon as the game was over to steal a little time at home with each other before their teens got back for the evening. Steve decided to share his angel experience with her when they were alone. After taking off their coats, Steve told Sara he had something special to tell her. He took her by the hand and led her over to the brick fireplace and invited her to sit on the floor with him. There, he relayed his encounter from the night before in as much detail as he could remember. Sara sat fascinated by what he was telling her.

"Oh my," Sara responded when he finished. "How awesome! I didn't hear Samson bark or even know you were outside last night. I must have really been out of it." Then she thought for a moment. "It had to have been real, Steve, and not a dream. What an amazing experience! I wish I had been outside with you."

"I wish you had been there too, Sara. The angel was so powerful looking. You could see his rippling muscles, but you could also feel a real tenderness when you looked into his soft brown eyes! I could feel the presence of God flowing through him. I knew he and the others were there to protect us."

Sara closed her eyes trying to imagine what Steve saw. What a comfort it was to know that God's hand, as always, was on her and her family.

"You should write this down, Steve, while it is fresh in your mind," she said, opening her eyes.

"Good idea. I'll do that before we go to bed."

Sara smiled. "If you hear Samson barking again tonight, please let me go this time."

"You got it, Babe."

They both laughed. The sound of their laughter brought Samson into the room. He had been napping in his bed in the family room and didn't realize anyone was home.

A couple of hours later, Peter and Mary arrived at the parsonage. When they settled in for the night, Steve decided to tell them about the angelic visitation the night before. They too sat transfixed as their father told them about his encounter with the angels.

"Can I camp outside tonight?" Peter teased. "Maybe I could have my video recorder with me."

"Don't you think it's a little cold to be sleeping outside tonight?" Sara asked.

"We could watch out the hall window tonight," Mary suggested. "You can get a great view of the yard from there."

"I know," said Steve. "We could also set up the video recorder in the yard near the trees and just let it run all night."

The family laughed at Steve's suggestion. After some more discussion on the angelic visitation, the family went to the kitchen for a midnight snack and then headed off to bed for another night of rest. Steve and Sara felt amazingly peaceful as they retired for the evening.

Steve woke up early the next morning feeling anxious, quite the opposite of how he felt the night before. He couldn't explain it, but there was a feeling of dread in the air. He tried not to say anything to his family. He didn't want them to be concerned. After breakfast, the phone rang. Sensing it was church business, he ran to his office to answer the phone. His instincts were right. It was Paul Samples.

"Steve," he said. "We've got trouble."

"What now?" Steve asked almost afraid to hear the answer.

"Got a call from Cheryl Petrie this morning. She's not going to stand by the statement she gave to our stenographer over the phone. In fact, she's retracting it all together. She told me someone called and threatened to go to her place of employment and her church congregation and cause her a whole lot of trouble. It was a male voice. He even threatened to tell her new boyfriend that she tried to proposition her former pastor and some other men in the church she used to work at."

"Oh no," Steve's heart sank. "That's low."

"It is," Paul agreed. "Steve, we've got nothing now. This is the same group we tangled with before. They will do just about anything to protect one of their own, right or wrong. They almost caused another good pastor to leave the ministry altogether."

Steve closed his eyes to pray for guidance. "What do we do now, Paul?"

"Wait it out and see what happens. Don't be surprised if they try to pressure you out. You got too close to exposing their dirty little secret. They're out for blood now. The district office had hoped this wouldn't happen again when they agreed to let you and your family go to Nordstown, but unfortunately, it has. Everyone thought Pastor Randy would take advantage of the second chance he had been given. It's hard to believe he risked everything again not long after the first scandal had settled down."

"I know . . . Thanks for all your help on this, Paul."

"No problem, Steve. Just remember, the district office is behind you. I don't want to sound defeatist at this point, but if things continue to escalate, we can try finding you another spot within the district if you feel you need to leave there. I remember what they did to the last senior pastor. As a matter of fact, if your board at Community attempts to push you out, they will have to go outside of the denomination to find a new pastor, because we surely won't supply them with another one not even temporarily."

"I appreciate knowing that, Paul. I will continue to be in prayer over this situation. Stay in touch."

"I will. And I will continue to be in prayer over this situation too," Paul responded.

After the conversation ended, Steve leaned back in his office chair and looked up to heaven for guidance. Then lowering his head and closing his eyes, he sat there quietly for what seemed like hours. Then he got up and went to the living room to talk with Sara. The kids were out on a walk with Samson, so he and his wife were alone again in the house. When Sara heard the news she put her arm around Steve and the two just sat quietly together on their sofa, each with their thoughts and prayers on the situation. Suddenly, Mary and Peter came bursting into the house with Samson. They were laughing and joking, and Samson was barking in excitement and running in circles around the living room.

"Well, it looks like you all had a good time," Sara tried to smile, moving her arm from around Steve.

"We played Frisbee in the park," Mary giggled. "Some of the other dogs that were there wanted to play too, so we had a regular competition going on for a while."

"We got to meet some of our other neighbors while we were there as well," Peter added as he removed his coat and put it on the hook in the hallway. Then the teens quickly realized something was wrong. Usually, their father was at the church on Saturday mornings, praying in the sanctuary or working on his sermon. Steve looked at them with a serious expression on his face.

"Sit down kids, I want to fill you in on something." Looking at each other, the two unquestioningly sat down in the two recliners across from the sofa. The room fell silent as Steve relayed his conversation with Paul to his children, leaving out the details he felt they didn't need to know. Samson, sensitive to the gravity of the conversation, settled himself down next to Steve's feet.

"This doesn't make any sense," Peter finally said when his father was finished.

"Evil doesn't make sense, Son," Steve responded. "We may be in for a rocky ride here for a little while, but we'll get through. I promise you that."

"Yes, we will," Sara added. "We are children of the living God and He will stand beside us the whole way! He showed us that the other night."

Mary and Peter felt encouraged and got up from their chairs to hug their parents. At that moment, deep pride welled up inside Steve and Sara's hearts. They were blessed. Their family lived and moved together as a strong unit. They would come out on top when the storm had passed. There was nothing to fear in that regard. Samson came over for a hug as well.

"Hey, Samson," Mary said as he nudged her for a hug. "We didn't put a new bandana on you today. Let's go get one."

Samson eagerly ran to his bandana drawer in the living room. Everyone laughed as he sorted through the collection to find just the right one for that day. Steve went to his home office to finish his sermon, and Sara, Peter, and Mary went over to the church to practice a new worship song they were going to present at Sunday's service along with the worship leader. They had been rehearsing together every evening at home for a couple of weeks and felt they were ready for their performance the next day.

The Sunday morning services went on as usual, but there was a certain coldness in the sanctuary that day. Even those who were warming up to Steve and his family again seemed miles away. There was a definite disconnect. A sinister presence was starkly in their midst. When Sara and her teenage children got up to sing and lead the congregation in a praise song, it was almost as if they were the only ones truly singing to God. Just a few, here and there in the pews, were engaged in the music. Steve's sermon comments on compromising Biblical principles to please others were met with frowns and shaking heads. A couple of people in the back even got up and walked out during one service when he started talking about how people can be deceived. What had happened to the congregation he thought he had? Where were their hearts? Didn't they realize that they would someday have to account for their actions?

That evening proved to be even worse. Mary and Peter came home from youth group vowing that they would never return. Mary was in tears. As they were coming down the basement stairs of the church to the fellowship hall that night, they overheard the youth leaders in the kitchen telling a few of the kids that Pastor Steve was trying to ruin Pastor Randy's life. They were both dumbfounded. These were people they had looked up to. As they entered the hall, some of the teens were friendly as usual, but during the meeting, Peter and Mary were met with icy stares from some of the other kids. In addition, the youth leaders did not ask them to play their guitars to help lead worship songs as they usually did. And when Peter went to the men's room during a break, one of the older teens who was just leaving, intentionally shoved him into the wall as he passed him.

"Oh, I'm sorry," the teen said sarcastically. "My fault. I didn't see you there." Peter glared at the other teenager, wanting to push him back, but decided it would cause more problems for his family, so he let it go. Peter, though, was starting to become angry inside. He should not be treated like this by other teenagers who were supposed to be Christians, especially those he worshipped with each Sunday morning. And his youth leaders should be setting a better example for others. They could start by keeping their divisive comments, based on gossip and personal opinions, to themselves.[2]

After hearing what happened that evening, Steve and Sara decided it would be best if their teens skipped the next youth meeting or so until things cooled down a bit. Perhaps they could visit a youth group at another church with some of their friends from school. Steve would have a talk with the youth leaders that week about what had happened. That kind of behavior had no place in the church, ever.

The next couple of weeks went from bad to worse. Sara was getting the cold shoulder from several of the women in the congregation and her attempts to talk with Carol Nelson were fruitless. She soon realized that it was best to continue to keep her distance from Carol for a while. Sadly, her friendship with Carol Nelson was gone as quickly as it had begun. This deeply grieved Sara.

Steve tried to help diffuse things and bring unity back into the church by calling a special meeting of the ministry staff, pointing out to them what was taking place within the fellowship, and emphasizing scripturally what was expected of them. It was important for them to be a light to others and not participate in the gossip mills or be guilty of intentionally hurting someone with a differing view on the situation at hand. Most of the members nodded in agreement with what he said, but in reality, his efforts to reason with them brought about very little change. Their allegiance to Pastor Randy, who no longer attended staff meetings, strongly influenced what they ultimately did or did not do to help foster peace and unity within the church congregation.

At the next regular board meeting, Steve again was taken aback. The group shockingly laid out a list of grievances they compiled concerning his recent performance at the church. They told him he wasn't doing enough visitations of people in the congregation, he was late for committee meetings, and that his financial reports indicated an excessive amount of expenditures. They also told him his sermons were dull, no longer inspirational, and people were complaining about them to the elders. Many, they said, were not wanting to hear about things they couldn't understand, like spiritual warfare, bondage, taking authority, and deliverance, and expected his sermons to relate more to their everyday lives. They wanted more humorous anecdotes and less of the serious stuff, better suited for seminary students.

"This is outrageous!" Steve said loudly, after listening to their trumped-up complaints and accusations. He stood to his feet and continued. "I have been a good pastor to this church, and you know it! How dare you accuse me of not doing my job! That's a lie! I know what this is really all about, Gentlemen. Before this thing with Pastor Randy happened, you were all singing your praises about everything my family and I did for Community Church. And now because I choose to stand for righteousness and holiness, this is what you give to me in return? For doing my job? You should be ashamed of yourselves. Everyone last one of you! You are cowards, and your disgraceful tactics tonight only amount to wickedness and sin, brothers, SIN! And to make things worse, you have opened this church up to the enemy, encouraging everyone in it to sin as well, all to cover up something that needs to be investigated and dealt with scripturally head-on! You have taken the Bible, the precious word of God, and stomped on it!"

Steve could tell what he was saying was affecting some of the board members, but the others, most of all Tom Black, sat stone-faced and still. Praying and trying to take control of himself, Steve took a deep breath and started lowering his voice.

"When I interviewed with you some months back, I specifically asked if there were any unresolved issues here, and you said, 'no.' Now you find yourselves in the same boat you were in a few years ago, and you want to blame me for this current scandal? If things had been handled correctly the last time this happened with Pastor Randy, I wouldn't have had to deal with this situation now. This could have been taken care of quietly and professionally, but NO, you had to pull the whole congregation in on it before we had a chance to sort things out!"

"You've been acting as if you're judge and jury of Pastor Randy," Tom Black barked back. "You want to ruin his life."

"I am trying to find the truth here, Tom! Don't you want that?"

Steve looked around the conference table.

"Don't you all want that? You seem to be afraid of what might be uncovered here. And obviously, at least one person here is afraid."

Tom Black shifted nervously in his chair. Steve took another deep breath and went on.

"Why are the women who talked with me suddenly afraid to talk now? I'll tell you why! Because they have been harassed into silence! And I am convinced more than one of you had something to do with that. How could you?"

"Those women changed their minds because they know they were lying," another board member spoke up. "They don't want the public to hear their wild accusations."

Steve stared angrily at the group, trying hard not to say something he would regret later. His stomach was churning inside, but he was not about to back down.

"Pastor Steve, why don't you just do us all a favor and resign?" Tom Black suggested sarcastically.

"And why would I do that?" Steve asked angrily, looking directly at Tom.

"I think this has gone far enough," a voice from the back of the room suddenly broke in. The group members grew quiet and turned to see Attorney Paul Samples at the door.

"Yes, gentlemen, I heard everything. And let me assure you, the superintendent of the district will hear what you said as well. Now, I would suggest that you adjourn at this time and go home to think about what transpired here tonight. You will accomplish no good thing this evening. I also strongly suggest that you dust off your Bibles and review the Scriptures as to what is expected of you, the leaders of the church. You are the ones who should seriously consider resigning, not your pastor. Some laws have been broken here gentlemen, and you are going to have to answer for that."

The room was now silent, and some of the elders dropped their heads. One by one, the members got up from the conference table and left the room, not willing to look Steve or Paul in the eyes as they exited.

Disgusted, Tom Black shoved his chair into the conference table as he left the meeting. Some of the other board members avoided him in the hallway as they headed for their cars. They were thinking about what Paul had just said to them.

When the last member left, Steve looked at Paul. "How'd you? . . ."

"I remembered that your regular board meeting was scheduled for tonight, and I just had a feeling I should be here with you."

Steve exhaled loudly. "Thanks, Paul," Steve managed to say. "Thank you, Lord," he said looking up.

"No problem. And I *will* be talking about this to the superintendent in the morning. Now, I have a few minutes before I have to get back on the road, do you think we could go over to the parsonage and see what Sara has in the cookie jar?"

Steve started to laugh. "I do think I remember her putting something in there yesterday. And I also believe there's some leftover pizza."

"Sounds good to me," Paul chuckled. "I'm starved."

Eager to leave, Steve collected his things and headed out of the conference room. He and Paul turned out the lights in the church as they went through the building and headed for the front door. They went over to the parsonage and were soon enjoying a snack in the kitchen with Sara. Paul left shortly afterward to go home.

The next day, Paul Samples reported to the district superintendent what had taken place at Community Church. Remembering what happened to the previous pastor, the two began to discuss where they might be able to move Steve and his family if things got worse. Perhaps there might be a district position they could consider placing Steve in, at least temporarily.

As the weeks went by, the pushback from certain influential members of the congregation; came in many forms, and became worse for Steve and Sara and their children. It was particularly hard for Sara whenever she encountered Randy's wife, Carol, at the church. Carol had made it very clear to Sara one day that she was no longer welcome to be a member of the Hospitality Committee. Carol and the other committee members had unanimously decided that the situation with Pastor Randy was reason enough to force her off the committee. This hurt Sara deeply. It was so unfair and unChristlike of them to make that decision, yet it was one she decided not to fight. Sara so wanted to connect with Carol again and even tried to reason with her, but it was to no avail. Their friendship was over, and so was her friendship with some of the other women in the church.

Steve and his family had some allies among the members of Community Church, but those who worked against them seemed to outnumber those who were for them. At times, members from the two camps clashed, dividing the congregation even more. Though the best attempts were made to keep peace and encourage unity among the church members, it was hard for Steve and his family, particularly during the holiday season. The church Thanksgiving dinner, though, offered a bit of a reprieve for them. It was celebrated as usual on the Tuesday evening before the actual holiday. Even though attendance was down significantly from years past, most everyone who came was cordial and even friendly to the Hansons. Some disgruntled members also came but made it clear that they weren't happy to be there. Steve wondered why they even bothered to show up. Somehow, they all made it through the evening, and most of the people told him they had a good time once things got going. The Hansons were thankful for a mostly positive evening.

The next day, Steve sat in his home office and picked up a book on God's calling. While skimming through it, he was reminded of how dissenters came against Moses and his brother, Aaron. He also thought about Jesus and how His own people rejected Him. Then, he thought of the Apostles and the early church and what they had all endured for the Kingdom of God. Steve knew that one had to "count the cost"[3] when going into ministry. It would always have its spiritual challenges.

Steve then began to reminisce about how he and Sara were taken out to eat, given gifts and encouraged to come to Community Church when they were being interviewed by the board. He also thought of the warm welcome they received when they first pulled into the church parking lot there in Nordstown. It was a joyous occasion. Yet, he knew from the very beginning, it would not be an easy ride. He questioned himself as to whether he had adequately prepared his children for this fierce spiritual attack. *Perhaps I should have told them more about what could happen. Maybe?* . . . No, he would not go there. This is where they were now, this is what he would deal with.

In spite of what Paul Samples had said to the board at Community, during the next board meeting a couple of weeks later, Steve was informed that there would be a significant reduction in his salary. The board told him that giving was down because of the controversy. Steve began to worry about how he would make ends meet. He thought he left that worry behind in Ohio. Perhaps Sara could work part-time. *Yes, she would do it, but was it worth it?* She might have to give up some of her time at the nursing homes. That was her first ministry, and she needed to be able to fulfill her commitment to them. Steve found out later from Mrs. Hellinger that members of the board and ministry staff had encouraged many people in the congregation to intentionally withhold their tithes so that the financial reports would show a decline in giving. Such an evil plot, designed to starve the pastor and his family out of the church and Nordstown, was having a successful impact on its intended targets.

The last straw came when Steve received an anonymous letter in the mail, telling him and his family to leave town or suffer more consequences. As a result, Steve found himself feeling lower than he ever had before in his life. It was a chilling place to be. He knew God loved him and that he had a pastoral calling on his life, but at this point, he wasn't even sure he wanted to be a pastor anymore. He never thought he would feel that way after all his years in ministry, but he just couldn't stand by and see his family hurt or harassed another day. Steve was tired of hearing Sara and Mary cry themselves to sleep at night because of being rejected by former friends. He was especially concerned when he heard his son punch the wall in his bedroom out of frustration after coming home from a church function. He knew Peter was being bullied by some of the other teens and that he was standing down from retaliation out of respect for his family. This had happened on several occasions. Steve feared that Peter would soon resort to physical violence toward those taunting him if he did not take his son away from the church soon. Peter was only going to turn his cheek for so long. He did not want to see him end up in jail. Weakened by the relentless pressure, Steve began to pray for release from his assignment at Community Church.

Finally, one Saturday morning, when no one was around, feeling extremely depressed, Steve went to his church office to be alone with God. He pulled the blinds and closed the office door, thinking he had locked it behind him. When he sat down on his black leather chair, all of the pain, bitterness, and discouragement from within him started to gush out. He could not hold it back any longer. He had had enough. With his head down on the desk, he began sobbing like a child praying for an answer, praying for relief. He cried so hard that his lungs and stomach began to ache. He had given all he could to this church. He just was not able to give any more. Nor was his family.

As Steve was pouring out his heart to God, suddenly he heard a soft voice come from the doorway.

"Pastor Steve?" It was his neighbor and church member, Bob Brown.

Steve stopped crying, and trying to pull himself together, he lifted his head from his desk. He looked up at Bob, who now too had tears streaming from his face. Steve tried to speak, but couldn't.

"Pastor Steve," Bob choked. "I'm so sorry. I didn't realize how the situation with Pastor Randy was affecting you. I've had enough too. I want to ask for your forgiveness."

Nervously wiping his face with a handkerchief he pulled from his pants pocket, Steve felt a calm moving over him. Forgiveness found its way into Steve's heart. His old friend was back. The test of fire had proven the friendship stronger than either realized and the healing power of God brought restoration. Steve stood up from his chair and walked over to Bob. The two hugged each other for a few moments and then patted each other on the back, wiping their eyes as they pulled away. From that time forward, Bob became one of Steve's best and closest friends. Bob and Lucie would always be there for Steve and Sara and their family. They would prove to be two of their staunchest allies in the years to come when the Hansons faced other challenges and spiritual battles in ministry.

When Steve left the church later that morning, he knew in his heart that God had answered him. He and his family had been released to go on to another assignment. They had completed what they had been sent to do at Community Church. Someone else would be sent later to Community Church to help take it where it needed to be.

Steve felt alive again as he walked home to share the decision with Sara and the kids. There was a spring in his step once again. And as he entered the church parking lot, light snow began to fall softly on him. He looked up at the sky and smiled. The new year was not far away, and it would bring fresh and wonderful things for him and his family. Next week, though, was Christmas, and he planned to enjoy it. Not even the controversy at the church could ruin that.

Chapter 8

Forgiving and Moving on to a New Call

*C*hristmas day at the Hanson house brought a much-needed celebration. The midnight candlelight service the evening before was
beautiful and well attended by the members of Community Church.
Many people from their Nordstown neighborhood came to the service
as well. Even those who had worked against Pastor Steve came in with
smiles on their faces, as if nothing had happened. Several supporters
brought gift baskets for him and his family. Steve graciously accepted
them and the Christmas check he was given by the congregation. His
monetary gift, collected by Bob and Lucie Brown, was somewhat
meager compared to what Community had collected for their pastor
in the past, but it was still a nice-sized check. It saddened Steve to know
that those who staunchly supported Pastor Randy did not contribute to
the fund this year. Not that he cared about the amount he received. He
was thankful for anything. It was the reason why they didn't give that
concerned him. They were spiritually blind to the matter concerning
Randy — believing and supporting a terrible lie.

The Hansons sat around a brightly decorated Norway Spruce that
Christmas morning, opening their presents, talking and laughing
together as they always had in the past. Samson sat happily in the corner
of the living room, chomping on his new chew bone and wagging his
tail contentedly. He was wearing a special red and white Christmas bandana that Mary had made especially for him. When all of the presents

were opened, Mary and Peter picked up the torn paper left on the floor and put it in large plastic garbage bags to be taken out to the trash. Sara headed for the kitchen to get lunch ready and tend to last-minute details for their company who would be arriving later that afternoon. Steve's parents were on the way from New York State to spend the holiday with them. His brother Mike and wife, Marcie, who lived in a neighboring city in New York, were driving in the car behind them. The four travelers would spend a few days with the Hansons before going to Kentucky where they would be spending New Year's Eve with Marcie's family. While there was some snow on the ground that morning, the sun was shining brightly and the highways were clear. It was a perfect day for traveling.

At 3:00 p.m., there was a knock on the front door. Mary and Peter jumped up from their chairs in the family room and raced toward to answer it. Mary was the first one there.

"It's Grandma and Grandpa!" she squealed with delight, looking through the glass in the front door and jumping up and down with excitement.

Peter arrived slightly after her and teasingly pushed her aside, so he could be the one to open the door. On the porch stood Marianne and Joseph Hanson, an attractive couple in their mid-sixties. They were loaded down with presents, both big and small, all wrapped in colorful Christmas paper. Behind them was Steve's older brother, Mike, who looked a lot like him and was also a pastor. He too was carrying a variety of packages. His wife, Marcie, was just closing the back passenger door of their Ford SUV. She pushed back her long blonde hair and grabbed several Christmas gift boxes she had temporarily placed on top of the car. All of the travelers were dressed warmly, with heavy coats, hoods, and earmuffs, and had big smiles on their faces. They were anxious to be with Steve and Mary and the kids this holiday season. Steve had been filling them in on what was going on at Community Church. They also knew of his decision to leave Nordstown.

Peter quickly opened the front door of the parsonage. "Come in, come in," he and Mary said, almost in unison. Steve and Mary were not far behind their teens, and soon, everyone was greeting, kissing, and hugging each other. Samson came running into the room and jumped around the visitors in excitement. After hanging up the coats, everyone headed to the living room to find a comfortable place to sit. The fireplace, with stockings hung for everyone, was blazing brightly, and it wasn't long before hot chocolate and hot cider were being poured and served to anyone who wanted one or the other. Steve and Sara were so thankful for this special blessing of being with family. It was the best gift they had received that day. As everyone chatted and got caught up on family news, Samson went from person to person, trying to find someone who would invite him to sit next to them and rub his ears. Finally, he settled next to Steve's father who was always willing to pay attention to him. The room was filled with laughter as more presents were opened in the Hanson house.

Christmas dinner that evening was a true banquet. It included appetizers, soup, turkey, ham, and lamb, assorted vegetables and casseroles, fresh-baked bread and rolls, and lots of desserts. Marianne and Marcie brought some of their specialties adding to the already complete menu prepared by Sara and Mary, and even Steve and Peter. Red and white Christmas candles burned brightly sitting on the green tablecloth on the dining room table. Pine branches and holly leaves with berries decorated the room, and throughout the rest of the house, while sweet-smelling potpourri filled the air. Steve and Peter had put the extra boards on the dining room table the day before to accommodate the extra people at the table. Christmas music by the Gaithers[1] played softly in the background. Steve's father, a church deacon, said the prayer, and everyone ate until they could eat no more, chatting continuously throughout the five-course meal. Samson had his Christmas supper in the kitchen, where he found fresh turkey hotdogs in his bowl.

After dinner, everyone pitched in to clean up the dining room and the kitchen. Then, the group headed back to the living room to share

Christmas memories of the past. Steve's father read the first Christmas story from the book of Luke.[2] Then they all went over to the piano, where Sara led them in several Christmas hymns. It was a real old-fashioned Christmas, and it was also a healing time for the souls of four wounded Hanson family members. There was true peace that day, even amid the strife Steve and his family had endured within their church fellowship.

The next day, the sun shined brightly again on the town of Nordstown. Fresh light snow had fallen overnight, making the world around the Hanson home bright and cheery. After breakfast, Mary and Peter went to the family room to watch one of their new movie videos. Samson decided to go with them. The adults sat around the kitchen table to talk and enjoy a fresh pot of Christmas coffee. As they talked, the subject of Steve's decision to leave Community Church was brought up.

"Steve," Michael said. "Did you ever think about starting your own church?"

"There were times when I first became a pastor . . . But right now, Mike, I'm feeling like I need a complete break from ministry for a while," Steve replied, reaching for his coffee cup.

"I know you've had a bad experience here, Steve, one you didn't deserve, but I'm feeling that God has something more for you . . . actually, something in this very county."

"I don't think the district ..."

"I'm not talking district, Steve. I'm talking about you and your family. And maybe some of the people who still stand behind you."

"Start a church plant? How would we live? I would need another job."

"Well, it just so happens that I may have found a job for you." Steve put down his coffee mug to listen to what his brother was about to say. "Harold Cannon, an old friend of mine from college, lives in Anderson Hills. That's just the next town over from you. Anyway, I bumped into him at an interdenominational prayer conference I attended three weeks ago. He was there with a group from his church. And by what I consider a divine appointment, we had a chance to talk together over lunch. I hope you don't mind. I told him a little about your situation here, not going into a lot of detail, of course, and he said he would be interested in talking with you about working for him for a while. That could be your income while you start your new church."

Steve looked doubtful. "I don't know, Mike. I will have to pray over that one. I don't even know if we should stay in this area. The prospect of a job, though, would be worth considering. We could move to Anderson Hills. Even though it's just the next town over, that would put a little distance between us and Community Church."

Steve turned and looked at Sara. She was listening intently and shrugged her shoulders at him, indicating that it might be an opportunity worth considering. Steve took that as a cue to keep talking about it.

"What kind of business does your friend own?" Steve asked, a little curious now of the prospect.

"I believe they make difficult-to-find car parts. You know, for old or foreign cars. He says he needs someone to help manage some of the smaller accounts. His business is growing right now too, so the work would be steady. Maybe even some commission checks for the new accounts."

Then turning to Sara, Mike said, "And he also needs a part-time receptionist."

Steve was starting to see the possibilities, and looking at his wife again, he said, "I think this is something we need to look into, Hon. And Anderson Hills is part of the Tri-community school district. The kids wouldn't have to change schools."

"Yes, I agree," Sara returned, beginning to feel hopeful about their future again. "I don't like the idea of uprooting them from their school and their friends right now. They have been so supportive of Peter and Mary through all of this."

"I guess that means we're going to check out Anderson Hills."

"Yes," she nodded. "I believe that makes the most sense right now. Let's see if it's the door God wants to open for us."

Turning to his brother, Steve said, "Why don't you tell your friend that Sara and I would be interested in interviewing with him. We, of course, will be praying about the prospect, but I feel safe in saying that we would like to at least talk with him. Thanks for looking out for us, Mike."

"No problem, Bro," Mike said, patting his brother on the back. "You are much too good of a pastor to give up. What you need is a change of scenery to get that old fire going again."

"Your dad and I will be praying as well," Marianne broke in. "This opportunity couldn't have come at a better time for you and Sara and the kids."

"Indeed," Joe Hanson said, smiling as he wiped his mouth with his napkin. "I'm familiar with your neighboring town, and I know the people there are very warm and hospitable. It's worth talking with Mike's friend. I'm feeling that God is in this, Son."

Steve nodded at his father and smiled widely. In response, his father patted him on the back to encourage him even more.

"I'm so glad you are going to check out Anderson Hills," Marcie happily chimed in. "Mike and I have been praying for a new situation for the four of you for weeks now. It broke our hearts to see all of you hurt so, but God can make all things new again for you."

"I know," Steve nodded in agreement. "We really appreciate those prayers and your love and concern for us."

"Yes, we do," Sara added. "We love you all so much," she said, trying to hold back the tears forming in her eyes. Marianne, who was sitting next to Sara, put her arm around her daughter-in-law. Sara turned and smiled at her, wiping her eyes before the tears became too evident.

A fresh excitement began to well up inside of Steve. This could be God's answer for them. While he felt a release from Community Church, he was not feeling a release from the area. It was decided that Mike would call his friend that afternoon and arrange a time for Steve and Sara to meet with Harold after New Year's. When Peter and Mary were told about the possibility of a new start in Anderson Hills, they immediately agreed it was a good choice. They loved the idea of being in a new town but remaining in the same school district. That was the best news ever. They could graduate with their friends!

The rest of the family visit was a source of strength for Steve, Sara and their children. During the visit, the family group went on short trips in the area, ate out at various restaurants, and spent a good bit of time in prayer together. But all too quickly, the stay was over, and everyone was kissing and hugging each other and saying their goodbyes. Soon, the four travelers were on their way to Kentucky in their small motorcade. Mike had spoken with his friend in Anderson Hills, and a time was set for Steve and Sara to meet with him the second week of January. The couple began to pray over the interview.

One night after dinner, Steve decided to go outside to look at the stars. The temperature was unseasonably warm, so he just slipped on a light jacket. As he began to think on the vastness of God, his thoughts turned to the recent conversation with his brother. At that moment, he sensed that God still had plans for him and his family in that area. His children especially would benefit from being there. He knew, without a doubt, that he and his family would be moving to Anderson Hills. He also felt that a new church ministry was in store for them. One, for some reason, that needed to be built quickly. Steve also realized that to be effective in that new ministry, he had to forgive all those who had hurt him and his family at Community Church. No baggage could be taken to the new fellowship. This was something the whole family needed to do together.

The following evening, Steve called a family meeting in the living room. He talked with them about the move and what God had shown him about their next ministry assignment. He also talked about the need to forgive the people at Community Church who had wounded them. Sara reached for Steve's hand as she relived in her mind the cruelty they all had endured for the sake of truth. Yes, forgiveness was necessary, no matter how hard it was to do. After an hour and a half of discussion, the family of four knelt on the floor together, holding hands, and prayed for Pastor Randy, Carol, their boys, and the people at Community Church who had misguidedly followed a shameful lie. They prayed for truth to be exposed, justice to be served, sins to be confessed, and lives and relationships to be restored. They also prayed that God would help them completely forgive what had just happened to them and for them to be able to move on without hindrance to their next ministry assignment. Tears flowed freely as each one took their turn praying out loud. When the family finished, the room was filled with a feeling of supernatural peace. Samson, who had been lying quietly next to them, nuzzled next to Steve as if to say, all was complete, and it was time to move on.

The next couple of weeks went speedily by, and soon Steve and Sara were on their way to an interview in Anderson Hills. Peter and Mary stayed home to do their homework while their parents went out for the evening. The couple was scheduled to meet at Harold Cannon's office that evening at 5:30 p.m. When they arrived, wearing their Sunday best, Harold and his wife Francine were there waiting for them at the front door of the company building. After some brief introductions, Steve and Sara were soon ushered into a parked Mercedes, and the four were on their way to *Alexander's Cuisine Restaurant* at the edge of town. As Steve and Sara enjoyed their meal of Monterey Chicken and fresh locally grown vegetables, they talked openly with Harold and his wife, and soon felt like they had made new and caring friends.

After the evening ended, Steve and Sara left extremely hopeful. Both parties would take a couple of days to think and pray about the possibility of the Hansons working at the business, and then Harold would be back in contact with Steve and Sara. Later that evening, when they arrived back in Nordstown, Steve and Sara went to the church to pray over the job possibility. As they prayed together in the silence of the large sanctuary, like they had done so many times before, the two began to feel the presence of the Holy Spirit. And in the stillness of the night, they each heard the same message. "You are my pioneers. It is time for new territory close by. I have already gone ahead of you and provided for all your needs." A warmth came over both of them, and they knew it was time to move in a new direction.

When the phone call came from Harold indicating his interest in Steve and Sara becoming employees of *Cannon Parts*, Steve was overjoyed. Without hesitation, he told Harold that he and Sara felt strongly they were to accept the positions and would be ready to start at the beginning of March. They wanted to give Community Church plenty of time to arrange for a short-term pastor; however, Steve knew the district office would never allow their supply pastors to go to Community Church during the time they would be looking for a replacement. The church would have to reach out to another denomination or to a seminary or Bible college to find an interim and eventually a new senior pastor.

After the phone call from Anderson Hills, Steve decided to let the district office know about his decision. He spoke first with Dr. Schaffner and then with Paul Samples. Both, at first, tried to convince Steve to allow them to try to place him in another church in the district, but after talking with him more, and realizing that he was following the will of God, they promised to help support his decision in any way they could. They also confirmed that they would not be willing to place someone from the district in Community Church for any length of time. They would tell the Board at Community that they would have to get by with the staff they currently had or look to another source for a lead pastor. Until some things changed at Community, the district was going to step back from their situation. In addition, they told Steve that Paul Samples would be present at Community the following week at their annual congregational meeting after Steve told them he was planning to turn in his resignation that night. Before the conversation ended, Dr. Schaffner and Paul Samples prayed for Steve and his family and the new ministry that lay ahead.

The next morning, Steve called Mrs. Hellinger into his office at the church. She came in with pad and pencil, thinking he was going to dictate a letter. When she sat down in the chair in front of his desk, she saw a look on his face she hadn't seen for quite a while. The tension was gone. It was a look of relief. Mrs. Hellinger knew something was up when he got up and closed his office door.

"Margaret, I have something to share with you. It's something you need to keep to yourself until after next Thursday."

"You're leaving us, aren't you, Steve?"

"Uh, yes," he said, looking surprised. "Sara and I have new jobs in Anderson Hills . . . secular jobs. However, God has shown us that He has something more in store for us there, a church plant. We're taking the first step right now by leaving here and moving to Anderson Hills."

"So close to Community?"

"Yes, I strongly feel that we are still needed in this part of the county. And moving to Anderson Hills will put a little distance between us and Nordstown but still give the kids the chance to stay in the same school district with their friends."

"Steve, this is incredible. I had a dream just the other night that you and Sara and the kids were packing up and going to a new place. You all looked so happy. I didn't know it would be so close, but I knew it was from God."

Receiving this confirmation on the decision to leave his pastorate in Nordstown made Steve smile.

"Margaret, I am going to give my letter of resignation during the annual congregational meeting next week."

"Not to the board first?"

"No, I feel it more appropriate to give it to the church congregation as a whole. I believe they all need to know exactly why we are leaving. If the board gets the letter first, they may try to interfere with what I need to say . . . This is my chance to set the record straight before I leave, and I'm not going to hold anything back."

Mrs. Hellinger nodded in agreement, lifting her brows as she grinned.

"So, where exactly will you be working, Steve?"

"Sara and I have accepted positions at *Cannon Parts*. I will be working in accounts, and Sara will be a part-time receptionist."

"Oh yes, I am familiar with that company. They do quite well for being located in such a small town."

"They must do a lot of advertising," Steve suggested.

"I hate to see you and your family leave Community. It should never have come to this, Steve."

"I know. But it is for the best. God has something new for us, so it's time to move on. Now, what I would like you to do is let the board know I am going to be making a special announcement at the congregational meeting next Thursday evening, and I would like it added to the agenda." . . . "Last on the agenda," he added.

Mrs. Hellinger giggled. "You got it, Boss. This is a meeting I would not miss for anything in the world. And don't worry, my lips are sealed." She pretended to turn an invisible key to her lips and got up from her chair to contact the head of the board, Tom Black.

"Thanks, Margaret. I knew I could count on you."

"This is going to be fun," she laughed, as she left the room, closing the door behind her. He could hear her laughing even as she ran to answer the main office phone.

Grabbing a writing pad off his desk, Steve quickly jotted down some notes for his resignation speech. He knew what he said that coming Thursday had to have a lasting impact on those who would be there. His words had to be chosen carefully, but they must also speak the truth. When he was satisfied he had included everything he wanted to cover, he laid his pen down and said a quick prayer. Then rubbing his hands together to get them warmed up, he began typing on his computer. As he did, the words began to flow.

On Thursday evening, the church sanctuary was unusually crowded. Those who only seemed to show up for holidays, like Christmas and Easter, or didn't normally take part in congregational meetings, were there among the other congregants. Everyone was talking, anxious to hear what was going to be said that night. Paul Samples, from the district office, showed up early with a tape recorder in his briefcase. With Steve's permission, he was going to tape Steve's presentation and take it back for the district superintendent to hear. As expected, all of the board members were present. It would prove to be an interesting meeting.

Sara, Mary, and Peter found their places in the front row of pews next to Steve. They had been briefed on what Steve was going to say and were all silently praying over his presentation. The board members were seated in the first row across the aisle from them, to the right. Pastor Randy and his wife Carol sat behind the Board, and the other members of the church ministry staff were scattered throughout the sanctuary, sitting with their families. When the meeting was called to order, Paul Samples was introduced as a visitor from the district office. He sat in the row behind Pastor Steve and his family. Everyone clapped, not realizing what his real mission was for being there that evening.

The congregation moved swiftly through the items on the agenda as Tom Black, the head of the board, presided over the meeting. Issues that were up for a vote, passed easily. Finally, the last thing left on the agenda was Pastor Steve's presentation. When it was time for him to speak, he turned to receive Paul Samples' tape recorder, then walked quietly up the steps to the podium. Tom Black took his seat in the front row. He was visibly agitated but remained silent. He did not like not knowing what Steve was about to say to the assembly.

After reaching the podium, Steve adjusted the microphone, turned on Paul's recorder, cleared his throat, and began to address the crowd.

"Before we wrap up tonight, I want to thank all of you for being here. It was good to be among you this evening. I have a few words I need to say before we adjourn our meeting."

Steve paused for a moment. Nervous inside and praying for strength, he continued.

"As most of you know, a little over a year ago, my wife Sara and I were invited to come here to Nordstown, so I could interview for the senior pastorate at this church. When we came that day, we were impressed with the friendliness and the eagerness for us to come. During the interview process, I specifically asked the question, as I always do when I interview, if there were any unresolved issues in this church. In other words, were there any problems I should know about that have not been taken care of? I was assured there were none and that I was in a good position to start leading the church with no hindrances. After much prayer, consideration, and confirmation from God, we, as a family, agreed to come. Upon our arrival, we were greeted with lots of fanfare and loving kindness as we got settled in our new home. It was amazing how many of you turned out to help us. We will never forget that day. What a blessing!

"In just a short time, my ministry efforts at Community Church were being applauded, and you embraced me and my family as your own. The ministry team and I had an immediate connection, and we began working enthusiastically together on many ministry projects for the church and the local community. I was also making valuable connections with other churches and ministries in the area. Things couldn't have been better. And for those weeks of harmony, I will always be grateful.

"However, several weeks after our arrival, I was made aware of a situation that had allegedly taken place long before I came . . . one you were not aware of. The disturbing allegations made that day, strongly connected with a situation you were aware of, made the new accusations even more alarming. So, as overseer of this congregation, I was obligated at that point–legally, morally, and Biblically–to investigate the new charges. You all know what I am talking about, so I won't waste your time laying them out to you tonight. As I pursued the matter, I was met with great opposition. Biblical truths and rules and policies of the church and the district were ignored and even compromised. What should have been a private matter, handled discreetly by the board, your appointed leaders, turned into a major church controversy.

"To make things worse, some people, who wanted to have their voices heard, were silenced by questionable means. In addition, my family and I suffered numerous abuses from many in this very room tonight, simply because I chose not to bend to pressure and abstain from my quest to find the truth. For those guilty of such acts, I need to say that you have caused us much pain and grief, all of which we did not deserve, and you were not justified in afflicting on us. I also want you to know, I sincerely tried to be fair and not judge another member of this ministry staff until I heard from him and everyone else connected with the situation. But I was not given a chance to complete my investigation. The district office tried to intervene, and they were shut down as well. To top it off, the accused ministry leader refused to answer many of our questions, using legal means to interfere with proper church due process.

"As a man who has given his life to pastoral ministry, I am astounded by the unChristlike behavior exhibited in the last few months by many of you in the audience. While some of you may feel that you have won, you must remember that God sees all, and He will deal with anyone who does not repent and turn from this sin. God is the final judge, and you will have to answer to Him for any wrongdoing. In Luke 8: 17, our Lord told us very clearly, 'For there is nothing hidden that will not be disclosed, and nothing concealed that will not be known or brought out into the open.' "[3]

Steve could see that a number of people were starting to become uneasy, including some of the board members, but no one interrupted. He had everyone's full attention as he continued with his comments. Even Pastor Randy was sitting quietly in his seat, his wife, Carol, holding on to his hand tightly.

"A couple of weeks ago, Sara and I were offered jobs in Anderson Hills — secular jobs, if you will. And after some prayer, the Lord has shown us that our call to Community Church is coming to an end, and we are to take the jobs in Anderson. Therefore, effective March 1, 1998, I am resigning from my position of senior pastor of Community Church."

Surprise immediately fell on many people's faces. Some of them began looking at each other and at those who had been causing problems in the church. Some smiles came to the faces of those who opposed Pastor Steve, but quickly faded when they realized others were watching them. Steve waited a few seconds and then continued.

"I realize, of course, that not everyone here was part of that attack on me and my family, so I'd like to take this opportunity to thank, from the bottom of my heart, all those who stood with us throughout this ordeal, especially for your love. We will always remember your willingness to stand for what is right. . . . In regard to many others in this room, and you know who you are, I would like to say that my family and I choose to forgive you. However, I cannot in good conscience continue as senior pastor here at Community Church, knowing that you remain spiritually blind and unrepentant. I pray the next pastor will be treated more fairly and with dignity and respect. So, at this time then, I am submitting my formal letter of resignation to Deacon Tom Black, president of the board, whom I'm sure will not hesitate to accept the document for the congregation. Thank you for listening. And thank you again for coming tonight. Deacon Black will dismiss you in just a few moments."

At that, Steve turned off the tape recorder, gathered it and his notes and resignation, and left the podium. Walking down the steps and heading to the front row, where the board members were seated, he handed his signed resignation to Tom Black. The room was completely silent as he gave it to Tom. Deacon Black was now in the spotlight, and Pastor Steve had just subtly implicated him as the ring leader of all the trouble that had been caused. There were some slight grins among a few who welcomed his leaving, but no one said anything. Steve turned and walked over to Paul. He handed Paul the recorder, then went to Sara and offered his arm, which she quickly took, and the two walked down the aisle to the back of the sanctuary with Peter and Mary following close behind. Those in the assembly were quiet and remained seated in the pews, many still stunned. The four Hansons grabbed the coats they had purposefully placed at the back of the sanctuary before the congregational meeting and walked out the front door of the church, closing it behind them. Then they headed across the parking lot to the parsonage with no intention of coming back for the refreshments afterward.

The room remained deathly silent after the Hansons left. Deacon Black nervously got up and ascended the steps to the podium. He awkwardly thanked everyone for coming and then dismissed the crowd. Bothered by what had just taken place, many in the congregation left at that time as well. Pastor Randy and his wife decided it would be best if they left too and exited the side door of the sanctuary as inconspicuously as they could. As they reached the parking lot, Carol stopped by her open car door and looked over at the parsonage for a few seconds before climbing into the vehicle to go home. She was disturbed by what Steve said.

Steve and Sara were our friends. We trusted them. Why is this happening again? Is there something I'm not seeing? she thought to herself.

Randy tried to reassure his wife that everything was going to be alright as he pulled out of the lot, but Carol remained troubled as they drove away.

Paul Samples put his tape recorder in his briefcase and got up to leave like the others, but not before going over to Tom Black. Looking him straight in the eyes, he said, "I hope you're satisfied, Deacon. The district superintendent will have my report on his desk in the morning. . . And don't be surprised if you get a phone call from him in the next couple of days." With that, he left the building and joined the Hansons over at the parsonage. Bob and Lucie Brown were not far behind him.

Mrs. Hellinger wanted to follow Steve and his family out of the building as well, but she and her husband Frank were overseeing the refreshments afterward. So, they headed straight down to the basement where the other helpers were waiting for them. Margaret was proud of her pastor and knew they would have a chance to talk at the office the next day. Things were about to change in a big way at Community Church, and she prayed it would be for the good of everyone.

Paul Samples stayed at the Hansons for over an hour before he headed for home. He and Steve had become good friends, and he wanted to make sure Steve and Sara were doing okay after the presentation. Paul congratulated Steve on his speech and told the couple he would be including the recording and typed transcript of it with his report to the district superintendent the next day. The board of

Community Church would soon be receiving a registered letter and phone call from him.

The following day, Steve was greeted with a cheery good morning from Mrs. Hellinger as he entered the main office. She had certainly proven to be a strong supporter of him and his family, and he was especially grateful for her presence in the church office that morning.

"Could I have a moment with you in your office, Pastor Steve?" she asked. "Terri is answering the phone this morning."

"Certainly, Mrs. Hellinger. Come right in."

Steve hung his coat on the hook on the office wall, and then sat down at his desk. Mrs. Hellinger walked in with two mugs of hot cocoa and set one of them in front of him.

"That was a good speech you made last night Steve. Quite a few were talking about it at the reception. Some of the people didn't realize how nasty some things had gotten for you and Sara and the kids."

"Well, I'm glad it's over Margaret. In some ways, I hate to leave, but we can't go on as we have here."

"You know, Steve, I have been thinking about what you said about a church plant, and last night as I was praying, I felt the Lord telling me that you are to start a new church in this area. He also told me that you need to do it quickly."

Steve was taken aback by her statement.

"Steve, Frank, and I want to help. We talked about it this morning."

"But I'm not sure how fast …"

"Steve, you are being called to start a new church plant, and I believe the time to get involved is now. Frank and I want to help make it happen."

"But your job here. They won't let you stay if you go with …"

Mrs. Hellinger broke in. "I haven't had a chance to tell you yet, but Frank's doctor has just given him the all-clear to go back to work. No more disability checks. That last laser surgery he had did the trick. He not only can go back to work, but he found a new job at a company where he can work as many hours as he wants. What I am saying is, we can get by on just Frank's income. Our youngest is going away to college soon on a full sports scholarship, so it will just be the two of us. This way I can easily come and help you out with a new church."

"That would be wonderful Margaret, but we wouldn't be able to pay you for a while. That would still be a sacrifice for you two. We don't even have a congregation yet."

"Oh, you don't have to worry about us, Steve. Frank will be making more money than he ever did in the past, more than enough to make up for my income. And we still have most of the settlement money Frank received for his back injury at work. To top it off, our daughters, already in college, found some new work-study money, so the pressure is off there as well. Besides, I don't want to work for this church anymore. I've had enough too."

"Well, I guess all I can say is, when can you start?"

"Is tomorrow too soon?" she teased.

They both laughed, and Mrs. Hellinger got up to go back to her desk.

"Thanks, Steve. I just know it's going to be wonderful for you, Sara and the kids in Anderson Hills."

"No, thank *you*, Mrs. Hellinger . . . for everything." Steve sat back in his chair and thanked God for the new turn of events.

The next day, Bob Brown and his wife, Lucie, stopped by the church office to see Steve. They also felt prompted by God to encourage him to start a new church. And they, too, offered to help.

"I feel the Lord wants you to start this new church quickly," Bob told him. "Whatever we can do to assist you, just let us know. We're following you to Anderson Hills."

Before the week was over, two other couples came and told Steve that he was to build a new congregation. They also emphasized the fact that he was to do it quickly. Feeling the call was being overwhelmingly confirmed, Steve moved ahead with his tiny church plant, pulling together a committee comprised of those who had come to encourage him to start a new church.

Initially, when the members of the area ministerial association heard about a new church being planned, Steve was met with some opposition from some of the pastors. They didn't feel another church was needed, but after they saw Steve was determined to move forward with his decision, most of them just decided to sit back and see what happened. There were still a couple of naysayers, but Steve knew in his heart that God would soon prove them wrong.

In the weeks that followed, Steve and Sara began to prepare for their new life in the next town by looking for a place to live. They also met with their small church plant group each week. Paul Samples joined them on occasion. He offered his services free of charge to take care of all the legal aspects of starting the church. Soon, those things were in order and Anderson Hills Church Fellowship was born. They were a real organization now.

After many discussions and researching the possibilities of a place to hold worship services, the church plant group decided to hold their services in a Christian school on the far north side of Anderson Hills, putting a few more miles between them and Community Church. They were offered the first six months' rent for free, so they had some time to start building their congregation. The building was more than adequate for their needs, and the school board was excited about having Sunday renters. The anticipated future income would be a huge benefit to the school. Services would be conducted in the new gymnasium. The tiny church would be able to use the school's sound system, and several of the classrooms would be made available to the new congregation for Sunday School classes, whenever they were ready for them. Soon, the group began to pass out flyers on the new church plant to get the word out. The school helped get that information circulated as well. Mrs. Hellinger also did what she could from her home, until an actual office could be set up for her someplace else.

Even though they searched diligently, the Hansons had not yet found a home in Anderson Hills. Hearing about their plight, a contractor friend of Harold Cannon graciously offered to rent the Hansons a remodeled older house he owned in Anderson Hills. He would let them have it for just the cost of the property taxes on it each month for the first year, to help them get on their feet again. They would settle on a regular rental price the following year. Steve and Sara were amazed at God's wonderful provision for them and readily accepted his offer. As the time came close for the Hansons to move, they all grew anxious. The family was feeling a renewed pioneer spirit and were ready for the chance to help start something new from the ground up.

Despite all that had transpired, a group of people from Community Church and some of the local churches and ministries got together and planned a farewell party for the Hansons, even though they weren't going that far away. While many of the dissenters did not attend, it turned into a real-time of healing for those who did come. There were some tears and a few apologies, but most of all, for the Hansons, it was leaving a congregation knowing that their ministry efforts there were not in vain. God would bring forth some fruit. Maybe they couldn't see it now, but someday...

Moving day was much like it had been in Ohio the summer before. However, a U-haul and some pickup trucks were used instead of a large moving van. The Hansons filled their Jeep Cherokee with just a few boxes this time because their new home, a four-bedroom English Tudor, was just a little over twenty minutes away. No long trip this time. As the family started climbing into the SUV, Steve felt moved to go to the backyard once more.

"I'll be right back," Steve said, closing the driver's side door of the vehicle.

Walking around the house, Steve stopped and stood in front of the grove of trees where the angel had appeared to him. He wondered if he would see that angel again. Pausing for a couple of minutes, and thanking God for the new congregation, he turned and headed back to the car. Samson was already pushing his way to the backside window, so he could look out as the family pulled out of the driveway. So much lay ahead for this family. It was another adventure that would have a huge impact on all of them.

The Hansons began to sing some praise songs as they traveled through Nordstown. The familiar sites of the town, where they had just spent several months of their lives, would now only be revisited whenever necessary. That evening, they would have dinner in their new home in Anderson Hills with some of the new parishioners, and a new pioneer adventure would begin for them again.

Side Note...

A year after the Hansons left Community Church, Pastor Randy Nelson also left and became the assistant pastor of a larger church in another city in Pennsylvania, three and a half hours away from Nordstown. This church was with another denomination. They had accepted Randy's references from Community's board, a previous seminary professor, and his background check, which did not show anything, since no charges were ever filed against him. There was no need in their minds for recommendations from the district office. The only thing they needed from them was a confirmation that he was licensed through their denomination. Pastor Randy had decided, that with the past controversy still alive in his current church, he and his family would benefit from a new start. At least that is what his wife, Carol, and two sons believed they were getting.

However, after just a few months at his new church, Pastor Randy was accused of having an extramarital affair with a church employee, and this time, he was not able to cover it up. The woman he was having an affair with was the music ministry director. Without the strong support of a congregation and board that could be manipulated, he was forced to confess to the allegation. Shortly afterward, his girlfriend confessed as well. His marriage to Carol quickly ended in a divorce, his new denomination revoked his credentials, and the district office, after finding out, revoked his credentials with them as well. Randy and his girlfriend then moved to the state of Washington (leaving his children in the sole custody of their mother) where they married and started a dried foods company together. The couple split a couple of years later when Randy was caught in another adulterous affair with a female employee at their place of business.

Sadly, the board of Community Church, as a whole, never apologized for their retaliatory actions against Steve and his family. Some of the members even rebuffed Steve and Sara's attempts to help restore relationships with them. In addition, several more families left Community Church when they found out what happened to Pastor Randy and joined other congregations in the area. They finally realized that their board had not protected them from a ministry leader who was out of bounds and out of control, and they had lost more than one righteous pastor because of the board's actions to cover up Pastor Randy's sin. As the years went by, some other church leaders at Community, and another church in Nordstown, were also exposed for similar offenses. Most of those individuals were forced to leave their church congregations. One ended up in prison.

Sometime after the Hansons heard about Pastor Randy, Sara received an unexpected greeting card in the mail from Carol Nelson. On the front of the card, was a picture of two little girls playing dress-up together with a trunk full of old-fashioned clothes next to them. Inside the card, it simply said, "I will never forget you," and was signed, "Carol." The envelope was postmarked "Cleveland, Ohio" but did not include a return address. Carol had moved to that area after the divorce to start a new life with her sons, away from the gossip and rumors of her last church.

Sara stared at the card for a long time, and her eyes welled up in tears. She understood that it took a lot of courage for Carol to send it to her. Maybe someday they would talk and become friends again. Sara decided to try to find out Carol's new address but would wait until the Holy Spirit told her when the time was right to send something in return. Sara closed her eyes and, lifting the card towards heaven, prayed for Carol and her two children, asking God to watch over them. She also prayed that Randy would someday fully realize what he had done and seek the Lord's help to be set free from the spiritual bondage that had controlled his life and hurt so many people, ultimately destroying a myriad of relationships and the pastoral ministry to which he had once been called.

Chapter 9

A Time of Growth and Blessing

$\int$teve looked out over his new congregation from the portable lectern that stood on the stage of the gymnasium of Immanuel Christian School. It was now six weeks since services started there, and already, the tiny congregation of Anderson Hills Church Fellowship was setting up more folding chairs for new visitors. Harold Cannon and his wife Francine decided to join the new church plant as well. Steve thanked God for this new church ministry, now inching up to nearly fifty regular attenders. His face was bright that morning with the joy of the Lord as he delivered the day's message on the Body of Christ. Various people in the audience smiled, nodded, and shouted "Amen!" as he progressed through his sermon, which included a personal story. When he finished, everyone clapped, and Sara went up on stage to lead the congregation in a couple of hymns on her electric keyboard. The ushers collected the offering, and then Steve pronounced a short blessing on the group and dismissed them to go to the school cafeteria to enjoy a covered-dish meal together.

Steve and Sara stopped at the gymnasium doors to talk and shake hands with the congregants as they left the service. The group began to work their way down the main hallway of the school to where the cafeteria was located. It pleased Steve and Sara to see so many remain after church for the meal. This was true fellowship, and Steve felt a fresh zeal for ministry again. There was so much he wanted to see this little congregation do for the Kingdom of God. The newly formed church board at Anderson Hills wanted to see great things accomplished as well and strongly supported Steve's ministry efforts.

In just a few minutes, everyone reached the cafeteria and found their places at dozens of white paper-covered tables. As the members stood quietly behind their chairs, Steve led them in a prayer of thanks for the meal, and then everyone headed to form a line at the food tables, allowing the older people to go first. Mrs. Hellinger was in her element that day, supervising everything that was going on in the kitchen. Bob and Lucie Brown helped get the food that was still being brought in by other members ready for the food tables. Frank Hellinger and a couple of other teenagers supervised those tables out in the main room, removing empty serving bowls and replacing them with filled ones. Peter and Mary went around the tables where people were eating to see if anyone needed more coffee, tea, or milk for their children.

After the meal, the church group lingered in the cafeteria for a couple of hours, enjoying the fellowship and the delicious homemade desserts. Some of the children went back to the gym to play basketball and badminton, while their parents and grandparents talked. Sara and Steve went from table to table to visit with people and thank them for being a part of this church family gathering. Around 2:30 p.m., the group began to break up and go their separate ways, after picking up their freshly washed serving dishes in the kitchen. Several people stayed behind to help clean up the cafeteria and kitchen, so they would be ready for the staff and students the next day. Steve, Sara, and the Hellingers locked up after everyone left.

Later that afternoon, when they were back home, Steve and Sara decided to take a walk around the neighborhood before supper. It was a pleasant day, and the sun was shining. Mary and Peter were spending time with their friends from school, so it was a perfect opportunity for the couple to go off by themselves. Pulling on their spring jackets, they looked down at Samson, who was standing by the front door, waiting for them to attach his leash. His sad pleading eyes made them feel guilty. He didn't like being left behind. Samson was always ready to go on an excursion with any family member willing to take him along. It was his break from the house and a chance to see things he had never seen before.

"Okay, Samson," Steve said as he took Samson's leash from the hook on the wall and attached it to his collar. "I guess it's too nice of a day for any of us to stay inside."

Happily, Samson led Steve and Sara out the front door and down the porch steps to the sidewalk. Starting down the street, the Hansons waved at a church member who honked as he drove by in his utility truck. It felt good to be part of a church family again.

"I'm so glad we came here, Steve," Sara said as they walked.

Sara was hanging on tightly to Samson's leash as they strolled along the sidewalk. He was energetically pulling her, happy to be out with them and eager to explore the neighborhood again.

"Yes, it's certainly a welcome change," Steve responded as he looked at the houses along the way.

The Hansons' English Tudor was located in a neighborhood where the homes had been built in the 1950s. A number of the houses had originally been owned by some of the wealthier people in town at that time. However, many of them and their families had long since moved on to larger houses in other parts of Anderson Hills and even Nordstown, leaving their older homes for middle-class owners to purchase.

"I had an interesting dream last night, Sara," Steve said suddenly.

"Oh?" Sara responded as she looked at the houses on the street.

"Yes, I dreamt that we were having a groundbreaking ceremony for the church. We had a huge party when the building was complete."

"Really?" Sara turned to him, anxious to hear more.

"I don't think we are quite ready for that yet, but I believe God has plans for us to have our own church building at some point."

"Oh, wouldn't that be wonderful? That would be such an awesome blessing to the congregation! Let's post that on our prayer board and pray over it tonight," Sara suggested.

"It's already there," he chuckled. "I put it there this morning before we left for church. I also wrote Dad and Mike and asked them and Mom and Marcie to pray over it."

Sara smiled at Steve. He moved over to put his arm around her waist as they continued on their walk with Samson still leading the way. After they had gone several blocks and reached the downtown area, they decided to stop at a local old-fashioned drugstore to buy ice cream cones. Checking to make sure he had his wallet with him, Steve went inside to get the cones while Sara and Samson waited for him outside. They had been so busy talking with people at the church meal, they both neglected to have any dessert. Samson suspected Steve had a special purpose for going into the store and waited expectantly for his reappearance.

After a few minutes, Steve emerged from the drug store with two Rocky Road ice cream cones in one hand and a small Styrofoam bowl of vanilla ice cream in the other. Samson sat panting and wagging his tail as the dish was placed on the ground in front of him. Steve and Sara sat down on the wide cement steps of the store to eat their cones and watch the traffic go by. Feeling revitalized after their snack, the three were soon on their way exploring more of the town. When they returned home a couple of hours later, Steve and Sara decided to watch a movie and eat frozen dinners together in front of the TV. Samson went off to take a nap in his bed in the corner of the room. They all relaxed in the family room until Mary and Peter came home later that evening from their friends' houses.

The Hansons were quickly adjusting to and becoming known in their new Anderson Hills community. Even though they were only in the next town, it seemed so far away from Nordstown. The teens were glad to continue in their same high school and often invited other youth their age to visit their new church. Peter was given a spot on the high school wrestling team that spring, and Mary was invited to be on the school newspaper editorial staff because of the exceptional reporting stories she was submitting. It was then that she met Josh Franklin, a tall, slender, dark-haired, basketball star who also loved to write journalistic articles. Like Peter, he was finishing up his junior year. It was not long before the two teens were spending more time together. At first, it was working on the school paper, but soon they found other reasons to be together.

Sara, once again, found a nursing home that welcomed her ministry. Willow Place was located just blocks from the Hansons' home. Sara decided to let some women from Community Church take over the nursing home ministry she had in Nordstown. That helped make a cleaner break there. She only worked as a receptionist for Harold Cannon's company on Monday, Wednesday, and Friday from 9:00 a.m. to 2:00 p.m., so she had ample time to spend at the home during the rest of the week. The home also had assisted living apartments. Interested in her ministry, they asked her to do a regular Bible study for their clients two evenings a week.

Sara often took flowers to the home as she did in Ohio and Nordstown. Many were from her own gardens once the weather was warm. As a result of her visits, she became friends with Lisa Wright, the head nurse at Willow Place. Lisa was a widow in her mid-thirties. She lost her husband, Matt, in a military accident a couple of years earlier. The helicopter he and several other soldiers were in malfunctioned and crashed during summer maneuvers. The couple had no children, but at one time, had hoped to adopt a child or two from an Asian country. The two women soon found they had a lot in common and looked forward to Sara's visits at the home each week.

Sara invited Lisa to come to Anderson Hills on a few occasions, but Lisa declined the offers, finally admitting that she stayed away from churches for years because of some bad experiences she, her parents, and siblings, had had some years ago. Lisa felt the church was full of hypocrites, and, rather than opening herself up to being hurt again, she was better off just watching Christian TV at home. When Matt was alive, Lisa would only go to church with him on special holidays and occasions. He went by himself most of the time when he was home, but they made sure they studied the Bible together every night. She was living in another state at the time she lost him to the accident. Sara didn't push the issue but prayed for an opportunity to share her own recent church experience with Lisa. She was eager to tell how God provided a way to move her and her family on to a new and healthier congregation. Perhaps Lisa would realize that not all churches were alike and that a new church fellowship experience would be good for her as well. As time went on, Sara noticed that Lisa would stop and listen in on some of her Bible study sessions at the nursing home. This was encouraging to Sara, and she started to believe that maybe someday Lisa would change her mind and give Anderson Hills Church Fellowship a try. She thought Lisa would connect with the ministry they had there.

Steve was pleased with the growing interest among those in the church fellowship to participate in the various ministries being started. Someone was always stepping up to lead them. He was also excited about making some good connections in the small Anderson Hills community. He was getting to know people at the local hospital and the relief shelters and was being asked to speak at various clubs and associations in the area. Some of the local charities were also taking an interest in Anderson Hills and reached out to them for assistance. Anderson Hills Fellowship Church was making a significant impact in the county.

One day, another kind of opportunity was presented to Steve that would help the ministry of Anderson Hills. As Steve was working in his home office, the doorbell rang. Steve got up to answer the front door. It was Harold Cannon. He was now a member of the church board. While Steve worked on small accounts for Harold's business, he did a lot of that work from home, so he could be available for church business.

"Well, good morning, Harold!" Steve greeted cheerily. "Come on in."

"Good morning, Steve," Harold responded with a grin as he walked into the house. "Got a few minutes?"

"Sure," Steve replied ushering Harold into his office. "So, what can I do for you today?"

"Well, actually, I came to share a new possibility for the church. I wanted to get your opinion on it."

"Great! Tell me about it," Steve said as he took his seat behind his desk. Harold in turn sat down in the chair in front of him.

"A friend of mine, John Perkins, started an organization called *Expanding the Kingdom* (ETK) several years back, and after talking with him today, I thought it might be something we should become a member of. It isn't a denomination. It's more of a network of churches that share similar or compatible visions and missions. They have memberships all over the world and offer all kinds of services that are helpful to church plants like ours. Their membership fee is based on the number of people in a congregation. So, for us right now, that would just be a few hundred dollars a year."

"Sounds interesting."

"Yes. And they also have conferences each year for pastors and other church leaders. I was invited to go to one next month. I'd like to go to see what they're like. I'm taking Francine with me. She loves that kind of thing."

"I would be very interested in going to some conferences."

"I thought you would," Harold smiled. "Here is their website, Steve. There are lots of endorsements on it. Some people's names I think you would recognize."

"Well, let's take a look at it right now."

"Ok. I've got a few minutes."

Steve turned to his computer keyboard and typed the web address he had just been given into the search bar. An inviting and brightly-colored website for *Expanding the Kingdom* came up. Steve read the mission statement of the organization out loud and began going through the site as Harold looked on.

"You're right. They have some great endorsements," Steve said.

"Yes, they do. So what do you think?"

"I think I would like to talk with your friend on the phone. I have a few questions."

"Sounds fair. I just happen to have his phone number with me. He'll be in his office after two this afternoon," Harold said, handing Steve the man's business card.

"I thought you would," Steve grinned. "I'll give him a call this afternoon."

"Super! I look forward to hearing back from you on this."

Harold got up to leave. "Well, I better get back to the office. You know how it is over there this time of day."

"Yes, that's why I like to do much of my work at home. It saves a lot of time."

"You're doing a good job, Steve. Not just for me . . . the church, especially. We truly appreciate you and your family."

"Thanks, Harold. We are really happy we came here."

Spying some of Sara's fresh-baked oatmeal apple raisin cookies on the end table near the computer, Harold asked. "Ya mind if I take a couple for the road?"

"Help yourself," Steve chuckled. "They're really good."

"Thanks." Harold picked two of the larger cookies. Taking a bite of one of them as he was leaving, he said goodbye to Steve and headed to the front door of the parsonage. In just a few seconds, he was back.

"Perhaps I should take one more for later," he said with a boyish grin, reaching for another cookie from the plate.

Steve laughed. Grabbing a third cookie, Harold winked, turned and left the house to go back to his office several blocks away. Steve returned to his computer and began downloading the application form for *Expanding the Kingdom*. He wanted to look it over before calling John Perkins after lunch.

That afternoon, Steve was able to talk with John. They spoke for close to an hour. Steve wanted to make sure he understood what he might be getting his church into. John assured him his church would maintain its autonomy and that belonging to *Expanding the Kingdom* was just belonging to a ministry network and support system. They would not be submitting to a governing body. Pleased with what he heard from

John and read on the website, Steve called Harold at his office and told him he felt the membership possibility should be brought up at the next board meeting. Just to be on the safe side, Steve later called some pastor friends of his who were knowledgeable about other organizations. When he received the green light from them, he began to feel at peace about joining. He and Sara also prayed for clear discernment on the opportunity. Steve knew the members of the church board would be praying as well when they saw the proposal on the board agenda. The following week, the Board unanimously voted to join *Expanding the Kingdom,* perceiving it would give the church more credibility and praying the services the organization provided would help grow the congregation and expand their outreach programs.

Like the ministry at Anderson Hills, Sara's ministry outreach at the nursing home continued to grow. More doors opened for her there, including being asked to plan and direct a Christmas play on the birth of Christ. She also got to know Lisa a little better, and they became good friends. It was nice to have another woman to talk and share things with again . . . someone she could trust. The two would sometimes meet for coffee or go shopping together at the local stores or the mall just outside of town. Slowly over time, Sara began to see a change in Lisa's attitude towards church fellowship. At one point, Lisa opened up and told Sara about her church experience, where she and her family were deeply wounded by the leadership of their congregation. Her family had, at one time, been very active in their local church. Her father was even an elder. Understanding Lisa's pain, Sara shared what her family endured at Nordstown. When Lisa heard Sara's story, she began to have a change of heart, especially upon hearing the family had started a church plant so close to the church they had left. She realized it was time to let go of the past.

"I guess I need to forgive what happened, don't I, Sara?" she said one day. "That's what Jesus died for, isn't it? To forgive and restore. Matt tried to tell me that lots of times."

Sara nodded, knowing her friend was on the way to forgiving the past and trusting a church community again. That Sunday, Sara was not surprised when Lisa came and sat down in the back of the gym at Anderson Hills Church Fellowship during the worship music. It would not be long before Lisa became a regular attender. Several weeks later, she began co-leading the Senior Adults Bible Study. As time went on, she was even more active in the church. Lisa also became a dear and loyal friend, and a blessing to the Hanson family.

Steve and Sara were excited and thankful for Lisa's turnaround. It was an incredible feeling of joy to see someone find their way back to church fellowship.

It was even more thrilling for them when someone found Christ for the very first time, particularly one who had been trapped in a culture of deep spiritual darkness, with no seeming way of escape, at least from human eyes.

One evening, when Steve and Sara were watching the news in the living room, there was a knock at the front door. Steve got up to see who it was. Samson followed him. Steve opened the door to a tall, dark-haired man in his early twenties dressed all in black. The man's long duster coat was open, showing his jeans and T-shirt. His face was white and expressionless. Steve was hesitant when he saw the man. The young man reminded him of one of the three people he and Sara had seen standing across Community Church in Nordstown one night, a long time ago.

"Are you the pastor?" the man asked nervously?

"I am," Steve replied cautiously. "Pastor Steve Hanson."

"Could I talk with you?"

Sensing the man was not there to cause any harm, Steve replied, "Yes, of course. Please, come in."

The man quickly looked around outside and then entered the Hanson home. Samson watched quietly next to Steve as the man stepped into the house, and though he was uneasy about this strange visitor, he did not growl or bark. Sara, too, was a little nervous when she saw the young man enter the foyer of their home.

"I'm going to meet with this young man in my office for a little while, Sara."

Sara nodded and called Samson over to her. Then she turned off the television and began to pray. Steve directed the young man to his office at the end of the hall. The man was unusually quiet as they went. When the two were seated in the room, the young man reached into his duster and pulled out a tract on the life of Jesus. He tossed it on Steve's desk and asked,

"Is it true, Pastor?"

Steve reached for the crumpled booklet. Immediately recognizing it as one he had used in the past for street ministry, he answered, "Yes, it is."

"Then I want Jesus," the man replied, finally looking Steve in the eyes.

Sensing the kind of life the man was wanting to leave, Steve asked, "Are you ready to give your whole life to Him? To turn your back on satan and the powers of darkness?"

"I am," the man began to cry softly. "I don't want to serve them anymore. I hate that life."

"What's your name, son?"

"David."

"Is there a last name?"

"Just David."

"Ok, David. Let's pray. I can feel the presence of God in the room, and He's telling me you are ready."

David nodded.

Steve thanked the Lord for bringing David to him, and then led the young man in the Sinner's Prayer, renouncing satan and the life the young man had grown up in. As Steve led him, David asked the Lord Jesus to cleanse him with His blood, set him free from spiritual slavery, and for the Holy Spirit to come and live in him permanently. Then Steve told David how much God loved him and that he had been made in God's image. He was meant to live and serve Him only. Steve also told the young man that God had a plan and a purpose for his life. God would be with David forever, and He would never leave or forsake him. The Holy Spirit would equip him with spiritual gifts to do ministry and to help him fight against the attacks of the enemy. When Steve finished talking, there was a new look about David. It was a look of pure joy and serenity, and the young man began to smile. Color had come to his face, perhaps for the first time in years.

"Thank you, Pastor. I've been in torment for so long . . . I've always sensed that God was there, reaching out to me. I was just afraid to reach back. I didn't understand who He really was until I read that tract. I can hardly believe it, but I feel completely free right now. I've never experienced that in my entire life."

David sat back in his chair and was quiet for a while, smiling and taking in what had just happened to him. Then instinctively, he lifted his eyes and hands toward heaven. He had just experienced victory over the darkness. Steve prayed silently as the man worshipped his creator. Finally, David lowered his eyes, looked at Steve, and spoke again.

"You know, Pastor Hanson, I can't go home now, not even to pick up my things."

Steve looked at him with some alarm.

"If my family even senses the change in me, they'll kill me. Or have me killed, by someone in the coven . . . They will do that with no sense of guilt whatsoever."

Realizing the serious ramifications of David's decision, Steve asked, "Where will you go?"

"I don't know . . . I just have a few dollars on me. And the clothes on my back."

Steve asked God for wisdom. He sensed an urgency to help this young man leave the area as soon as possible. Then an idea came to him.

"I know of a place," Steve told the young man. "It's in Bakersfield, New York. It's a ministry focused on people in your situation. They can help you start a new life. They'll give you food and lodging, help you find a job, and train you in the Word of God. Their doors are always open to new residents with a sincere heart for God. Would you be willing to go there, if I paid for the bus ticket? I can give you some extra money for meals, too."

David looked surprised by the offer but eagerly accepted it. There was no other option.

"I'll be right back," Steve told him.

Steve got up and went into the storage room. He came back a couple of minutes later with a brochure on the ministry he had just told David about and some money. The money, from the church emergency out-reach cashbox, was enough to cover the cost of the bus trip, plus food along the way. He handed them to David.

"Thank you," David said, astonished by Steve's help. "I can't believe this is happening."

"You serve a great God now, David. He always provides. His power is mightier than anything you have ever seen or known before."

David nodded. "I know. I can feel it," he said. "I have so much to learn about Him."

"I can take you to the bus station if you want," Steve offered.

"I'm afraid that won't be possible, Pastor," David replied, getting up from his chair. "It would not be good for us to be seen together. It's possible that I'm being watched right now."

"Yes, of course. I understand."

"I need to go," David said suddenly, nervous again. "It's not safe."

"Do you know where the bus station is?"

"Yes, I've been there before. It's not that far from here."

"The Lord and His angels will be with you, my new brother."

David smiled and got up to leave.

"Wait! I have something else for you," Steve said quickly.

Steve pulled a new Bible off his shelf and handed it to David. David took it and slipped it into the inside pocket of his duster. Steve then handed David a handful of Sara's cookies that were laying on a tray near his desk and a bottle of water and led him to the front door.

"Go with God," Steve said, hugging him. "I'll give the ministry in New York a call after you leave to let them know you are on the way."

With his eyes full of tears, David nodded and hugged Steve back, then hurriedly left the house, disappearing into the night.

After he left, Steve went back to his office to call Bakersfield. When he finished talking with the chaplain at the ministry there, he went to the living room and told Sara what had taken place. The two knelt next to the coffee table and, with Samson laying close by, prayed that David would make it safely to his destination. They prayed he would be able to start his new life in Christ without fear. They hoped they would see him again someday. It would be such an honor to know how God had worked in his life. Perhaps, his family would find Christ as well.

For the next three years, the church congregation at Anderson Hills grew steadily. By then, they had 325 members and were still meeting in the Christian school gymnasium. Peter had graduated from high school and was attending classes at the local community college. He worked part-time for *Tom's Pizzeria* delivering pizzas, and to save money, he decided to live at home until after he graduated with his associate's degree in human services. He wanted to become a social worker but wasn't sure yet where he wanted to get his bachelor's degree.

Mary was still working on the high school newspaper and developing a stronger relationship with Joshua Franklin. He occasionally came to services with Mary at Anderson Hills. Steve and Sara liked Joshua and trusted him, but were concerned that Mary's relationship with him could become serious too soon. When Joshua left for college in another state to start a degree in journalism, they were at first relieved. But the young couple was soon talking online and were often together when Joshua was home for the holidays or the weekend. Distance did not seem to make a difference for them. Steve and Sara were thankful that Joshua was going to a well-known Christian college, but they still watched the pair closely, especially since Mary was still a minor and a senior in high school. They wanted to make sure the two stayed focused on their individual life goals. College degrees were important to their futures.

Since going to Anderson Hills, Steve was finding time to relax and enjoy watching the stars again. He kept his telescope set up in his office, next to the French doors that led to the back yard, and would take it outside on the deck on clear evenings. One night in particular, when he was looking up at the stars, he was reminded of his dream about building a new church facility. He and Sara had been praying over that dream for more than three years. The slip of paper Steve had written his dream on was still securely tacked to the bulletin board where it had originally been placed. As he looked up to the heavens, he felt the presence of God and began to realize that it was finally time to broach the topic of a new building to the board of Anderson Hills. When he went inside, he made sure the agenda for the upcoming meeting included a discussion item indicating a special project he wanted to discuss with the Board. He didn't want to be specific until that evening.

At the next board meeting, Steve finally got his chance to share the dream God had given him about a new building. The group, now consisting of eight members, including his friend Bob Brown, was a huge change from the board at Community Church. They were respectful, supportive, and a joy to work and pray with. Steve could feel the Spirit's presence when it came time for him to share about a possible building project. When he stood to speak, he was holding the piece of paper he had removed from the bulletin board at home that afternoon. The date of the dream was handwritten at the bottom of the paper.

"As you all know," Steve began, "our congregation has been growing steadily. I am full-time now. Mrs. Hellinger, our office manager, as well as our music ministry director, youth leader, and maintenance personnel are all on the payroll. We're holding our own and our building fund is up to $151,000 thanks to a very generous donor from a nearby community. I think it's time to start talking about a building of our own."

The group perked up at the notion of having their own building. It was something many of them had thought about at one time or another but were waiting for someone else to bring it up at a board meeting. Steve briefly told the group about his dream from a few years before and showed them the slip of paper he had written it down on. He passed the paper around the room, so everyone could see it. He also told them that he and Sara had been praying over the slip of paper ever since he had the dream. Then, he told the board that God had recently let him know it was time to start talking about a church building project. Each member smiled as he or she read the piece of paper when it came to them.

"What did you have in mind, Steve?" Harold Cannon asked curiously.

"Well, I think we should look at all the possibilities out there. We could buy a property and build on it. I'm thinking at least a few acres. *Expanding the Kingdom* has affiliate organizations that donate building materials to churches like ours. That could save us a lot of money."

The members of the board, which included six men and two women, looked around the room at one another. They were soon nodding and talking excitedly about the possibility of the church having its own facility.

"Or," Steve went on, "we could find an existing building and renovate. Either way, we have a lot of skilled people within our congregation who could help us, also saving us a *lot* of money. Of course, we will also have to start a capital campaign to raise the money we need to pay for the remainder of the cost."

"I could look into interest rates and closing costs for a bank loan," Angela Camp, a newer board member and the assistant branch manager of a local bank, eagerly offered.

"That's another possibility," Steve replied, seeing the energy in the room pick up. "If the board is open, I would like to suggest we move ahead with investigating our options for getting a church facility."

"I agree," Bob Brown put in. "I'm sensing that it's time as well, and from the reaction of everyone here this evening, it looks like we're all feeling the same way. I move that we start investigating the possibility of having our own building."

"I second the motion," Jerry Simpson, another board member, added right away.

"All in favor?" Harold Cannon asked.

In unison, the whole group said "Aye." Then smiling and laughing, they divided up into small groups to investigate the different building options. Steve was elated. Something wonderful was about to happen.

After a couple of months of research, the church board decided on a building plan and presented it to the congregation. An overwhelming majority of the members voted to pass the proposal. The church was able to purchase ten acres of land from a local farmer looking for some retirement money and willing to sell the land at well below market price. The parcel of land was partly wooded, with a large creek running at the back of the property. Shortly after that purchase, a capital campaign was launched. Money was gathered quickly, and a bank loan for the balance was secured at a local bank.

The church board found a Christian company through *Expanding the Kingdom* that built the foundation and basic structure of the church, finishing the outside, along with doing the plumbing, electrical, windows, and outside doors, leaving the rest of the work inside to the congregants to finish themselves or hire out. Supplies were donated from people and organizations the church never even knew existed. Finding out about the building project, a local company even offered to donate most of the gravel for the parking lot. The congregation was off to a good start. God was at work.

The architecture of the building was simple yet attractive. The structure consisted of a sanctuary and fellowship hall with a kitchen and church offices. Several classrooms and the restrooms were located in the back of the building. The structure also had a full basement, where some additional rooms were built out. There were plans to add on to the main building later, but this would be sufficient for now.

For several months, various crews had come to the church property and worked tirelessly on the new building. Steve was amazed at how fast the structure went up. Everyone in the congregation pitched in to help in some way. When everything was completed, the building was ready to be dedicated. Steve and the members of the board anointed all of the rooms and entrances of the building the night before there was to be a huge celebration. The following day, people from both the church and the Anderson Hills community flocked into the new building to attend the first service which included a building dedication ceremony.

Steve and Sara's families came from out of state for the special event. Steve's brother, Mike, gave the sermon that day and his father did the closing prayer. When the service ended, everyone headed to the fellowship hall in the church basement for a covered dish meal. Reporters were among the crowd from the local newspaper, radio, and television stations. They interviewed Steve and the members of the church board after the service and took pictures and footage of the new facility. The dream Steve had almost five years before was now a reality.

After the celebration, the board at Anderson Hills began to discuss and research other ways to grow the church ministry since they now had their building. In addition to Sunday services, they had numerous Sunday School classes and community outreach programs. Youth group and Bible studies were available for various age groups on different days of the week. Almost every evening, there were cars in the church parking lot. One of the board members suggested that the group seriously consider evangelistic outreach to the local community and to parts of the world where the Gospel message needed to be shared. Steve thought that was a logical area of ministry to add to their current programs and remembered that *Expanding the Kingdom* had an affiliate organization called *Hearts on Fire* listed on their website that specialized in evangelistic outreach ministry. Since Anderson Hills was not connected with a denomination at that time, ETK was the logical place to start. Steve told the group he would contact that organization to see what type of mission programs they had and how they could be involved. He also said he would see if someone from that office could come to their next meeting or talk with them via conference call, so they could all ask questions. Everyone agreed and looked forward to hearing about Steve's findings.

After revisiting the ETK website for information on the evangelistic organization, Steve decided to call the *Hearts on Fire Evangelistic Ministries* office. Their program seemed to be exactly what the Board was looking for. When the receptionist answered the phone, she immediately connected Steve with Pastor Adam Daugherty, who answered with a hearty greeting. Adam was elated to receive Steve's call. He was overwhelmingly friendly and eager to come to Anderson Hills to talk with Steve and his board about partnering in some way with his organization's ministry. Adam had been an evangelist in the United States and Canada for a number of years, spending a brief period in some Asian countries, and currently oversaw the *Hearts on Fire's* church evangelistic partner program. He had just been with them for a little over a year and had been praying for more church connections. He saw it as an answered prayer when Steve contacted him that day.

While talking with Adam on the phone, Steve decided to invite him to come to the next board meeting. Pastor Daugherty checked his schedule and confirmed his availability for the night of the meeting. Coming from the Pittsburgh area, about three hours away, he would need a place to spend the night. Steve quickly offered him the spare bedroom at the Hanson home in hopes it would give him more opportunity to discuss and ask questions about the evangelistic partnering program. Pastor Daugherty graciously accepted and insisted on providing the refreshments for the board meeting, which he would have delivered by a local grocery chain that had a catering service. The conversation ended with Steve thanking Adam for coming on such short notice to talk with the Board.

Steve was anxious to meet Pastor Daugherty and was grateful things were happening so quickly, but when he hung up the phone, he couldn't help but feel that something wasn't quite right. But he shrugged the notion off, believing that *Expanding the Kingdom* would only align themselves with reputable organizations. He then proceeded to let the board members know Pastor Adam was available to come to their next meeting to share information on the evangelistic partner program. The group was excited, understanding this could be an opportunity to embark on a powerful ministry that could potentially impact countless lives, both here in the United States and abroad!

Unable to shake the feeling he had after talking with Adam, Steve decided to touch base with John Perkins from *Expanding the Kingdom,* just to be on the safe side.[1] He wanted to be at peace before he jumped too quickly and allowed *Hearts on Fire* to talk the board into a contract they possibly shouldn't sign. John gave a glowing recommendation on Adam's organization, indicating he had received strong references before taking them on as an affiliate partner. He had met Adam on several occasions but never really had a chance to get to know him personally. John was more familiar with the organization's president, Don Williamson. However, he had no reason to doubt Adam Daugherty's character, otherwise, he wouldn't be on the staff of *Hearts on Fire*. Relieved by what John Perkins told him, Steve felt he had made a good decision by asking Adam Daugherty to come to Anderson Hills for a presentation.

Chapter 10

The Partnership

On the morning of the board meeting, Steve drove over to the church to just sit and pray in the sanctuary for a while. As he sat in one of the pews, he began to think back over the last few years. A lot had happened since coming to Anderson Hills. His thoughts soon shifted to the new building and everything that went into putting it together and decorating it. He was amazed at how fast it was built, everyone in the church family had contributed to the project in some way. Looking up at the lights, he thought of Larry and Karen Elterbridge, who donated the fixtures. Looking at the pews, he thought of Matthew and Daniel Gleason, brothers, who hand varnished every one of them carefully matching them to the woodwork throughout the building. Looking at the ceiling, he thought of the congregants who stood on tall ladders and scaffolding to paint it. These thoughts went on for several minutes as he looked around the room. Then Steve began to pray. Getting up, he went to each bench in the sanctuary, anointing it with oil from a small vial he always carried with him. As he came to each row, he thought of the people who usually sat there on Sunday and prayed for them, continuing until he reached the last pew in the room.

When finished, Steve sat down and prayed over the meeting that evening. Public evangelism on a large scale was not something he had a lot of experience with. As he prayed for guidance, he began to have feelings of doubt again. Could it be from God, or was he just being overly sensitive because he was about to enter unfamiliar territory? Then suddenly, Steve felt the Holy Spirit telling him that things were about to change for him and his congregation. Steve thought perhaps that meant the new ministry would add the missing dimension of the church. It could only be a benefit to their ministry, right?

Late that afternoon, Steve and Sara heard a car pull up in the driveway. Looking out the living room window, Steve spotted a man getting out of a dark blue Chevrolet sedan. He was a professional-looking man, medium height, and slightly overweight. He had brown hair and was wearing brown rimmed sunglasses and a dark hunter green business suit. The man opened his trunk and retrieved a black briefcase and a small brown flight bag. Closing the trunk lid, he headed for the front door of the Hansons' home.

"That must be Adam," Steve said to Sara. "I'll go let him in."

"Okay," Sara responded. "I'll wait here in the living room."

Steve reached the front door before Pastor Daugherty was on the front porch and opened it wide to welcome the new visitor.

"Hello there. You must be Adam," Steve greeted cheerfully.

"Yes, I am," Adam responded with a big smile as he walked toward the front door. "And I must be in the right place. I'm guessing you're Steve." Adam removed his sunglasses and put them in his coat pocket.

"I am, and you are in the right place. Please come in."

Pastor Adam entered the hallway of the Hansons' home. His liberally applied cologne soon permeated the air.

Steve held out his hand to shake Adam's. Adam eagerly grasped Steve's hand in response, shaking it heartily.

"Just set your things here and come join us in the living room," Steve said, indicating the entryway.

Pastor Adam put his briefcase and flight bag on the floor by the front door and followed Steve to the living room where Sara was waiting to meet him.

"This is my wife, Sara," Steve said introducing his wife.

"Good to meet you, Adam," Sara said, as she stood to shake Adam's hand. "We've heard a lot of good things about you."

"And it's all true, too," Adam teased. Everyone laughed.

"Won't you sit down, Pastor Daugherty?" Sara offered.

"Well, don't mind if I do. And you can call me Adam."

As he was about to sit down, Samson came into the room, his toenails clicking on the hardwood floor as he ambled his way over to the living room sofa. He wanted to see who had come for a visit. Perhaps they had brought him a treat. As he came closer, he stopped suddenly and looking at Adam, began to growl quietly.

Steve and Sara were surprised at Samson's reaction, but Adam didn't seem bothered by it at all. Instead, he reached out his hand to let Samson smell it. However, instead of accepting his gesture of friendship, Samson began to bark at Adam. Steve ran over and grabbed Samson by the collar and pulled him away from their visitor while he was still barking.

"Stop it, Samson!" Steve lifted his voice. "This is our friend."

Samson reluctantly obeyed and pulled close to Steve as he continued to glare at Adam.

"I'm sorry, Adam. I don't know what's got into Samson. He's never done that before to anyone. He's usually very playful with new people."

"Oh, that's alright. I get that all the time. Dogs just don't seem to like me. I think it's a territorial thing or something."

Hearing the commotion in the living room, Mary, who was working on homework in her room, came running down the stairs.

"What's going on?" she asked as she entered the living room.

"Oh, Samson just got a little excited," Steve said, attempting to make an excuse.

"He did?" Mary looked puzzled.

"Uh, Adam, this is our daughter, Mary," Steve said still hanging on to Samson's collar.

"Pleased to meet you, Mary," Adam said as he reached out to shake her hand.

Mary walked over to where he was standing. "Nice to meet you too, Pastor Daugherty."

"Mary, why don't you take Samson up to your room?" Sara suggested.

"Okay, Mom," Mary said, still looking confused.

"Go with Mary," Steve said releasing Samson to follow Mary upstairs. Samson started to follow Mary but then stopped and turned to look at the guest again. He snarled at Adam, this time showing his teeth. Mary quickly grabbed Samson by the collar and led him upstairs. He resisted part of the way, but she finally managed to get him up to her room and quickly pushed him inside. When she closed the door behind her, she could hear Samson whimpering on the other side. Then she went back down to the living room to talk more with the visitor.

"My apologies again, Adam. I don't know what came over him," Steve said, somewhat embarrassed.

"Uh, he just had his yearly shots at the vet this morning," Sara managed to say. "Perhaps he's a little cranky over that."

Steve rolled his eyes, but their guest seemed undaunted by the encounter. So they just began to talk about his organization, which Adam proudly expounded on for the next half hour.

After visiting for a little while more, Sara got up to go to the kitchen to start fixing an early supper. Mary followed her mother.

"Is everything alright?" Mary whispered to her mother. "I've never seen Samson act like that before."

"I know. Maybe he's starting to feel old."

"He's only seven and a half, Mom."

"I know, Honey. I don't know what set him off. Just try to keep him away from Pastor Daugherty tonight, okay?"

"Okay, Mom. Will do."

The two put the food on the table and called the men in to eat a light meal of soup and chicken salad sandwiches. The men would be eating more at the meeting that night. When the two finished, Adam complimented Sara on the meal and thanked his hosts for their warm hospitality. Steve then offered to take Adam over to the church a little early, so he could show him around the building before the others arrived. Adam welcomed the offer and quickly grabbed his things to go over to the church. He wanted to be there early to meet the caterer anyway.

As soon as Steve parked the car in his reserved spot at the church, the caterer drove up behind them. In the brightly colored company van were two women dressed in company uniforms, one in her twenties, and the other in her thirties. They were a half-hour early, but Adam seemed pleased that the food had already arrived. Steve let them into the building and showed them where they could put the food in the kitchen refrigerator. The delivery people went back outside and brought in a fruit plate, a veggie plate, a cracker and cheese plate with various kinds of sausage, and some apple strudel. There was enough food for twenty people. They also brought in plastic plates, cups, and silverware. No detail was missed.

"Wow," Steve exclaimed. "You didn't have to do all this."

"Oh, my pleasure, my pleasure," Adam responded with a big smile. "I have a lot to share tonight, so I want everyone to enjoy themselves."

"Well, that's very nice of you, Adam. I'm sure everyone will appreciate it."

Adam gave each woman a generous tip before they left. Since they had some extra time, Steve took Adam for a tour of the facility, going outside at one point to show him the size and boundaries of the property. After seeing most of the church, they headed for the classroom where the board meeting would take place. Tables and chairs were already set up. The two men covered one of the long tables with a tablecloth for the food to be set out on. They also set up the coffee and other beverages on another small table. Steve found a projector for Adam's slideshow and set it up for him, while Adam put information on *Hearts on Fire* at each of the places where the group members would be sitting. They were ready for the meeting.

At 7:00 p.m. the board members started entering the classroom. Adam greeted them all warmly and encouraged them to partake of the small feast he had brought in for them. When everyone was settled,

Steve led the group in a word of prayer and then invited Adam to give his presentation on his evangelistic organization.

Adam talked about the history of his organization and gave a short bio on each of its leadership staff members. He shared their vision and mission and told the group how his organization had worked with many other churches over the past decade with great success. He also gave an emotional presentation on their evangelistic efforts, pointing to the vast number of people in the world today living in spiritual darkness and the many signs pointing to the second coming of Jesus. Adam concluded his presentation by explaining how they could work together.

"*Hearts on Fire* would become partners with you for an agreed-upon period of time to help develop the evangelistic outreach side of your church ministry. We can be involved as much or as little as you'd like, depending on what you want to accomplish in this area of ministry. We lead that part because that is what we do best. Our organization does not take part in the other ministries of your church. We also set up crusades. More than one church is generally involved together in sponsoring those."

"How much is this going to cost us?" Bob Brown questioned.

"That depends on what we work out with your church personally. We ask churches to add evangelistic ministry to their yearly budgets. How they raise that money is different in each situation. Some churches take special collections throughout the year or have other outlets to bring in monies to help feed the evangelistic side of the ministry, like holding revival events or having a bookstore. Most of our churches have gained members because of the evangelistic ministry. That also brings in extra money. So, to answer what I think you are asking, it doesn't affect your bottom line unless you are struggling financially. And if you were, you wouldn't be asking me to talk tonight. Our online store is also connected with your website, and you are given credit for the money coming in from that link to go towards this ministry. You can also sell some of our evangelistic products right here at your church."

"Are there other churches we can talk with to see how things have worked out for them?" another board member asked.

"Why, of course," Adam replied. "I have a list of a few different places you can contact in the packets I gave you tonight."

When Adam finished his presentation, and everyone had asked their questions, there was a definite excitement in the air. Steve himself was completely convinced at this point. Harold Cannon led the group in a closing prayer. The board decided to leave their other church business for the next meeting when they would also decide whether or not to take this potential partnership to the congregation for a vote. Everyone left the room enthusiastic about the prospect of having the church involved in evangelism on a larger scale. They each promised to pray over the matter and get back to Adam with any additional questions within the next week.

After everything was cleaned up and put away, Steve drove Adam back to his house, talking excitedly along the way about the evangelistic opportunities that might lie ahead. When they arrived home, Sara had a kettle of hot chocolate warming on the stove and had popped some fresh popcorn. Peter was still at work, and Mary had gone to bed early because she was taking the college SAT in the morning. Samson was back in her room for the night. He had been allowed to roam the house while Steve was at the meeting, but was confined again to Mary's room when it was almost time for Steve to come back home with their houseguest. Steve had called Sara before leaving the church to give her a heads up on their return. Steve, Sara, and Adam stayed up that evening for another hour and talked about Adam's presentation. Then Steve led Adam to the spare bedroom upstairs. Sara had taken his flight bag upstairs while he was gone, so everything was waiting for him in his room that night, including fresh towels and soap. Soon, everyone was in bed and the house was silent.

When Steve finally crawled into bed, he and Sara were able to talk more candidly about Adam's organization.

"So, what'd ya really think, Honey?" she asked curiously.

"I'm feeling good about it. It could be a real blessing for Anderson Hills," Steve answered. "But even though it looks good, I am going to do a little more research. I also want to pray over this some more. Let's talk about it more tomorrow morning after our guest leaves, okay?"

"Sounds good," Sara agreed. "I'll turn the lights out. Goodnight, Sweetie."

"Goodnight, My Love," Steve said kissing Sara on the cheek. He turned over, pulled the covers up to his neck, and fell fast asleep.

In the middle of the night, Adam Daugherty woke up to the sound of someone coming up the stairs. It was Peter. He had just gotten home from work. Now awake, Adam remembered he had forgotten to bring a glass of water to bed with him, so he got up to go downstairs to the kitchen. Slipping on his robe and slippers, he soon realized that he had to walk past Mary's bedroom where Samson was also sleeping, so he went as quietly as he could. He didn't want the dog barking and waking everyone up. As he crept gingerly past her door, Samson, who was also awake at the time, sensed Adam's presence and growled under the door as he went by. Adam picked up his pace and headed down to the kitchen, not wanting to wake anyone. Upon his return upstairs, water glass in hand, Adam tried to move even more carefully past Mary's door, but Samson, spying Adam's shadow, started to growl again.

Finally, safely back in his room, Adam laid down on his bed again and began to think about his presentation to the Anderson Hills board. He would have no problem convincing them to join his organization's evangelistic efforts. Adam was more than pleased with that thought as he looked out at the moon from the bedroom window. Evangelism was his passion, and unbeknownst to Anderson Hills, their partnership would help launch him into the personal ministry he had dreamed of ever since he was in Bible college. It was there Adam was told he had a special gift for evangelizing others. In truth, he did not see himself staying with *Hearts on Fire* forever. He wanted more. He was destined for more! Like the other churches he had worked in, Anderson Hills was a stepping stone to his world ministry. Certainly, God had orchestrated him coming there that evening. This particular church was special. It could be the door for him to fully realize his divine calling. Feeling satisfied that he had completed what he had come to do, Adam rolled over to try to go back to sleep.

Adjusting his pillow, Adam began to imagine himself standing on the stage of a large auditorium in front of a huge crowd, including many well-known world evangelists. He was receiving a prestigious honor for his evangelistic efforts overseas. Adam's parents were there in the front row, beaming proudly at their younger son. His brother, Noah, was sitting next to them with his wife, Kate. Adam was finally being recognized instead of his older brother. Growing up, Adam and Noah always seemed to be competing with each other, but for some reason, Noah was constantly the one coming out on top. He was the obvious favorite of the family. Noah had gone to an Ivy League school and graduated from a distinguished seminary where he received his PhD. in Theology. He had written several theological books and was on the teaching faculty of a well-known Christian university. Noah had received many accolades over the years, but now, finally, Adam was getting the recognition he so deserved. His family would certainly give him the respect he craved for so many years. Adam continued envisioning his day of recognition and soon drifted off to sleep.

The next morning Sara got up early to prepare breakfast. Adam wanted to get an early start back home. When he came down to eat, Sara already had eggs and sausage and waffles on the table. Steve was close behind him as he entered the room.

"I thought I smelled a heavenly aroma when I came down the stairs this morning," Adam said, smiling as he took his seat at the kitchen table. "Thank you, Sara. You and Steve have been most hospitable."

"Oh, you're quite welcome Adam," she returned. "We were glad to have you stay over with us last night. I hope you slept well."

"Yes, quite well. Thank you."

"You're welcome to stay here again," Steve added, "if the board decides to connect with *Hearts on Fire*. And I think they will."

"I think so too," Adam said smiling. "They're a great group of people, Steve. You work very well together."

"Yes, they are. We are very blessed," Steve said proudly. "Why don't you lead us in a word of prayer this morning?"

"Why thank you, Steve!" Adam replied. "Such an honor. I will be glad to do that." After his inspirational prayer, the three began serving themselves from the food plates on the table. They enjoyed breakfast together, talking more about a possible future partnership. At that point, Mary came down to have breakfast with them. Samson was still up in her room and would stay there until after their guest left the house. Peter would be in bed for another hour or two. Since he had come home from work in the early hours of the morning, Adam would not have a chance to meet him during this visit.

After breakfast, Steve and Adam went into Steve's office. Steve wanted to show Adam his collection of resource books he had accumulated since entering seminary. He even mentioned one he still wanted to purchase. When it was time for Adam to be on the road, he thanked his guests profusely and gave them each a big hug before leaving.

"I am really looking forward to coming back here to Anderson Hills again."

"We look forward to your next visit," Steve replied.

"Bye now," Adam said as he went out the front door.

"Goodbye, Adam. Safe travels," Sara and Steve said as Adam walked toward his car.

They waved as their new friend pulled out of the driveway.

"Is it okay for Samson to come out of my room now?" Mary asked.

"Go for it," Sara said smiling. Soon, the playful beagle came barreling down the stairs, almost sliding as he went. Samson headed straight to his bowl in the kitchen where he found some scrambled eggs on top of his dog food. He was glad to be free to roam his house again.

"I still don't know what got into Samson yesterday," Steve thought out loud.

"Yes, that was weird," Sara replied. "Hopefully, that was a one-time incident."

"Really," Mary said as she walked by. "That dog snores. I love him to pieces, but I don't want to sleep in the same room with him again. He was even growling in his sleep. He must have been having a bad dream."

"Well, the next time he can sleep with Peter," Steve responded. Then they all laughed. Mary went into the kitchen and opened the refrigerator door looking for some things to put in a lunch bag to take with her to the testing site. It was SAT day, and she wanted to make sure she had plenty to eat since she would not be going to the high school cafeteria that day. As she packed the food, there was the sound of a car honking outside in the driveway.

"That's Sophie!" she exclaimed. "Time to go!" Grabbing her jacket, purse, and lunch bag, and giving Samson a quick pat on the head, she ran for the front door. "Bye, Samson, see ya later!" she called out. "Goodbye, Mom and Dad!" Mary raised her voice as she went hurriedly down the hallway.

"Goodbye!" they both called out from the living room.

"We'll be praying you do well today," Steve said loudly as he got up to make sure the door was closed tightly after her.

"Thank you, Daddy!" Mary called back as she left. She was excited about the exams. She knew it wouldn't be long until she was in college working on a degree like her brother Peter.

That afternoon, Steve picked up the list of church references Adam left him from his desk and began to call each one of them. As promised, they all gave glowing reports on Adam's organization. A few did not know Adam, because their dealings with *Hearts on Fire* were done long before he was on staff. The other two churches were just getting to know Adam. Convinced the churches he spoke with were working with a good organization, Steve sent out an e-mail to the rest of his church board, letting them know what he found out. One by one, he received return messages from the members indicating they wanted to talk more seriously about a partnership with Adam's organization at the next board meeting.

Wanting to get one more reference on *Hearts on Fire*, Steve contacted Paul Samples at the district office. Glad to hear from Steve again Paul offered to do a little research for him. After a couple of days, he too was able to give some good feedback on the organization, but he wasn't able to comment much on Adam Daugherty. All he knew was that Pastor Daugherty had been involved in evangelistic efforts both in the U.S. and in Canada, and his career had been favorable. He was not able to find out anything else about him personally.

At the next board meeting, Steve shared everything he found out on Pastor Daugherty and *Hearts on Fire* and his conversation with Paul Samples.

"It looks like we have an all-clear, everyone. I move that we arrange for Adam to come and give a presentation to the church congregation, and then call for a congregational vote on this possible partnership."

"I second the motion," Bob Brown said, lifting his right hand.

"All in favor?" Steve asked. There was a resounding "Aye" in the room. "Opposed?" There was silence. "Ok, the aye's have it. I'll give Adam a call tomorrow and see when he can do a presentation for the church."

The following morning, Steve arrived at the church early. He was eager to start the day and talk with Adam about the board's decision. As Steve pulled into the parking lot, he noticed an old charcoal Chevy pickup parked across the street. He thought that was unusual since the building was situated out in the country where there weren't a lot of houses or traffic going up and down the road each day. Why was it there? As he parked his car, he saw two dark figures sitting inside the vehicle. They were staring coldly at the church. Steve perceived an evil presence and immediately thought of the strangers that once stood across from his church in Nordstown as he and Sara prayed over it. Were these some of the same people? Steve became uneasy and decided to head straight to his office, praying as he went and trying not to look hurried. No one else was at the church at that time. Mrs. Hellinger would not be there for at least another hour.

As he entered the hallway of the church, Steve quickly closed and locked the front door behind him. More questions began to run through his mind. Was this a sign that the enemy was about to attack their new ministry effort? Or maybe, those people were some of David's family. Had they somehow found out that David had gone to Steve for help? Steve decided to call the police and walked quickly to the main office. When he entered the room, he went right over to the window to see if the pickup was still there. Not surprisingly, it was gone.

Steve immediately called Detective Jamison Fee at the sheriff's department. Detective Fee oversaw the occult investigations for the county. Fee took down the information Steve gave him, but could only offer to send out a patrol car to see if there was any sign of occult activity on the church property. The deputies would be looking for occult symbols or signs of any satanic rituals. Steve was told to keep a lookout for those things as well in the weeks to come. When the two peace officers arrived, Steve walked the building and grounds with them. Nothing suspicious was found, but the deputies promised to drive past the church more frequently just to be on the safe side. As they were finishing up, Mrs. Hellinger arrived for work, wondering why the deputies were there. After the officers left, Steve filled her in on what had just happened and also the situation with David. Realizing nothing more could be done at that point, the two took time to pray together for the strangers in the parked pickup and protection for the church and its members. Then they went to their separate offices to start their work for the day. Steve would tell Sara about the parked car when he got home that evening. She would want to know about the situation, so she could be praying as well.

Seeing that it was almost 9:00 a.m., Steve decided to give Adam Daugherty a call. Adam was elated to hear from Steve. Looking at their calendars, a presentation was soon scheduled for the Sunday after the next. Steve once again extended his offer for Adam to stay at his house, but Adam insisted on a hotel room this time, stating that it would give him more time to work on his presentation. He liked to update it for each church so it connected with the interests of the congregation. He didn't want to ignore Steve and his family while staying in their lovely home. Adam told Steve he would like to take him and Sara out to the restaurant at the hotel instead of putting Sara out on preparing a meal for him. Steve reluctantly accepted Adam's reasoning for not taking advantage of his invitation, thinking it was due to Samson's unwelcoming response to him the last time he was there. He also felt that Adam had a right to decide which arrangement was best for his overnight stay in Anderson Hills.

On the Saturday afternoon before the church presentation, Adam Daugherty checked in to the new hotel in downtown Anderson Hills. Once settled in his room, he called Steve and Sara and invited them to join him that evening for dinner at the hotel's restaurant. They would meet there at 6:30 p.m. When the Hansons arrived at the restaurant, dressed in their best Sunday clothes, Adam ran over to greet them as soon as he spotted them coming in. Being his usual overly-friendly self, Adam shook their hands with great energy, and then escorted them to their table, where he had already been seated. Appetizers soon arrived at their table. A young man in a black tuxedo with a red bow tie sat at a shiny black grand piano in the middle of the room playing soft dinner music, creating an atmosphere that was warm and inviting. When their waiter came back to take their orders, Adam encouraged Steve and Sara to have whatever they wanted on the menu. After the three had placed their orders, Adam reached under the table, pulled out two colorful gift bags and handed them to the Hansons.

"What's this?" Steve asked surprised.

"Oh, just a little thank you from *Hearts on Fire*," Adam replied, with a big smile.

"You didn't have to do that," Sara said, looking at her flowered bag.

"We just wanted you to know how much we appreciate the chance to talk with your congregation tomorrow."

"We're looking forward to your presentation," Steve responded. "The whole board is."

Pulling the carefully arranged pink tissue paper aside, Sara looked inside of her bag and found a large two-pound box of assorted chocolates from her favorite candy store. Steve found in his bag the Bible commentary he mentioned he wanted during Adam's last visit.

"Thank you, Adam," they both told their dinner host almost at the same time.

"This was very thoughtful," Sara added.

"You're welcome," Adam said warmly. "It gave me great pleasure to bring those things to you."

As the evening progressed, Adam was very charming and flattering to his guests and did most of the talking. He complimented Steve and Sara on what their church had accomplished so far. He talked enthusiastically about what a great board they had. Some of the people sitting close to their table turned for a moment when he raised his voice in excitement. Now completely animated, Adam gushed about some of his evangelistic experiences from over the years. Steve and Sara were drawn into his thrilling descriptions of some of his past revival events. Salvations and healing miracles were realities in all of his crusades. Certainly, the church in Anderson Hills would want to be a part of this exciting ministry as well. Adam asked the couple to join him on a couple of upcoming evangelistic events some other churches were having. That way they could get some first-hand experience on what went on in them. Steve and Sara eagerly agreed to join him. Perhaps some of the board members would want to go as well.

By 9:00 p.m., the three were finishing up their dessert of chocolate mousse when Steve and Sara decided it was time to head back home. They took a moment to pray together with Adam over the presentation on Sunday, and then the Hansons left for home so their host could finish preparing for the next day. On the drive back to their house the two talked with great fervor about all the things the partnership could bring to Anderson Hills. When they got home, they found it hard to think about going to bed. Mary and Peter were still out with their friends from school, so they decided to watch one of the VCR tapes Adam gave them on *Hearts on Fire*. Samson came and lay next to them as they did. When the video concluded, they took a few minutes to pray over Adam's presentation and then went up to bed.

That Sunday morning, Adam gave an emotional appeal to the congregation on evangelistic ministry. His PowerPoint presentation included numerous pictures of lost souls on big city streets. Gangs, drug dealers, and prostitutes were featured in many of them. The pictures of homeless people and children with sad, dirty faces tugged at the heartstrings of many in the audience. Those people needed to hear the good news of Jesus. When his presentation was finished, the congregation broke out in applause. Steve followed up on the idea in his sermon, and Sara and the worship leader led the group in inspiring worship songs that also focused on evangelistic outreach. The members of the congregation would go home to pray about the partnership opportunity and then vote on it the following Sunday. Many stopped to talk with Adam after the service at his table set up in the lobby. They were eager to grab more of his literature and free VCR tapes and ask more about how the church could be involved. Steve and Sara were encouraged by the number of people that lingered at Adam's table long after the service was over. Adam then packed up his things, and after hugging Steve and Sara, headed back home.

The following week the church membership voted almost unanimously in favor of the partnership with *Hearts on Fire*. There were a few dissenters, worried about the cost to the congregation, but the majority of the people were satisfied that the church board would work out the details to the benefit of everyone concerned.

After Steve contacted Adam to let him know of the positive outcome, Adam made arrangements to come to the board's next meeting to work out an agreement with *Hearts on Fire*. Steve asked a lawyer from the congregation to look it over after the draft has been agreed on. Once some minor changes were made, the board voted to accept the contract. Then the group authorized Steve and Harold Cannon to sign the agreement for the church. The temporary partnership, which would last three years, was now a reality.

The next Sunday when the church board announced the partnership at the morning service, the decision received a standing ovation from those in the audience, many cheering, and whistling. The board then announced a celebration for the whole congregation to attend the following week. It would be a covered dish meal after the service. Steve had already let Adam know and asked him to be there as well. Adam graciously accepted, telling Steve he wanted to supply a large cake and some ice cream for the celebration and that he would not take "no" for an answer. Steve welcomed Adam's offer and said that the church would greatly appreciate his donations. Adam also let Steve know the president of *Hearts on Fire*, Don Williamson would accompany him to personally thank the church for becoming a partner.

When the day of the celebration arrived, it was a festive occasion with lots of fanfare. The local newspaper was there to do a press release. Some of the other local pastors came with their wives as well. Anderson Hills Church Fellowship was about to take on their biggest ministry project ever, and they wanted the community to know about it. God had greatly blessed this church plant, and its pioneers, Steve and Sara Hanson were overjoyed. They could see more blessings coming down the road for this ministry and thanked God for the new partnership. Steve and Sara hoped their children would catch the evangelistic vision and be a part of that ministry as well. Things couldn't be better, or so they thought.

Chapter 11

New Trouble

One morning, a few days after the celebration, Steve was alone in his home office, reading a theological journal while relaxing in his favorite recliner. As he became engrossed in an article on evangelism, the sunlight coming through the doors and windows started to fade, and the sky became unusually dark. Steve continued to read, unaware at that point, of the change taking place outside. Suddenly, there was a great gust of wind. Steve looked up for a moment to see the strange transformation in the weather, but thinking it was just an oncoming rainstorm, he continued to read. Seconds later, there was a loud crash outside. Lightning had hit the ground somewhere close to the house. The jolt made the room shake. Steve jumped up to look out the glass-paned French doors of his office.

Quickly opening one of the doors, Steve stepped out on the back deck to make sure nothing was on fire. When he did, he was met with another strong gust of wind. Steve lifted his hands to block some dirt and dried leaves from flying in his face. At that moment he began to imagine (or was it a vision?–he wasn't completely sure), a supernatural struggle of gigantic proportion between an army of heavenly warring angels and an army of opposing warring demons, more than he could count on either side. Engrossed in this unusual daydream, Steve's mind shifted from one part of the battle to another. Most of the beings were mammoth in size. It was an incredible scene, more graphic than any movie maker could create. The struggle was fierce. Steve could hear loud shouts and the clanging of swords. He envisioned bright sparks flying as heavy blades clashed together. Steve could also see some hand-to-hand combat. Spiritual creatures of great strength and incompatible allegiances wrestled intensely, each side determined to keep the other from advancing into their territory. Their faces were full of passion and resolve.

The angels were bright, beautiful, and muscular, wearing white tunics and shining silver and gold armor. Many were holding shields and wielding huge fiery swords. A bright light streaming from heaven was upon and glowing through them. The demons, on the other hand, were dark and hideous in features and wore shields and breastplates, as black as they were themselves. Saliva drooled from their mouths. There was no light in, on, or around them, and all were frightening to look upon. Steve's thoughts suddenly shifted when he felt Samson nudge up against him. Looking down, he was glad for his dog's company. When he looked up again, the sky was clearing and the sun began to shine again.

Steve shook his head and went back inside. As he sat down in the recliner again, Samson came over and sat at his feet. Feeling unsettled, Steve prayed for peace and understanding of what had just taken place. From the Scriptures, he understood how powerful God and His army of angels are against the attacks of enemy forces. Reflecting on that, He soon realized the Lord was showing him he and his family were about to engage in another harsh spiritual battle, fiercer than the last one. This battle, though, he was not sure he was ready to fight, yet he and his family had to trust God and walk by faith and not what they could see in the natural.[1] He had to remain obedient and do whatever needed to be done for the ministry he was called to.

When Sara returned from the nursing home, later that day, she found Steve on the phone with his brother, Mike. As she stood by the door of his study, she could tell the conversation sounded serious. She decided to go upstairs and change her clothes, so she wouldn't interrupt their conversation. Just as she turned to leave, Steve spotted her at the doorway and motioned for her to come in. Sara saw his gesture in time and went in and sat down on the brown leather sofa in his office. Steve held up his index finger, indicating that he would be just a minute more. Sara nodded, picked up the journal Steve had been reading earlier, and started going through the table of contents. Samson went over to greet Sara and then headed for the kitchen to find his water bowl.

"Thanks for talking with me, Mike. That helped a lot. Looking forward to seeing you and Marcie again this fall. Love you guys. Okay, I will. Bye now." Steve put the receiver down.

Sara looked up at Steve concerned. *Is someone ill?* She wondered.

"What's happening, Sweetie?" Sara asked as Steve reached for a glass of water on his desk. "Your parents okay?"

"Everyone's fine," Steve said, after taking a big swallow. "And Mike said to say hello. I called him because I just had a strange experience. I didn't want to bother you at the nursing home, so I thought I would talk with him about it."

"Is everything alright?" Sara asked.

"Yes. At least for now, I should say."

"Did you have another angel encounter?" Sara asked, discerning something supernatural had taken place.

"More of a revelation," Steve smiled at her. He began to tell her about what happened that morning. When he finished, Sara sat and reflected on what Steve had just shared with her, trying to grasp its significance.

"My goodness," she finally said. "I don't know what to say . . . You know, I didn't see it storm today. At least not where I was. The sun was shining all morning, and there was no strong wind. I know, because all of the rooms I was in at the nursing home had windows in them, and I could see what was going on outside. What do you think God is telling us?"

"Well, after talking with Mike, I'm feeling God is telling us that evangelistic outreach ministry, on a large scale, is not going to be without its pushbacks . . . We're about to engage in some serious spiritual warfare again, Babe."

"Yes," Sara replied. "I'm feeling that too . . . Wow . . . We need to really bathe this venture in prayer, don't we?"

"Yes, we do. Periods of fasting are going to be important too. And not just us, the board and congregation as well . . . Let's just keep this vision between us for right now, until we have had more time to pray about it."

"I think that's wise," Sara replied.

Just then, Samson came strolling back into the office, and Steve turned his attention to his canine friend as he came around the desk to see him. "You were with me when it happened this morning weren't you, Buddy?" Samson looked up at Steve, wagging his tail as if he knew what Steve was talking about. Steve patted Samson on the head, and their beloved beagle headed over to the corner of the room to lay down.

Sara reached down and rubbed Samson's ears as he walked past her. What a great comfort he had been to the family in times of trouble.

"You always seem to be around when God is telling us something very important, aren't you little one? If only you could talk," she said wistfully.

"Ruff!" Samson barked playfully at her and began to wag his tail again. Steve and Sara laughed.

Turning back to Sara, Steve said, "Let's go to the park and find our favorite spot. I'm feeling a need to be in prayer right now . . . both of us . . . together."

"I'd love to," Sara responded, without hesitation. "Just let me change my clothes real quick," she said, as she got up from the sofa.

"That's fine. I'll finish up my journal entry on the vision while you're upstairs," Steve told her.

Sara left the room and ran up the stairs to their bedroom. In just a few minutes, she was back down in jeans, a T-shirt, and hiking shoes. The two were ready to leave for their favorite place in the woods to talk with God alone, but before they could go out the front door, once again, they gave in to Samson's sad eyes, and he happily escorted them to their car. Then Steve drove them all to the city park, less than two miles away.

When they arrived at the park, the couple headed for their special spot in the woods, a lookout point on a hill along the heavily wooded park trail. There they found a bench and sat down. No one was around, so they had the privacy they were hoping for. Samson laid down by the park bench. Steve took Sara's hand in his and began to pray for protection, strength, courage, and discernment in what was about to come. They also asked God to move them and their family up to a higher level of spirituality and intimacy with Him. Steve and Sara sat quietly on the bench and waited for God to respond. Remaining silent, yet expectant, they soon sensed a divine presence.

Closing their eyes and enjoying being outdoors amongst nature, peace came upon them. A moment later, they felt compelled to look up at the sky, and there they saw something like a blue and white blanket coming down from heaven, landing softly on their heads and shoulders and enfolding them. The words of the Psalmist came to their minds as they encountered this spiritual covering, *"God is our refuge and strength, an ever-present help in trouble."*[2] That protection, they knew, was for their whole family. Steve and Sara began to sing the hymn, "It Is Well with My Soul,"[3] and as they did, they felt carried away supernaturally. Still holding hands, they soared to a place where there was perfect peace, a place where there were no tears, but instead, pure joy. The feeling was overwhelming yet exhilarating. Then all too soon, the moment faded and Steve and Sara found themselves back on the park bench with Samson laying quietly at their feet. God would be with them, no matter what happened. That they could count on. He would equip them with all they would need.

The next day, Steve received a call from Adam Daugherty. He wanted to schedule a Sunday morning sometime soon when he and a fellow evangelist could give the congregation at Anderson Hills a taste of a real evangelistic sermon. Steve was always willing to accommodate Adam, whenever he could, so he penciled him and his friend in for the last Sunday in June. These guest presentations would be announced in the bulletin, on the church website, in mailings, and on the local radio station.

The church's evangelistic ministry was about to begin.

The following week, Steve and Sara accompanied Adam on a major evangelistic event in northern Canada, sponsored by *Hearts on Fire*. Adam, and several well-known world evangelists, led the crusade. Steve and Sara were utterly amazed at what took place in the large public stadium where the event was being held for two days. The atmosphere was electrifying, and the amazing presence of the Holy Spirit was indescribable. People of every age were crying out to God and experiencing His incredible love and forgiveness. Some were even being healed. Steve and Sara were blessed by what they saw and prayed for the same kind of experience for the people of the Anderson Hills area. They went back home that week with the unbelievable mountain top experience still very much alive in their minds.

When the week of Adam's revival service came, the church was packed . . . standing room only. Steve was a little nervous when he saw the size of the crowd that showed up that day. But the ushers managed to seat everyone, and the service went on without any problems. Perhaps the next time, they would rent the gym at the Christian school for this type of event. The service was met with great enthusiasm by all who were present. It was something many of them had never experienced before. Adam and his co-evangelist were in their element and on fire for the Lord. The presence of God was undeniable in the sanctuary that morning, and many walked forward to receive Jesus Christ as their Lord and Savior.

After the service, when most of the congregation had gone home, Adam came up to Steve and put his arm around him.

"Steve, my friend," he said. "It was apparent to me today that this community is passionately open to the new evangelistic ministry you have here at Anderson Hills. Since I will be coordinating other events here as well, what would you and the board think about me having an office here at Anderson Hills? Just a place to hang my hat, if you will. It would give *Hearts on Fire* a stronger presence at the church, and I wouldn't have to do as much traveling. It would also really help you expand your evangelistic outreach ministry."

"Well . . . sure . . . I think we could do that. I guess we never really thought about it," Steve responded, slowly trying to think the matter through quickly. He did not like being caught off guard by anyone when it came to making an important decision for the church. "I'll talk with the board about your request this week."

"Wonderful! Wonderful, Steve!"

Adam patted Steve on the back and then continued down the hall to retrieve his notes and anointing oil from the sanctuary, and to say goodbye to his friend who had come to preach with him that day. He was pleased with Steve's response to his request.

A couple of weeks later, a small construction team was working hard putting in a small office in a section of the church basement that hadn't been finished yet. Adam would have a place to work from when he came to Anderson Hills. He would also be able to connect more directly with the congregation and the church board as the evangelistic ministry grew.

As the summer months went by, more people were coming to Anderson Hills. Some came from the next county. Before they knew it, the church was adding two more services, one in the morning and one in the evening. It was soon decided by the board that Adam Daugherty would preach at one of the services every other week because of his popularity. By late August, Pastor Daugherty was preaching at even more of the services. The partnership agreement with *Hearts on Fire* was being redefined and stretched to the limit. Steve began to wonder where this would all end when the three-year contract had been fulfilled. Would the church be able to continue with the work Adam had started there? He also worried about some of the families who had been with the church from its very beginning but had left the fellowship because they didn't care for Adam's style of preaching. Had the church changed too much?

As the church grew more rapidly, the board hired two administrative assistants. Nancy Flanagan for the main office, and Bridgett Crumbly for the evangelistic outreach ministry. Mrs. Hellinger was glad for the additional help. The church board also expanded, with two more members. The newest additions were particularly interested in the evangelistic outreach ministry, led by Adam and seemed to spend a lot of time talking with him at the church after Sunday services and weekday meetings and events.

Adam continued to be his usual charming and charismatic self, but at the same time, something seemed to be changing in him. He was making more and more requests for his ministry at Anderson Hills. He was also spending more time there. When Steve asked Adam about the other churches he was supposed to be helping, Adam just brushed the questions off, saying that someone else was handling them now. *Hearts on Fire* was so excited about Adam's success, they wanted him to stay close to Anderson Hills so he could plan some large-scale crusades with them in the state of Pennsylvania. No one seemed concerned that Adam was taking on more of a pastoral ministry role at the church. Many just accepted him as part of the staff. Some people were even seeking him out for private counseling. Seeing all this, Steve became more concerned.

Steve and Sara attended a couple of other evangelistic events with Adam. However, the excitement they felt at the first crusade was not there anymore. Something didn't seem right now. They also saw a side of Adam Daugherty they had not witnessed during other events. At times he was moody, distracted, and self-absorbed. On occasion, he was arrogant and rude to others attending an event and would even dress down someone on the evangelistic team, for no apparent reason. Twice, he was short with Steve but later apologized, indicating that stress was the contributing factor.

To Steve and Sara, Adam's Sunday sermons didn't seem as inviting as they once were either, and the luster of the evangelistic outreach ministry was beginning to fade for them. Perhaps, they told themselves, it was just because Adam was pushing himself too hard. However, as the weeks passed by, Steve became more aware that something was genuinely amiss, especially when Adam decided he didn't have time to mentor a seminary student interested in helping with Anderson Hills' evangelistic outreach ministry. This was something the board had included in their written agreement with *Hearts on Fire*. The student was the pastoral candidate Steve and the board had hoped would take over the evangelistic outreach ministry after Adam was gone in three years.

In addition to what they were seeing in Adam, Steve and Sara sensed a different attitude towards Steve from some of the board members. Those individuals were undoubtedly enamored with Adam and blind to the fact that his personality was evolving into something very different. Or perhaps . . . Adam was just now showing his true self. While members like Harold Cannon and Bob Brown were still loyal to Steve's leadership and the original vision and mission of Anderson Hills, others were beginning to see things from another perspective. They were so taken with Adam, they were siding with him on more and more church decisions, even though he was not their pastor, or an employee of the church, and did not have the right or authority to be involved in those decisions. On top of that, the music ministry leader was consulting and collaborating more with Adam on the weekly music, than he was with Steve. Steve's concern for the ministry of the church was deepening, and soon he would find that some others in the church were feeling the same way.

Late one evening, when Steve was working on his sermon notes for the next Sunday, there was a knock on the French doors of his office. Steve looked through the glass panes to see Bob Brown standing on the deck. Surprised to see him there, he got up and opened one of the doors to let him in.

"Well, this is a pleasant surprise," Steve exclaimed. "What are you doing at the back door?"

"I was out for a walk and saw your office light on," Bob said, as he walked in. "Do you have some time to talk?" Bob and Lucie had sold their house in Nordstown and bought a house in Anderson Hills on the next street to be closer to the church. Bob had walked over to Steve's house from there.

"Yes, of course. Is everything ok?"

"I'm not sure. That's why I came to talk with you."

"Please, sit down."

Bob walked over and sat on the sofa next to the wall, moving some pillows out of the way as he did. "Steve, I don't know how to say this, but I think Adam has his eyes on your job," he quickly blurted out.

Steve looked surprised at his close friend. "What would make you say that, Bob?" Steve asked, taking his seat behind his desk.

"Well, quite a few of things. He's been getting awful pushy lately with the board"

"True, but he's always been a little expectant . . . I *have* been noticing some changes in his behavior, though. Perhaps he's getting some pressure from his boss."

"That might be true, but it's gone beyond that. You need to know that Adam has been taking some of the newer board members out to eat. He's meeting them for lunch or whenever they have time to get together with him. He's been feeding them a line that maybe he should be full-time at Anderson Hills and on our payroll."

"Why would he say that? His employment is with *Heart's on Fire*."

"Then why is this the only church he is working with right now? And why isn't he doing any evangelistic outreach training for us like his organization contracted with us to do? Everything he does seems to be for him and his aspirations for evangelistic ministry."

Steve sat back in his chair not knowing what to say. Bob was a good and loyal friend. He trusted his judgment, but was there really a sinister side to Adam Daugherty? Was taking over the church his ultimate goal?

"I think we need to keep an eye on him, Steve," Bob continued. "I have to tell you that Harold is concerned as well. We talked about this for quite a while this morning, and I told him I would come over to talk with you today for the two of us."

As he listened to Bob, Steve suddenly remembered the vision he had weeks before. Was this the battle he was about to engage in? A fight to keep his position at the church? Steve had to admit to himself that he had been seeing some significant changes in Adam, but his evangelistic ministry partner always seemed to have an excuse for them. The red flags had been there for quite a while now. Perhaps it was time to take them more seriously.

While the two continued to talk, Mary, unexpectedly walked by the office. She had been out shopping for fall school clothes and had just gotten back from the mall. When she saw that her father had company in his study, she looked in to see who was there for a visit. Mary was clutching an opened letter in her hand. Since her high school graduation, she had been eagerly awaiting news on a special scholarship she had applied for at the college she would soon be attending. To be granted the scholarship meant she would not have to work and go to school at the same time, at least not until the summer term. She knocked quietly on the door.

"Excuse me. Can I interrupt for just a minute?" Mary asked shyly.

Steve looked up. "Well, of course, Mary. Come right in." He seemed glad for a change of subject matter.

"Hello, Mr. Brown. Good to see you," Mary gave a big smile as she entered the room.

"Good to see you, Mary. You look like you have something important to share," Bob said spying the letter.

"Actually, I do," Mary said, trying to control the excitement in her voice. "Daddy, Mr. Brown, I was granted a full scholarship to Christ's College!" She squealed with delight, jumping up and down.

Both men caught up in the emotion stood up and went over to give Mary a congratulatory hug.

"That's the same college Josh Franklin goes to, isn't it, Mary?" Bob asked, already knowing the answer.

"Yes," Mary replied, trying not to blush. "He will be a junior this year. He's studying journalism, and I'll be going into the college of education.

I'm going to be a high school literature teacher someday! Maybe even teach at the college level!" Mary loved both writing and reading books.

"We're proud of you, Mary," her father told her. "You worked hard for the grades you received in high school. The principal at the senior high told me just the other day at a Chamber event what a great reporter you were for the school newspaper. You are well respected at your alma mater, you and your brother."

"Thanks, Daddy. That was nice of Mr. Wilbur to say that to you."

"When do you leave for school?" Bob asked.

"In just a couple of weeks," she said, realizing how close it was.

"We're going to miss having you here. Samson is going to miss you, too," Bob told her.

"I know. I hate leaving him, but I know he'll be good company for Mom and Dad."

"My goodness. Where does the time go?" Steve mused. "Our little girl, going off to college. It seems like just yesterday I was teaching you how to tie your shoes."

Mary giggled.

After a few more minutes of college talk, Mary excused herself and ran upstairs to call Joshua. She wanted him to know that she would be seeing him in Ohio soon. There was so much to do before fall. When Mary left the room, Steve closed the office door, and the two friends sat back down and resumed their conversation about Adam.

"Do you think I should confront Pastor Daugherty?" Steve asked his friend.

"I would. He's got no business having private meetings with board members. And if he continues in that vein, I will personally call his boss at *Hearts on Fire*."

Steve knew that Bob meant what he said. This was a situation that had to be taken care of soon. Who knows what else might be happening behind their backs? After some discussion on how the situation should be handled, Steve and Bob prayed together for a few minutes, and then Bob got up to leave. At that same moment, they heard the front door open. Sara had returned from grocery shopping. When the two men saw her carrying things in from the car, they went to help her out. Mary came running down the stairs to tell her mother her good news and to help bring in the food as well.

That evening, Steve and Sara took Mary out to dinner at her favorite restaurant to celebrate. Peter joined the group as soon as he got off from work. It was an exciting time in the life of the Hanson family, a change of season for the youngest member. Steve and Sara understood that their children were moving on beyond the walls of their home to become what God had created them to be. Their role in their kids' lives would be different now, and they would have to let them go, so they could fly on their own. They were adults, and Steve and Sara had to trust God to take care of them.

The next day when Steve entered the main office at the church, Mrs. Hellinger was eager to talk with him in his office.

"Of course, Margaret. Come on in."

Steve knew that whenever Margaret requested a private meeting, it was something important. She had always looked out for him and his family.

Before Mrs. Hellinger closed the office door behind her, she looked back to make sure her assistant had returned from her break. When she saw Nancy at her desk, she pushed the door closed. She had already let Nancy know she would be in a conference with the pastor when he came in that morning.

"Steve, this may sound kind of *déjà vu*, but there's trouble brewing," she said, before taking her seat.

Steve looked at Mrs. Hellinger unsure of what to say. This was the third person now sharing a concern with him. Steve settled into his desk chair.

"This wouldn't happen to have something to do with Adam, does it?"

"As a matter of fact, it does. How did you know?

"Someone else talked with me last night about him. In a way, two someone else's."

"Did they tell you about Rick?" Rick Radcliff was the music ministry director at Anderson Hills.

"Well, no. Our conversation dealt with another issue."

"Oh, you mean the board members," she shook her head.

"You know about that too?"

"I pay attention, Steve. You know that."

Steve smiled and nodded.

"So, what's going on with Richard?"

"Well, he's been spending an awful lot of time with Adam lately. He seems mesmerized by him. Like Adam's some kind of rock star or something."

"Yes, Rick is young and somewhat impressionable."

"Well, I followed him down to Adam's office the other day. I hid in the youth ministry storage closet in the basement and stood where I could hear what they were talking about together."

"Margaret?!"

"Oh, don't worry, Steve. They didn't even know I was there. And besides, you'll be glad that I listened in."

Steve knew it was fruitless to argue with Margaret about spying on other members of the staff. He also knew she did it with good intentions, so he just sat and listened.

Mrs. Hellinger continued, "Adam was going on and on about how wonderful he was and how Rick would be a great addition to his evangelistic ministry team as they traveled around the country. He told Rick that he felt he (Rick) was being called to join him. He also said he had plans to step up the evangelistic efforts here at the church, and that he would be in a position sometime soon to take a more permanent role at Anderson Hills. Rick was elated because he thought he would be able to 'accomplish more' here if he had the freedom to be as creative as he wanted to be."

"Meaning, he could bypass me on some decisions."

"Exactly. Steve, I think Adam is bucking to take over here. He has been schmoozing with a lot of people in the congregation. You know he's bringing in a lot of money. Money talks to a lot of people these days, more so than spiritual issues, unfortunately. He seems to be charming his way into their good graces. He's also dropping little hints here and there that maybe we need a different kind of leadership at this church — one that he's capable of providing to the good people of Anderson Hills."

Steve was starting to become uneasy with the thought of someone intentionally trying to take over a congregation he and Sara had been called by God to help build from the ground up. This was a church that defied the criticisms of many naysayers in the surrounding community, and one that was growing and thriving.

"Well, it looks like it's time to have a talk with Pastor Daugherty, Margaret."

"I think so. Especially since we are so close to voting on new board members. As you know, some of our older ones are up for re-election soon. The reason he's romancing some members of the congregation could be that he's trying to sway the election, so he can boot some of your supporters off the board."

Those possibilities had never entered Steve's mind. Why was this happening? Was Adam truly that devious? That calculating?

"I would appreciate it if you and Frank would be praying over this Margaret. Sara and I will be praying tonight. I think I will talk with Adam when he comes in on Friday morning. That needs to be done soon. I should probably talk with Rick too, but I'm not sure what to say to him at this point. . . I may wait until I talk with Adam."

"We will certainly be praying Steve," Margaret gave a hopeful smile. "And as far as Rick goes. I uh…" she hesitated. "I had a little talk with him myself about protocol within the church."

Steve lifted his eyebrows. "Oh?"

"Well, he looks at me like a mother. And he was out of line. I believe I got through to him, though. He should be coming to you more often now with his questions and suggestions. If he decides to follow Adam to his ministry team at some point in time, well, that's his business. But while he's working here, he owes you the respect you deserve as leader of this congregation. And I made sure he knew that."

Steve started to chuckle. "Thanks, Margaret. And thanks for bringing this to my attention. I'll follow up with Rick the next time we meet."

"I thought you would," Margaret smiled as she stood to leave. "Back to work now. Let me know how your meeting with Adam goes."

"I sure will."

Mrs. Hellinger went back to the main office where Nancy already had a small pile of messages waiting for her on her desk.

That evening, Steve and Sara prayed in their bedroom face down on the floor for over an hour before going to bed. They asked God for wisdom and clear discernment on how to approach Adam. If he was indeed conspiring against Steve's leadership, they would have to start praying in the defensive. Steve did not want to say too much to his father and brother just yet until he knew exactly what he was dealing with. He and Sara were thankful, though, that several people had begun to intercede on their behalf.

On Friday, Steve arrived at the church early to make sure he caught Adam before he got too busy with his work. At nine o'clock on the dot, Adam came in the front office with his usual "hellos" to everyone and then headed downstairs. Steve was in the sanctuary praying when he heard Adam's voice. Getting up quickly, he hurriedly followed Adam down to his basement office.

"Good morning, Adam," Steve managed to say, trying not to cause alarm.

"Well, good morning there, Stevie," Adam spoke back almost condescendingly.

"Do you have a few minutes to talk before getting started for the day?" Steve asked, trying to ignore how Adam had just addressed him.

"Well of course. I always have time for you. You are the leader here."

At least for now, Steve thought to himself.

"Let's talk over some coffee, okay? I think I smell a fresh pot brewing in the kitchen," Adam suggested.

"Sure, why not?" Steve responded.

After getting their coffee and one of the cookies Mrs. Hellinger had left on a plate in the kitchen, the two headed downstairs to Adam's office to talk. When the men finished some polite conversation on the weather and their favorite sports teams, Steve broached the subject of Adam taking board members out to eat.

"Well, Steve Hanson. I'm surprised at you," Adam responded sounding a little sarcastic. "Why would you be concerned about that? Those people had questions for me. I just thought we could talk about those questions over a meal and get to know each other better. I don't see the harm in that."

"That may be your intent, Adam, but it is raising questions among some of the people in the congregation. More than one has talked with me about it now. They are also concerned about your growing presence here at Anderson Hills and your numerous requests to the board."

"Oh? I detect that you are concerned as well."

"I am concerned that what we originally talked about concerning your role here at our church is continually changing and expanding. I am glad for the evangelistic outreach part of the ministry here, but it was my understanding that you were sent here to help us develop that side of the church's ministry for ourselves. To date, I have not seen you do any kind of training here since you came, so others can help with the ministry and take over when you've moved on to another church. When I asked you to mentor an intern we want to hire from the seminary, you said it was too early to have someone work beside you and that you didn't have time now to do so. You've also been making requests that seem to be more helpful in expanding your personal ministry rather than ours at Anderson Hills. You have even tried to influence how the church runs in general. I'm sorry, but that is not why you were brought to Anderson Hills."

"Is that what you think I am doing, Steve?"

"I think you are zealous for your calling, which is admirable, but that has colored your thinking on why you are here."

"I see. Hmm. Are you feeling a little bit of jealousy there, Stevie?" Adam said with a smirk.

Steve bristled. He did not like being called, "Stevie." And he certainly was not jealous, so he decided to ignore Adam's disrespectful comment for the moment. "This has nothing to do with jealousy, Adam. I am just concerned about what's happening to the ministry here. This is not what we talked about. It is not what our agreement with *Hearts on Fire* says we will do together. I am still the pastor of this congregation, and I have the right to investigate any concern that has been brought to my attention, no matter who it pertains to." Steve could tell that Adam was not pleased with where the conversation was going.

"Your congregation is growing, Steve," Adam pointed out, "by leaps and bounds."

"Yes, but why are new people coming? Are they coming to seek God and to serve others, or are they intrigued with a ministry that is getting a lot of attention right now? Frankly, Adam, I am feeling that we need to slow down, pray over this partnership, and regroup. Things are getting out of hand. You and I also need to meet sometime soon and really talk through some things."

Adam sat quietly with his arms folded in front of him until Steve finished talking, obviously annoyed. Then, not wanting to continue with the conversation any longer, Adam suddenly announced he had a lot to do to get ready for Sunday. He thanked Steve for stopping by and told him he would prayerfully consider what Steve said to him that morning. He would check his calendar to see when would be a good time for Steve and him to meet and discuss some things in more detail. Steve left Adam's office feeling like he accomplished very little. He also felt that this would not be the last conversation he would be having with Pastor Adam Daugherty. A great spiritual battle was about to ensue, and he knew it. Why hadn't he done something sooner to help head it off? What he didn't realize was that he would soon encounter battles from other spiritual fronts as well. It would soon be an all-out war against his ministry at Anderson Hills.

Chapter 12

A Roaring Lion Seeking to Devour

*T*hat afternoon, Steve called Bob Brown from his cell phone, while he was out picking up some communion supplies at the local Christian bookstore, and asked if he and Harold could meet with him at his home office early the next morning. When Bob heard the topic of discussion, he readily agreed and assured Steve that Harold would want to come as well. Steve wanted to tell them about his brief meeting with Pastor Adam and discuss his growing concern with Adam's influence on others in the congregation regarding the upcoming November elder elections. Adam Daugherty's meddling could result in a dramatic shift in the make-up of the Anderson Hills Board and the direction of the church.

On Saturday morning, Bob and Harold arrived at Steve's house at 8:00 a.m. Bob walked over from his house, so there wouldn't be two visitor cars in the driveway. The men didn't want to draw undue attention to their meeting with Steve. Sara had some fresh donuts and hot coffee waiting for the men in the home office when they arrived. After Bob and Harold took off their fall jackets, grabbed some refreshments, and selected a comfortable place to sit in the study, they began talking about the problem at hand. Steve decided to close the door before he sat down. As he started to do so, he noticed that Samson was standing in the hallway, wanting to come in as well.

"Sorry, not this time, Buddy," Steve smiled. "Why don't you go see what Sara is doing in the kitchen?"

Understanding what he was just told, Samson reluctantly moved away from the door and went back down the hall to find Sara, his tail wagging behind him. Steve shut the door, grabbed a jelly donut and coffee, and sat down in an overstuffed recliner in the corner of the room. He wanted to be relaxed for this meeting. Steve entered the conversation already started by telling the men about his discussion with Adam the day before. Harold and Bob then shared their continued worries about Adam.

"This is not what we bargained for when we signed up with *Hearts on Fire!*" Bob said emphatically. "That man is on some kind of glory trip, and he's using us to promote and build his own personal ministry."

"Unfortunately, not everyone is seeing that side of Adam," Steve said, before taking a sip of his coffee. "Many are taken in by his charm and fiery evangelistic sermons. He's got their attention right now. They think they're donating to a worthy cause. And more of his followers are joining our church family every week."

"I know," Harold replied. "This certainly isn't the same church we started a few years ago."

"I think we should call *Hearts on Fire*," Bob suggested.

"I agree, but that may be a little premature," Steve responded. "Adam is on the agenda for the next board meeting. He has some kind of new plan he wants the board to consider. Let's see what he is up to with that before we call his boss."

"I suppose we should," Bob said. "But we need to call *Hearts on Fire* after that. Adam's gaining more and more ground here at Anderson Hills, and I don't like it."

"I don't either," Harold chimed in. "That guy can't be trusted."

The three men continued to talk for an hour more about the problem. Then they prayed together for a long time. When they finished, the small group decided to meet again after the board meeting that Thursday evening. The two visitors got up to go, firm in their resolve not to let the situation get any worse. A few minutes after Bob and Harold left, there was a knock on the front door. Steve went to the front door and looked out to see if Harold had come back to get something he forgot. Instead, he saw Mrs. Hellinger standing on the porch. He opened the door quickly and let her inside.

"Good morning, Steve," Mrs. Hellinger said, as she entered the hallway. "The guys told me about your meeting with them this morning. I just wanted to stop by with a follow-up."

"Glad you came," he smiled.

Steve started to usher Mrs. Hellinger to his office, but she grabbed his arm and insisted that Sara be included in this meeting with her as well. So they went to the kitchen where Sara was standing at the counter, looking through her favorite recipe book.

"Good morning, Sara!" Mrs. Hellinger greeted her, as she entered the kitchen.

"Well, hello, Margaret," Sara said, turning around. "I'm sorry, I didn't hear you at the front door."

"Oh, that's ok. Pastor Steve heard my knock. I would like to talk with both of you if I could. This concerns you as a couple."

"Certainly," Sara responded. The three friends sat down at the kitchen table.

"Well, there's no sense beating around the bush. As you know, our beloved Pastor Adam seems to be working for himself and not the church. And he's doing it non-stop. He's been cozying up to a lot of influential people in the congregation lately. Been taking people out to eat and meeting some in their homes. He even invited Frank and me to breakfast yesterday morning at our favorite restaurant downtown, but we declined. We're getting worried. You folks went through so much at Community, we don't want you to go through another horrid mess."

Steve and Sara nodded in agreement but knew inside that another fierce battle was just ahead of them.

"He's supposed to talk to the board about some new venture on Thursday," Steve responded. "Harold and Bob and I thought we should wait until after the meeting before we do anything more. We're thinking about calling his boss at *Hearts on Fire* shortly after that meeting."

"You should," Margaret insisted. "This guy's way out of control. And that doesn't speak well of *Hearts on Fire* either, does it?"

"No, it doesn't," Steve said. "Unfortunately, he has a lot of supporters here in the church, so this is not going to be easy. People will stand up for him."

"What about our contract with *Hearts on Fire*? Can we get out of it?" Mrs. Hellinger asked.

"I don't know. I could give Paul Samples a call."

"That's a good idea," Sara responded. "I'm sure Paul would be willing to give you his opinion."

"I'm sure he would. I'll give him a call later this morning. In the meantime, I suggest we all continue to pray over this situation."

"Agreed," Mrs. Hellinger responded. "Frank and I are already doing that."

"You two are such a blessing, Margaret," Sara said, squeezing Mrs. Hellinger's hand. "What would we have done without you these past few years?"

Mrs. Hellinger smiled. "You and Steve are special to Frank and me. We know you and your family were called here. No one has a right to interfere with that calling. We don't want to see you all hurt again." Mrs. Hellinger shook her head. Then looking at the clock on the wall, she started to get up from her chair. "Well, I better head for the office. Lots to do today."

"Thanks for stopping by, Margaret," Steve said, as he stood to see her to the door.

"Yes," Sara agreed.

"Don't mention it, you two." Mrs. Hellinger replied.

Samson, who had been resting on the floor next to Sara, went over to Mrs. Hellinger to help Steve escort his friend to the front door.

"Why thank you, Samson," Mrs. Hellinger laughed. She quickly rubbed his ears and headed for the front door.

After Mrs. Hellinger left, Steve and Sara sat and talked about the situation with Adam a little longer, and then Steve headed back to his office to call Paul Samples at the district office. Paul was in a meeting when Steve called but would get back to him afterward. A half-hour later, Paul called on the house phone. Steve filled Paul in on what was going on. Paul asked Steve to fax a copy of the agreement with *Hearts on Fire* to him. He also told Steve he would do some additional background checking on Pastor Daugherty. He had a friend in another city who was equipped to do a more in-depth investigation than he had the resources to do. Paul told Steve that it could take a few days or more to get back with him, but would do so as soon as he found something out. His friend might still be out of the country on business, so it depended on when he got back. Steve thanked Paul for his help. After the call was finished, he went back to the kitchen to let Sara know what Paul had said.

"I'm glad you called him," Sara told Steve, as she wiped the kitchen table with a dishcloth. "He's been a good friend and supporter."

"Yes, he has. He's been great for the district office as well."

Steve decided to spend the rest of the morning and early afternoon doing hospital visits. He had a few people to see that day. Since there was not much more he could do about Adam at that point, Steve chose to focus on other issues for the time being. He knew he would need to confront Adam again, but for now, he would just pray for guidance.

The next day was filled with all kinds of church business and events, including Mom's Club, Bible studies, planning committees, and choir practice in the evening. Steve stayed at the church for most of the day, breaking just to go out to eat for lunch and to grab a snack for supper. After everyone had gone home for the evening, Steve was left alone to lock up. Finally ready to go home himself, Steve walked down the main hall of the church to turn off the remaining lights in the building. Whistling a favorite hymn as he went, he was enjoying the quietness of the night. Then, out of the blue, he thought he heard Samson bark. It was the kind of bark he had heard Samson make when he wanted to warn a family member of impending danger. Steve looked around and shook his head.

"Samson's at home," he told himself, and then laughed out loud.

As Steve rounded the corner after coming out of the choir room, he suddenly heard the sound of a great rush of water. He stopped to determine where the sound had come from, hoping they didn't have a broken water pipe somewhere in the building. At that moment, at the end of the hallway, there appeared out of nowhere, a vision of a huge, terrifying, brown-gray sea creature, with a long dragon-like neck and powerful jaws, forcefully pushing its way to the surface of a great body of water.[1] It twisted and turned as it fought to loosen itself from a tangle of seaweed so that it could stay afloat on top of the water. While doing so, it screeched the most dreadful and piercing cry Steve had ever heard, until it was free of its restraints. Then spotting Steve, the great beast hissed at him, reared back with its eyes blazing red and full of hate and vengeance, and started swimming towards him with incredible speed and energy. Horrified, Steve stood frozen in fear, unable to move in any direction.

"Lord!" he finally managed to cry out.

Just then, the angel Steve had seen in his backyard in Nordstown, stood before him once again. He was positioned between Steve and the beast. Drawing his sword that glistened like the light of heaven, he turned toward the creature. Seeing the threat at hand, the beast stopped abruptly, retreated, and dove back into the water. Water splashed everywhere as the creature submerged into the deep, its tail visible for only a moment. Steve could feel a spray of water on his face. When it had disappeared, the angel walked toward Steve, took a second sword from his silver scabbard, and laid it down on the ground, motioning for Steve to pick it up.[2] Then he too was gone, and the entire vision vanished.

Breathing heavily and feeling overwhelmed, Steve braced himself against the wall of the hallway and forced himself to go into a nearby classroom to sit down until he could regain his composure. He didn't even notice that the chair he sat down on was made for children. He just wanted to get his bearings and pray. Wiping his forehead with his handkerchief, he sat for a few minutes in the dark room, his heart racing and pounding in his chest. Soon, he was praying in the spirit. A peace came over Steve, and he was finally able to stand up again. Steve decided to go and sit in the church sanctuary for a little while before attempting to drive home.

When he reached the dimly lit room, Steve slid into the first pew he came to.

"Lord, show me how to fight this one," he asked, looking up to heaven.

Steve sat and prayed for another half hour with tears running down his cheeks. As he prayed, he sensed the presence of the Holy Spirit filling the room. A greater feeling of peace quickly enveloped him, and he began to smile. His strength returned. Soon, Steve felt he was able to drive back home. He stood up and finished turning out the lights in the building. After locking the front door, he got in his car. Starting the engine, all he could think of was being with Sara.

When Steve walked in the front door of his house, Sara came running. "Where in the world have you been?" she asked, almost in tears. "I've been worried about you! I tried calling you on your cell phone several times tonight, but you didn't pick up."

"I'm sorry, Hon. I … I …" Steve started to shake as he was still reliving the vision he just had at the church. "I couldn't…"

"What's wrong, Steve?" Sara asked becoming scared.

At that moment, Samson came in from the living room to see what was going on. He went right over to Steve and licked his hand. Appreciating the welcome, Steve quickly rubbed Samson's ears. Then he reached for Sara, who was trying to get past Samson to get to him, and pulled her close. They stood quietly, holding on to each other in the hallway until Steve felt at peace again. When he was able to speak, Steve took off his coat and hung it up on the coat rack in the hall, and led Sara to the kitchen table where he proceeded to tell Sara what he had seen that evening at the church.

Sara was stunned. The battle they were engaged in was going to be worse than she thought. The two decided to go into the living room to pray before Steve ate the supper that was still being warmed in the oven for him. There seemed to be an urgency to do so. When they finished praying, both agreed that some kind of fast was in order. They would start the next morning. Steve needed to replenish his system right then. God would show them what to do about this trouble that had darkened their path. They needed to be ready and armed for the vicious advancing attacks.

All of the board members of Anderson Hills were present at the board meeting that Thursday evening. Without exception, each member arrived early, eager to hear what Pastor Adam had in mind for the next step in their evangelistic outreach ministry. Adam was wearing a new dark blue suit, a white shirt, and a red power tie. His hair had the look of a recent cut, and he was wearing his usual cologne, slightly on the heavy side. He was poised and ready to make the best sales pitch of his life. When it came time for Adam to speak, he almost jumped out of his chair when he heard his name announced. His enthusiasm was more than evident. After thanking everyone for being there, he began to expertly present his vision for a new building project, which as they soon found out, would result in an evangelistic building complex. One that would service evangelistic efforts around the world.

Steve, Bob, and Harold closely watched the reaction of the other board members as Adam rolled out his five-year multi-million dollar plan, complete with PowerPoint and handouts filled with all kinds of charts, graphs, and financial projections. The bottom lines looked overwhelmingly inviting. Many of the members sat mesmerized and quickly grabbed on to his vision in a big way. Some of them were nodding and saying "Amen!" and "Praise the Lord!" After forty-five minutes of his emotional appeal, Adam finished his presentation and opened the floor for questions and comments. No one spoke at first, because they were still taking in what he just presented to them.

Steve took a deep breath, and spoke up first, "Adam this is all great. No one can deny that. And I don't want to burst any bubbles here, but as I mentioned to you the other day, I think we are moving just a little too fast. My understanding when we contracted with *Hearts on Fire* a few months ago, was that you would help us start an evangelistic outreach program, not promote your personal vision or become the hub of activity for the entire *Hearts on Fire* ministry in this part of the country."

Adam stared at Steve. It was evident he was becoming agitated. He reached up and nervously adjusted his tie.

"I don't think you understand what I am proposing here, Pastor Steve. " 'The harvest is plentiful but the workers are few.' "[3] This is a chance of a lifetime!"

"Yes, it would be an exciting venture, but before we get a little carried away, everyone," Steve said, turning and looking around at all those sitting at the board table, "we need to be in prayer and seek God's opinion on this proposal. This is a huge undertaking, and we have to consider that we also have a lot of other ministries to tend to here as well. We've only been at this evangelistic outreach program for a short time and we're just getting our feet wet. With all due respect, we cannot allow one person's enthusiasm to cloud our judgment. The impact on the world, yes, could be huge, but I'm feeling we're just not ready yet."

"But I say we are!" Adam came back defensively, his eyes were intense. Everyone looked surprised at his dramatic response. "What are you afraid of, Pastor Steve?" he chided him and began to pace the front of the room. "Are we getting you out of your comfort zone? Are you underestimating God?"

"Excuse me?" Steve raised his voice. "This is not a matter of comfort zone, Adam, nor am I putting limitations on God," Steve said, looking Adam straight in the eyes. "I know what the Lord can do when He is behind something. I've seen Him build this very congregation from the ground up. My concern is a matter of timing and discernment. Is your proposal in fact in alignment with the will of Almighty God? Is it also what's best for this congregation? Don't get me wrong, we are sincerely grateful for what you have done so far, but not everyone here at the church shares your whole vision. You're making some huge assumptions here. That is not what we contracted with your organization to do at Anderson Hills."

Harold Cannon broke in.

"Adam, I agree with Steve. We need to give your vision a little more time and prayer. I, for one, would like to see you work with the seminary student we were supposed to have hired a while back and build our program from there."

"But I have been on the front lines," Adam quickly shot back. I know what is needed out there." Then turning to everyone at the meeting, he almost begged, "Please don't let this opportunity slip through your fingers. The time is now. I can feel it! I know I am right on this. God has given me this vision for Anderson Hills. You have been chosen 'for such a time as this!' "[4]

Bob Brown was about to speak when another voice spoke out.

"I agree with Adam. I'm feeling the same thing." It was Angel Gonzalez, one of the newer members of the board. "With all the things happening in the world today, I believe the Lord is coming back soon. How can we ignore such an opportunity, especially when someone is willing to lead us in it? Adam Daugherty has clearly been sent here from heaven. I have to support him on this one. The iron is hot. The time to strike is now. We cannot show any fear." At that point, her eyes were full of tears, which she quickly wiped away with a Kleenex she retrieved from her purse.

At that, all of the board members began talking amongst themselves, most excited about the possibilities, while the smaller part of the group tried to encourage their fellow board members to slow down. The group was drastically divided on the issue, and Adam was visibly delighted with the division.

"Yes, we cannot stand in the way of God's purposes," another voice lifted above the talking. Others responded in agreement.

Bob Brown made an effort to calm the group down and was soon able to speak. He raised the motion to table the discussion until the same time the following year when they had more time to see how things went with the current evangelistic outreach program. Another member quickly motioned to continue discussions at the next meeting and to take a vote then. After an emotional tug of war, the side supporting Adam's venture won out to continue the discussion at the next meeting, and then the group moved on to other church business.

Adam was overjoyed and thanked his supporters profusely for answering God's call. But Steve and his friends were shocked and deeply troubled. The door was now open for Adam Daugherty to have a stronger foothold in Anderson Hills. His charm, emotional pleas, and manipulations had worked. He had most of the board members eating right out of his hands.

After the meeting, Steve, Bob, and Harold met in Steve's office at the church. Angela Camp and Jerry Simpson, two other long-term elders, joined the group when they saw them in there talking. They too were concerned about what was happening at Anderson Hills and had voted against proceeding with Pastor Adam's proposal. Together, the small group decided it was time to contact Don Williamson, the president of *Hearts on Fire* to fill him in on what was going on at Anderson Hills. Pastor Steve would be the one placing the call, but Bob and Harold would be on the line as well. Angela and Jerry would be praying over the conversation during that time.

Later that evening, Steve sent an e-mail to Mr. Williamson, requesting a conference call with him and a couple of board members of Anderson Hills. When he received a reply, he set up a time for Friday afternoon. The three were hopeful that Mr. Williamson would soon intervene. When the phone call took place the next day, the three men started by expressing their thanks for what *Hearts on Fire* had done for the church so far. They immediately followed with their concerns about Adam. Mr. Williamson listened intently and promised to get back with them the following week after he had spoken with Adam. He wanted to make sure there were no misunderstandings. The only thing that Steve and his group of supporting board members could do now was to sit back and wait.

The church services that Sunday were packed as usual. Word continued to go out into the community about Adam's fiery and inspirational sermons. The local radio station aired some of his sermons at a reduced cost to Anderson Hills, to help build the church's evangelical outreach ministry.

Unfortunately, Adam was avoiding Steve now. The two had made their positions very clear to the board, and the opposite camps were quietly beginning to form within the church body when the members found out what had happened at the meeting. It was hard at times for Steve to even be in the same building with Adam because he knew what his real intentions were. Although the two were able to put on a false front for a while for the sake of the church family, their private interactions were not as amicable as they had once been.

As Steve sat in his church office after the second morning service reflecting on Adam's sermon, there was a knock on his door. Steve got up to see who it was. Sara's friend, Lisa Watson, was standing there with a troubled look on her face. Steve invited Lisa to come in.

"What can I do for you today, Lisa?"

"Well, I feel funny about coming here," she said, as she entered the room. "Almost as if I'm tattling on someone, but this is something that can't be ignored."

"Oh? What's going on?" Steve replied as he headed back to his desk chair.

"It's Susan Pillar, one of our newer adult Sunday School teachers. She's been teaching some really strange stuff in her classes. I know, because I sat in on more than one of them myself. I'm afraid some people are buying into what she is saying. And she seems to be bringing in others to her classes with the same mindset."

"What is she saying?" Steve asked uneasily.

"Well, some of it is New Age, and she seems to have meditation confused with prayer. She's also saying that all roads lead to God and that Jesus is 'a way' and not 'the way' to God. One day, she even endorsed reincarnation."

"How long has this been going on?"

"I'm not sure, but people are starting to talk about it. I heard a couple of new members say today that they were leaving the church because of the heresy that is being taught at Anderson Hills. They were pretty mad. I tried to tell them what she said was not the church's position, but they argued back that she still represented the church. I don't know how she got that teaching position, but she shouldn't be here, Steve. She's dangerous."

"I don't know either, but I am going to look into it right away. We don't need that kind of theology going around this congregation."

At that moment, Tina Burger, the Sunday School director walked into the main office to drop the Sunday School attendance folders off to Mrs. Hellinger's administrative assistant, Nancy. Spotting her, Steve called her into his office.

Looking at Lisa, Steve said, "You need to tell Tina what you know."

"I understand," Lisa replied.

When Tina came into the pastor's office, Steve offered her a seat and then Lisa told her about Susan. After she finished, Tina's face was flushed with embarrassment.

"I don't know what to say, Steve. To be honest, I did get a couple of comments about her a few weeks ago, but it didn't sound serious at the time. I thought maybe they misunderstood her comments. I guess I should have followed up with Susan. This lady came to us well recommended by another Christian education director and Susan's former church pastor. You know we check out everyone who wants to teach here, and Susan has been attending Anderson Hills for several months now."

"And to this point, we've had some very good teachers," Steve replied. "But we can't allow this woman to teach as long as she purports this kind of doctrine."

At that moment, Brice Holly, another Sunday School teacher in his thirties came flying into the office. When he saw the group meeting in Steve's office, he hurried in, thinking that his emergency overrode anything they were talking about.

"Pastor Steve, I'm sorry to interrupt, but we've got a problem," Brice blurted out.

"Does it happen to have anything to do with another Sunday School teacher?"

"Actually, yes it does. How'd you know?"

"Lucky guess." Steve motioned for him to take a seat while he got up to close the office door.

As each member of the group relayed whatever they knew about Susan's class, Steve carefully jotted down some notes. He realized he needed to confront Susan as soon as possible, but he wanted to know exactly what was being said. He also asked Lisa to identify the members who had said they were leaving the church. He then asked the group to give him the names of anyone else they could think of who might be espousing the same false teachings in the church.

After the group shared all that they knew, they left the meeting to head home. Steve looked up Susan's contact information and sent her an e-mail, indicating that he wanted to meet with her sometime that week, and to please give him a phone call.

He also looked up the phone numbers of the members who had angrily left the church that day. He would give them a call later that afternoon before the evening service. Steve knew how critical it was to get this situation under control before it grew into a bigger problem. *If only he had taken more precautions concerning Pastor Daugherty.* Thinking back on the vision in the church hallway, Steve realized he was being warned of a myriad of attacks from the enemy, simultaneously coming against the church. As the appointed shepherd of the flock, he had to protect the members of the fellowship from any kind of distortion of the truth. Steve also decided to email Bob and Harold to let them know what was going on, and ask them to touch base with the people he was told might be spreading some false doctrine as well.

That afternoon, Susan Pillar responded to Steve's e-mail and said she could stop by his office on Wednesday morning. Steve set a meeting for 9:00 a.m. She was curious as to why she was being summoned to his office, but Steve decided to be evasive in that regard until he was able to talk with her in person.

As the day went on, Steve managed to get a hold of the two new members who wanted to leave the church. They were cordial but offended that Susan had been placed in a teaching position when she obviously did not have her theology correct. They thanked Steve for calling but had already decided to start looking around for another fellowship to be a part of. When the conversation ended, Steve sadly put down the phone. He and the board had worked so hard to help build a good reputation for the church. The presence of just one person had begun to change all of that. The next day, Steve received phone calls from several other members of the church, complaining about Ms. Pillar's lessons. He assured them he was aware of the situation, and it was being taken care of. Fortunately, they weren't threatening to leave the church. They trusted Steve and the work he had done there since the ministry started.

Tuesday morning, Steve received a phone call from Mr. Williamson from *Hearts on Fire*. While he was polite and friendly, he was adamant that he was not willing to intervene in the problems the group had shared with him concerning Pastor Adam. After talking with Adam, he felt that there was simply a conflict in personalities and suggested that they work things out directly with Adam. Their organization was excited with what Adam had accomplished there and did not see how Adam could be overstepping his bounds.

Steve was flabbergasted. What had Adam told him? He could just imagine Adam's conversation with the president. He was certainly good at twisting the truth and covering his tracks.

On Wednesday morning, Susan Pillar came into the main office and let Mrs. Hellinger know she had an appointment with Pastor Steve. Susan was dressed in a rose-colored sweat suit and her shoulder-length brown hair was pulled up in a ponytail. She explained to Mrs. Hellinger that she was going to be teaching an aerobics class later that morning. When Mrs. Hellinger let Steve know that Susan was there, he came out right away to greet her in the main office.

After Susan went into Steve's office, he shared with her the concerns he had been getting about the content of her teaching. He asked her directly if she had been bringing those ideas into her classes, and if she believed them. When she confirmed that she had and that she was convinced those things were true and accurate, Steve told her that he had no choice but to remove her from her teaching duties. He offered to enroll her into an online Christian theology class that a nearby seminary was offering, but she declined even though Anderson Hills would be paying for her to take it.

"I don't understand this at all, Pastor Steve. I was invited to teach here. I was interviewed, and I signed the statement of faith you have everyone sign. I taught at another church last year and no one complained there."

"I hear what you are saying, Susan, but obviously, your interview did not disclose your thoughts on certain issues. And as for the other church, they either didn't pick up on what you were teaching or they, unfortunately, agree with you. I'm sorry, but we cannot have that kind of worldview taught here."

Susan quickly became defensive and angry.

"This isn't right, Pastor. You can't do this to me!" she almost shouted.

"Actually, yes we can. You are teaching against church doctrine. If you would just listen to-"

"No, I don't have to listen!" Susan raised her voice. "I don't have to be treated this way either! I spent a lot of time preparing those lessons! I sacrificed personal time. And what thanks do I get?" She stood up angrily. "I'm out of here!"

When she got to his door, she turned and said, "I'm calling my lawyer this afternoon! This is censorship!"

With that, Susan left Steve's office and stomped through the main office, slamming the door behind her. Mrs. Hellinger and Nancy jumped in their seats at the sound of the door banging in its frame as it closed.

As Steve stood at his doorway, Mrs. Hellinger turned to him and said half-teasing, "Something you said?"

Steve rolled his eyes, shook his head, and then went back into his office. He felt bad about what had just happened, but he knew something had to be said. Heretical teachings could not be tolerated in the church. Susan was responsible for how she reacted to his decision. There was no way to cushion the blow. If she took the time to think about it, she would understand he was right.

Steve sat back down in his chair and started to type an email to Tina Burger. He mentioned that the meeting did not go well with Susan and that she should not be returning to teaching the adult class. Tina could follow up with Susan if she thought it would help, but she might want to wait a day or two. Tina emailed back a few minutes later and thanked him for talking with Susan. She would follow up with Susan in a couple of days to see if she could reason with her a little more.

Susan did not return to Anderson Hills, but began telling others she knew how she was mistreated, emphasizing that Pastor Steve Hanson was a controlling individual. Steve and some of the board members soon found themselves putting out fires here and there because of her teachings. Unfortunately, even though Steve had removed Susan from the Sunday School teaching staff, the damage had been done and would take some time to undo. Steve made sure he addressed her erroneous teachings (not mentioning the source) in the next few sermons, to hopefully counter some of the confusion Susan's statements had created for some people in the congregation. Susan's lawyer threats were never followed through, but her verbal bashing of the church within the local community continued for months.

The next couple of weeks went by quickly. It was time for Steve and Sara to drive Mary to school in Ohio. They helped Mary pack and get ready for the big day. Filling the Jeep Cherokee with all of Mary's things brought a wave of emotions inside both of her parents. They were letting go of their little girl so that the Lord could bring about His purposes in her adult life. Prayerfully, they had done everything to help prepare her for this very moment. How proud they were of their daughter and her accomplishments. They were also thankful for her faith in God and her choice of schools.

Climbing into the vehicle, packed to the brim, Mary turned and waved goodbye to Samson, who was looking sadly out of the front window of the living room. She wiped away the tears, forming in her eyes, as they pulled out of the drive and shifted her mind to the new adventure that lay ahead for her. She was also thinking of Joshua Franklin. He would be meeting her and her parents at the girls' dorm when they arrived. That would be the best part of being at Christ's College that day.

Mary's thoughts then turned to her brother Peter. He was at school, but the two had arranged to spend the afternoon together at the mall the day before, where they just kicked around and had fun, like when they were younger. It seemed strange that they would now be separated, but they understood it was time to follow the call of God on each of their lives. They said their goodbyes just before Peter left the house that morning, promising to email and call each other as often as they could.

The ride to Christ's College was three hours long. The trio decided to drive for half an hour and then stop by a small family restaurant they had enjoyed eating at after moving to Nordstown. When they reached the restaurant, Steve pulled into the crowded parking lot, and the family went inside. An old-fashioned jukebox was playing a fifties song by Frank Sinatra when they entered. The large open room smelled like fried food and baked goods and was packed full of customers. Fortunately, there was an empty booth near the front entrance and cash register. As the three sat down and made themselves comfortable, they began to look through the menus already placed in front of them by one of the waitresses.

A minute later, Mary suddenly said, "Hey, isn't that Pastor Daugherty over there?"

Steve looked across the room to see Adam Daugherty and one of the members of his church chatting away over lunch. Adam was facing the other way, but it was unmistakable that it was him. The man who Adam was talking with was Alex Keys, a big giver and a very respected member of the church fellowship. He was also running for an elder position. Steve looked at Sara. She nodded.

"Should we go over and say hello?" Mary asked as she placed her napkin in her lap.

"Uh, no. As a matter of fact, I think we should leave," Steve told her.

"Why?" Mary looked puzzled.

"I'll tell you in the car. Let's try Bob Evans in the next town. Sorry, Angel."

"Well, okay. But this is really weird."

At that moment, a waitress in her mid-forties with blonde curly hair, came over to the table to take their orders. She had a pleasant smile and was dressed in a light blue-gray uniform. Her silver wire-rimmed glasses hung from a chain around her neck, and her perfume smelled like lilacs. She pulled her pen and an order pad out of her white apron and flipped the pad open.

"What would you all like to have today?" She said, looking at them expectantly.

"I'm afraid we won't be staying, Ma'am," Steve said, getting up. "Sorry. Unfortunately, we have to leave."

"Oh, I'm sorry to hear that," the waitress responded. "I hope it wasn't anything we did."

"No, no," Steve replied. "It's just one of those things."

"Ok then," she said, closing her order pad and putting it and the pen back in her pocket. "Please come back again soon."

"We will. Thank you," Steve said handing the waitress their menus. He hurried his wife and daughter out of the restaurant, so they would not be spotted by Adam and Alex.

After leaving their booth unnoticed by the two men on the other side of the restaurant, the three Hansons headed for their car and were soon on their way to Bob Evans. Steve explained to Mary that there were some concerns over Pastor Adam and it was best he didn't run into him that day. Mary accepted her father's explanation and promised to pray over the matter. Steve did not want to say too much because he didn't want her to worry, especially since she was moving away from home. Nothing more was said about Pastor Adam, and the three enjoyed the rest of their trip to Christ's College, talking excitedly about Mary's future.

The family arrived at the college just in time to check Mary in, take a tour of the campus, and have an early supper with Joshua. It had been an emotional day for the family, and aside from the fact that her dorm room wasn't completely ready when they got there, all else went well for the new student. Before leaving, Steve and Sara prayed with Mary and Joshua, and the two promised to be home every weekend they could manage to get away from school. As Steve and Sara pulled out of the dorm's parking lot, they waved goodbye to Mary and Joshua and headed for the expressway.

By now, Steve and Sara were anxious to get back home. When they were almost at the turn for the highway, Steve's cell phone began to ring. Sara reached over to answer it because Steve was driving. It was Paul Samples. Sara asked Paul to hang on for a minute so they could stop and change drivers. Steve quickly pulled into a gas station he spotted nearby and took the phone from Sara as he got out of the car. He talked with Paul as the couple changed places behind the wheel. Paul had found out some interesting information on Adam Daugherty.

"Sorry, it took so long to get back to you, Steve. As I mentioned, my friend Darrel was out of the country for a while."

"No problem. What did you find out?"

"It seems that your friend, Pastor Daugherty, has been somewhat of a troublemaker in the past. The reason he left his work as a traveling evangelist around six years ago was because he couldn't get along with some of the people in his organization. He also tried to take over the ministry of another evangelist he was working with on his last Asian tour. After that, he had a couple of other ministry jobs before landing his current job with *Hearts on Fire*. How he did that, I don't know. It appears that he had some problems with the two previous employers as well. I don't know who vouched for him this time. Maybe someone gave him a glowing report just to get rid of him. Steve, from what you've told me about Adam, I would have to agree that he wants to take over your church, so he can build his own ministry again and in a big way."

"What would you suggest I do?" Steve questioned.

"Well, according to the contract your church signed, you have agreed to certain things. If he does not fulfill those areas and you can show that he has intentionally overstepped his bounds, then you can petition *Hearts on Fire* to release Anderson Hills from your contract. Of course, since *Hearts on Fire* seems to be oblivious to what is going on with Adam, it's not going to be easy to prove your point. You are also going to be at odds with half of your congregation. If *Hearts on Fire* still refuses to listen, that's when I get involved. I would suggest you keep good notes on the situation. Get a few written statements too regarding concerns with Adam. He's a sly one, Steve. He's left quite a trail of messes behind him. We'll have to handle this very carefully."

"Thanks, Paul. We really appreciate your help. It seems like you are always bailing me out of some kind of trouble."

"Well, at no fault of your own, Steve. Besides, that's what friends are for."

"You're the best kind of friend anyone could have. I'll let the others know what you found out. Have a good week!"

When the conversation ended, Steve put his phone back in its holder. He turned to Sara and sighed. "Well, Babe, here we go again."

Chapter 13

Another Dream Fades

$\mathcal{F}$all was passing quickly, and the congregation of Anderson Hills Church Fellowship would soon be voting on the elders who would be serving on the board for the next four years. Current church elders were allowed to run for re-election for one additional term, which would include those who served on the original board, but then would have to sit out a term before running again. The new elder board would be installed at the end of December to prepare for the New Year, so it would not be long until a new board was in place.

Adam Daugherty was working overtime to influence the election by endorsing candidates who supported his evangelistic vision. He continued to meet with numerous people in their homes and bought gifts for them to try to sway them into voting for people who embraced his agenda. Steve, on the other hand, continued to encourage his congregation to vote for members who were loyal to the original vision and mission of Anderson Hills, which was strong on discipleship and individual ministries. Despite Adam's obvious campaign efforts, he was also being unusually nice to Steve and Sara at this time. They surmised he was doing that to keep Steve from contacting *Hearts on Fire* again before the election.

One evening, Adam showed up at the door of the Hansons under the guise that he was dropping off the new *Hearts on Fire* crusade schedule. Peter was home alone up in his room, working on a term paper for his psychology class. Steve and Sara were over at the Browns' house, enjoying an evening of fellowship with them. As Peter was finishing up his assignment, the front doorbell rang. Peter stood and stretched, glad for the break, and ran downstairs to answer the door. Samson came running out of the family room to join him. As Peter reached the door, he saw who the visitor was through the glass in the door. Adam Daugherty was not one of Peter's favorite people. He had heard enough from his parents and some of the board members, to know that he could not be entirely trusted. Yet, even before his parents had trouble with the man, he was leery of anyone who was constantly flattering others and giving them gifts.

Realizing what Samson's response might be to Adam's visit, Peter turned and told him to go back to the family room and lay down. When Samson obeyed, Peter opened the front door to see what Adam wanted.

"Hello, Pastor Adam," Peter greeted half-heartedly. "What can I do for you?"

"Well, hello there young Mr. Hanson. Are your parents at home?"

"No, they're over visiting some friends."

"Ah, could I leave some information with you for your dad?" Adam asked, being overly nice.

"Sure," Peter replied, reaching out for a manila folder Adam was handing to him.

"Thank you, Peter... Ya know," Adam said, scratching his head. "Now that I think about it, your dad mentioned he had something for me he was bringing to my office tomorrow. He said it was in a large white envelope on his work stand. If I could pick it up today, that would be even better. Could I come in? I bet I could spot the envelope right away."

Peter hesitated. There was something fishy about Pastor Adam's request. Curious, though, as to what he was up to, Peter decided to let Adam in to see if he was telling the truth.

"I don't remember Dad saying anything about a white envelope, but I could look for you."

Peter opened the front door for Adam to step in. He then started down the hall to his father's study.

Adam, without hesitation, followed close behind Peter to Steve's home office, carefully watching to make sure Samson wasn't hiding behind some corner, ready to jump out at him. When they reached the office, Peter began to look through his father's things on the work stand near the sofa. There were a number of papers and files stacked there. As he looked through the pile, his back was turned to Adam. Pastor Adam began to wander around the room, pretending to look at the myriad of books in the bookcases covering two of the walls.

"Boy, your dad sure has a lot of great books!" he noted, as he began looking at the shelves and working his way over to Steve's desk.

Making sure Peter wasn't looking, he quickly began to sort through some of the things there. Spotting something of interest, Adam lifted an opened black notebook to read the contents of the pages a little closer. They were notes on a recent meeting Steve had had with Harold Cannon and Bob Brown.

Adam was ready to tear a few pages from the notebook, so he could put them in his coat pocket when Samson came into the room. Spotting Pastor Adam, he began to snarl at him, showing his teeth. Peter turned around to see Adam holding something in his hand he had obviously picked up from his father's desk. Adam hurriedly dropped the notebook back onto the desk as Samson began to bark at him. Peter grabbed Samson by the collar and told him to be still. Samson unwillingly did what he was told, but kept a watchful eye on Adam.

"I'm sorry, Pastor Daugherty. I just don't see that white envelope. You'll have to come back when Dad is here or wait until tomorrow. I'm sure he will have it for you then. I don't think you'll find what you are looking for on Dad's desk."

"Uh, yeah. I see that. Just thought I'd check since I was in here," he smiled sheepishly and then moved away from the desk.

Samson was becoming restless. It was obvious he did not like Adam Daugherty being in Steve's office. He began to growl with his teeth clenched, the whites of his eyes turning red. Peter told Samson to be quiet. Adam smiled and thanked Peter for his time. Then looking down at Samson, he quickly moved past him and Peter and headed for the front door.

"Please tell your dad, I was here."

"I sure will, Pastor Daugherty," Peter said, with a grin on his face. "Thanks for stopping by. I'll make sure he gets this folder too."

"Thank you, son. I'll just let myself out. Bye now." Adam couldn't move fast enough to get away from Samson.

After Adam closed the front door, Peter let go of Samson's collar. Samson immediately ran to the door barking the whole way, jumping up on the glass pane, and clawing at the wood. After seeing that Adam was in his car and leaving the property, he stopped barking and ran back to find Peter, wagging his tail as he went. He almost looked like he was smiling with his mouth stretched wide and his tongue hanging out.

"He's gone now, old friend," Peter told him, as he walked down the hall to join him. Rubbing Samson's ears as the dog panted, he said, "Yes, I know Sammy. I don't like that man either."

A couple of hours later, Steve and Sara returned home from visiting the Browns.' Peter was sitting in the family room watching TV, and Samson was lying in his bed in the corner of the room. When he saw his parents come in, Peter got up and quickly told them about what had happened earlier that evening.

Steve shook his head, "I find it disturbing that he was rummaging through the things on my desk and reading my journal notebook. . . You know, I'm not sure what he was referring to regarding a white envelope. It must have been some stats I offered to share with him some time ago. I had forgotten about getting them to him."

"Maybe," Sara said thoughtfully. "I think he had another reason for coming." Sara looked at her husband. "What's particularly unsettling is that we thought it was odd when Samson acted so vicious toward Adam the first time he was here. It looks like our little friend had that guy pegged long before any of us did."

"I have to agree with you on that, Sara," Steve replied. "All the more reason to keep an eye on him now."

The three decided to have a snack and watch the news together before getting ready for bed. Samson, waking up from a nap, met them in the kitchen, where Sara was popping some popcorn. He was greeted with hugs and ear rubbings, then Steve gave him his favorite treat, a turkey hotdog which he quickly and happily consumed.

The day of the congregational meeting at Anderson Hills soon arrived. The new elders would be elected that evening. Steve and Sara fasted the day before, praying for God's will to be done in the church they helped start. The sanctuary was packed to capacity that night, so some folding chairs were placed in the lobby just outside of the worship center for the overflow. Pastor Daugherty was seen milling around the congregants as they entered the church doors, talking excitedly with them. This was a big day for him. The election was one of the early items on the agenda so that the votes could be counted before the meeting was over. Before the ballots were passed out, the congregants were reminded that only members could vote. This seemed to frustrate Adam, as he anxiously waited for the results from his seat in the first row of the pews.

At the end of the meeting, Harold Cannon stood in front of the congregation to share the results. He, Bob Brown, and Angela Camp had not been re-elected. However, Jerry Simpson maintained his position on the board. A couple of other older elders were not re-elected either. And not to Steve's surprise, Alex Keys was elected to the board, along with some other new people. In sum, the board was now drastically stacked in favor of Adam's vision for the evangelistic outreach program at the church. Adam was beside himself after the announcement. Later, he was seen vigorously shaking the hands of all of the new board members at the reception in the fellowship hall after the congregational meeting.

Steve stood back from the crowd and lamented the fact that the original vision and mission of Anderson Hills was fading. A shiny new vision was taking its place, one that had questionable origins and intentions. Steve wondered if the congregation realized what they were trading for. He dreaded the first board meeting of the New Year. Adam Daugherty would then have more control over what happened at Anderson Hills than he would. Steve was beginning to wonder what his role at the church would end up being. Would he continue to lead the congregation?

When Steve and Sara got home later that evening, Steve placed a call to his father, Joseph Hanson, in New York. It gave him comfort to talk with the man who had had such an impact on his life. Joe wasn't just his father; he was his mentor and devoted friend. When they finished their conversation, he talked with his mother for a few minutes as well. He was always moved by her sweet spirit and strong faith in the Lord. Marianne was the encourager of the family. No one ever left her presence without a kind or uplifting word from her lips. How blessed he and his brother had been to be raised by such special parents. He then called his brother, Mike, and talked with him. All of them promised to be praying for him and Sara and Anderson Hills.

Sara sat and played the piano as Steve talked with his family members. As she played softly, she closed her eyes so she could escape, if even for a few moments, from what was happening at the church. She was also trying to push back the memories of what had happened at Community Church. After playing for a while, Sara decided to call Mary at school when she heard Steve hang up the phone in his office. Sara didn't tell her daughter everything that was going on, because she didn't want Mary to worry and not be able to study. Final exams were coming up soon. She just asked her and Joshua to be in prayer. Mary said they would be praying and promised to be home early for Christmas.

In December, the new members of the board were installed during a special ceremony at the second service. Adam insisted on some fanfare and paid for another reception following the service. Steve wondered where Adam was getting all of his money. It seemed like he had a never-ending supply. After that day, Adam began to ignore Steve and Sara again. He spent a lot of time socializing with the people of Anderson Hills, promoting his dream to all who would listen. It was almost as if he was running for political office. His sermons became even more passionate as he pushed to get more new members excited about his vision for an evangelistic building complex.

Steve's parents and his brother and wife came that year for another visit at Christmas. Mary and Joshua also came home early, as promised, and were seen a lot together by their parents. On Christmas Eve, the Hansons invited the Browns, the Hellingers, and the Cannons over for a festive celebration with their visiting out-of-town family members. Paul Samples came with his wife, Mia. Sara's friend, Lisa Wright, was also invited and she brought her new boyfriend, Dr. James Lin, a man in his mid-forties and a heart surgeon, originally from Taiwan. Lisa had met Dr. Lin at a hospital in Philadelphia during a nursing conference. He was lecturing on the importance of good aftercare for heart patients and took an interest in Lisa when she approached him with more questions after his presentation. What was especially attractive to each of them as they talked was that they were both Christians. He asked Lisa out that evening, and their relationship grew steadily from there. James was a widower with an eighteen-year-old daughter, who was just starting college, and like Lisa, he was looking for love again. After seeing the two together, Sara and Steve anticipated a wedding before the end of the coming year. Perhaps Steve would be performing it.

Steve dreaded going to the first board meeting of the New Year. He knew Adam had been gearing up for another emotional plea to the board. Adam was also becoming more critical of Steve, not only to him directly, but in his comments to others in the congregation. He wanted everyone to know that Steve was not a supporter of his God-given dream. That night, Adam was ready to start talking about a capital campaign. He came equipped with an architect's vision of the complex. It was three times the size of the building they already had. His hard work had paid off. Before the end of the meeting, he was awarded the go-ahead to start promoting the building project to the congregation. They would have a chance to vote on it in a couple of months. Steve knew at that point that the new board would never support getting out of their contract with *Hearts on Fire,* so he needed to find other ways to convince the congregation they were being used.

That night, though, Steve did have one breakthrough. He managed to convince the board to hire Jonathan Wells, the seminary student who was interested in evangelistic outreach, as a part-time associate pastor. Thirty hours a week would greatly benefit the congregation and give Steve more help. Jonathan's office would be located directly across from Adam's office in the church basement. Fortunately for Steve, this young man took a liking to him right away and was willing to do whatever the senior pastor expected of him. His loyalty was never to Adam, whom he viewed as being a little too pushy and controlling. He sensed right away that Adam had his personal agenda for the church, after first meeting him, and wanted no part of it.

As the winter weeks went by, Adam did his best to try to make Steve look as bad to others as he could behind Steve's back. He maintained a more positive and cooperative exterior when he was in front of a large group or when Steve was present but was very different around smaller groups of people when Steve was not close by. His advantage was that many of the new people didn't know Steve as well as those who had helped found the church. Fed up with the abuse, Steve decided to approach Adam again one morning in Adam's office. He had waited for Adam to arrive that day, and after saying a quick prayer, he headed down to the basement to talk with him.

"Adam, I would like a word with you," Steve said forcefully, as he stood at Adam's office door."

"Certainly, Pastor," Adam responded, annoyed at Steve's unannounced meeting, not looking up from what he was working on.

Steve went into Adam's office and closed the door behind him. Taking a seat in front of Adam's desk, he began the conversation. Looking directly at his colleague, he said, "I think it's time we talk about a few things, Adam. And I am going to be frank about them . . . It is more than apparent now to almost everyone in the church that we have some differences. That, at least for now, we won't be able to change. However, I would greatly appreciate it if you would stop trying to put me down to others. I know what your game is, and I don't like it. If you don't stop interfering with my ministry here, I will be forced to take action against you and *Hearts on Fire*."

Adam looked up from his paperwork, not surprised by Steve's words, "Why Stevie, are you threatening me?"

"I don't threaten, Adam. Not about things that affect my ministry at this church. I am disgusted and fed up with your smear campaign."

"I have no idea what you are talking about," Adam said with a smirk. "But as for you, my friend, I don't have to say anything. People see you for what you are."

"What I am?" Steve was taken by surprise. "I have worked hard at building a strong and respected ministry here at Anderson Hills! We had a wonderful congregation with a minimum of problems until you came!"

"Like the reputation, you had at Community Church? From what I heard, you failed miserably there."

"How dare you criticize something you know nothing about!" Steve shot back.

"Oh, don't I?" Adam smirked again. "And how about that little fiasco here with the Sunday School teacher who was teaching heresy? What was her name? Aw yes, Mizzzz Peeelaaar. People left here because of your mistake to allow her to teach adult classes."

"I did not invite that woman to teach here, and I took care of the situation as soon as I found out about it. I even followed up with sermons against those heresies, and you know I did, Adam!"

"I know people are still talking about it."

"They're talking about it or you are talking to them about it?"

Adam was becoming agitated. "So why did you really come here to talk with me today, Stevie? To intimidate me?" he almost shouted so anyone nearby could hear.

Then he lowered his voice.

"People are getting tired of your whining and false accusations about me. They are also tired of your dull meaningless sermons. They're here to hear me, Stevie. Me!"

"They come to hear from God, Adam, not you. You're not as popular as you think."

Adam glared at Steve. It was obvious that Adam was jealous and had every intention to continue to do what he could to build his evangelistic empire there at Anderson Hills. It was the perfect setup. Steve, recognizing his words were having no effect on Adam, switched to another topic.

"You know, Adam, I would also appreciate it if you would stay out of my personal things when you are in my home. As a matter of fact, don't come to my house unless I am there."

"I don't know what you are talking about," Adam lowered his eyes and pretended to be reading something on his desk.

"Yes, you do. You may think you're pretty shrewd, but I know what you are. And God knows what you are too. There's a lot of people who have been taken in by your charm and your wit, but not everyone has been duped by your so-called 'evangelistic complex vision.' And someday, your schemes to further your ministry ambitions are going to backfire on you. I only pray you realize that before you split this congregation in half."

"I think you better leave now, Pastor Hanson," Adam said, as he slammed down the pen he had in his hand on the desk. "The board and I are going to be moving forward with the capital campaign whether you like or not. You are standing in the way of a God-ordained project!" Adam said, raising his voice again.

"You mean an Adam-ordained project," Steve said, raising his voice as well. "How can you be so self-centered?" he demanded, his eyes fixed on Adam's. "Who gave you the right to take over this congregation? This is not your ministry! What you are doing is just plain evil!"

At that Adam jumped to his feet. "Leave!" he responded loudly, pointing irately at the door.

"Gladly," Steve said as he got up from the chair, feeling his face becoming hot. "One more thing, though, my name is Steven, not Stevie. Show some respect, you egotistical jerk!"

Steve turned and left Adam's workspace and angrily headed back upstairs to his office, wishing he and the board had never invited Adam Daugherty to come to Anderson Hills. When he reached the top of the stairs, he slammed the basement door. Those in the building within hearing distance stopped what they were doing and got up to see what was going on. Steve then proceeded to the main office, blowing past Mrs. Hellinger, and slamming his office door behind him.

Infuriated, Adam picked up a heavy dictionary and threw it across the room, hitting the wall with a loud bang, resulting in a large hole in the wallboard. Steve Hanson was not going to stand in the way of his dream becoming a reality. He had worked too hard to let that happen. It was time to push ahead with full force, and he knew what needed to be done.

As the next couple of months went by, Adam began to win over more and more of the church congregation to his vision. New visitors were still coming in each week. The church membership was now close to 700 people. Adam's disdain for Steve was becoming more apparent, especially to those who supported the senior pastor. Steve tried to keep his distance, understanding that anything he said would be manipulated to be used against him, but some encounters were unavoidable. Many people, drawn in by Adam's charisma, never suspected what

Adam was really up to. Before the church knew it, large sums of money were going into Adam's *Hearts on Fire* evangelistic ministry fund. He would soon have everything he had dreamed of for years.

Steve, Bob, and Harold attempted once again to talk with the organization's president. This time they were able to make a little headway. However, Adam soon convinced the president of *Hearts on Fire* that the board at Anderson Hills wanted this project, and Steve was trying to interfere. Adam brought up the conversation with his boss to the board to try to convince them Steve was jealous of his success and that he was being harassed by Steve and his cronies for his staying the course of his divinely inspired vision. Blinded from the truth, the majority of the board began to see Steve in a different light. In their eyes, he was a person standing in the way of the will of God.

The tension between the two men continued to mount, so the president of the board decided to call a special board meeting to discuss the matter with each of them present. Several people had sensed the tension and recently left the church. Steve was glad for the chance to air some concerns and contacted Paul Samples to see if he could be present at that meeting. Steve wanted to convince the board that something was greatly out of order, and they weren't getting it. Perhaps they would listen to what Paul had found out about Adam.

The special meeting was scheduled for the following week. At that time, Steve and Adam were each allowed to share their grievances concerning the situation with the board. Steve was allowed to speak first because he was the senior pastor. Steve was concerned when it was his time to speak that Paul Samples had not shown up for the meeting yet, but proceeded on his own, hoping Paul would soon arrive. In his comments to the group, he stated that Adam and the board had gone way beyond the original agreement with *Hearts on Fire,* and the church was standing behind a person who had intentionally hijacked the original vision and mission of the congregation for personal gain and fame. In addition, Adam was constantly trying to usurp Steve's authority as senior pastor.

Steve went on to say that Adam had also made numerous attempts to damage his reputation, both within the church and in the Anderson Hills community, giving several examples to support his claim. In addition, Steve told the board that Adam used private meetings and gifts to try to influence others to join in his vision and to influence the elder election, pointing out that even some of them had participated in those meetings. While the board respectfully sat and listened to their senior pastor's comments, Steve sensed that they were not convinced by everything he was saying. Adam had done a good job of distorting their view on many things.

When he concluded his remarks to the board, Steve wished that Paul Samples could have been there to share some of his findings on Adam, to help strengthen his case, but unfortunately, as Steve found out later, Paul was caught in traffic for almost two hours as the result of a multiple car pileup. Miraculously, no one was seriously injured, but the delay prevented Paul from making it to Anderson Hills until after the meeting had adjourned, and everyone left for home. Steve was not able to present the information himself at that time because the board would have considered it hearsay. Paul would have to share his information at a later time. While he spoke, though, Steve could feel the prayers of his supporters and supernatural confidence in telling the truth. He knew he wasn't alone in the room. He also knew that Sara was at home praying, as usual, for him at that very moment, and the thought of that encouraged him even more.

After Steve sat down, Adam was allowed to speak. In his comments, he reiterated that he believed he had been given a vision from God Almighty to build a home base for major evangelistic activity in the world and that Anderson Hills was part of that commission. He had not hijacked the original vision and mission, he just expanded on it. He skillfully avoided addressing Steve's claims that he had been attacking Steve's character but instead implied that Steve was the one hindering the ministry at Anderson Hills. He went on to use a few examples from the Bible, showing how others who stood in the way of God's plans, paid the price for their interference. He claimed that everyone he had talked with on a one-on-one basis was interested in his evangelistic vision, many seeking him out and that he had done nothing improper. He wrapped up his presentation by saying that Steve did not understand the powerful anointing he had on his life and was short-sighted and blind to the will of God in this situation. He then picked up his Bible and read from Acts 5, which was Gamaliel's (a respected Jewish religious leader) statement about some of the Apostles of the Church.

> But a Pharisee named Gamaliel, a teacher of the law, who was honored by all the people, stood up in the Sanhedrin and ordered that the men be put outside for a little while. Then he addressed the Sanhedrin: 'Men of Israel, consider carefully what you intend to do to these men. Some time ago Theudas appeared, claiming to be somebody, and about four hundred men rallied to him. He was killed, all his followers were dispersed, and it all came to nothing. After him, Judas the Galilean appeared in the days of the census and led a band of people in revolt. He too was killed, and all his followers were scattered. Therefore, in the present case I advise you: Leave these men alone! Let them go! For if their purpose or activity is of human origin, it will fail. But if it is from God, you will not be able to stop these men; you will only find yourselves fighting against God.'[1]

When he finished, Adam turned to Steve and said, "Pastor Hanson, I believe you are fighting against God."

At that last statement, those board members who supported Adam began to applaud him for his courageous statement. A few others, like Jerry Simpson, just sat there and shook their heads, knowing the truth about Adam and his plans to take over the church. Adam Daugherty had just successfully manipulated the majority of the board again into thinking they were on a great God-ordained mission.

After the meeting, Steve went home feeling discouraged and found himself beginning to think about resigning from that church before things got any worse. He did not want to leave, but he also did not want to be viewed as the cause of another split, which could very likely happen. Steve had been fervently praying for an answer from God for some time on what to do. He was growing weary and losing his will to fight. Adam Daugherty had essentially just taken over Anderson Hills Church Fellowship that evening.

Paul Samples went over to the Hanson's house as soon as he arrived in town. Steve shared what happened earlier that night with him and Sara. Steve and Paul decided to try to present the information Paul had obtained on Adam at another meeting with the board. The three were then moved by the Spirit to pray together over the situation. They passionately poured out their hearts to God, asking for Him to expose Adam Daugherty for what he was and to let Steve know whether or not he should stay at Anderson Hills. They also prayed for the congregation. Samson came and laid down by them as they prayed. Steve and Sara couldn't explain it, but there again, they could feel God's peace even stronger when Samson lay near them as they prayed. When they finished, Paul Samples left to go home.

The next day, Steve called another special board meeting with just him and Paul addressing the group. Adam would not be included in this session. It was set for two days later. When the board members heard what Paul Samples had to say, some were resistant to accepting the claims. They felt there was more to the story than what they were told. They also felt Adam should have a chance to read and defend himself against the accusations. Pastor Adam met with the board two days later and after all was said and done, he managed to convince the majority of the board members that the information Paul Samples presented had been largely distorted. Incredibly, they sided with Adam and continued to support his evangelistic ministry campaign at the church.

Early one morning while working in his church office, when it seemed like things couldn't get any worse, Steve suddenly felt a tremendous sense of loss. The feeling was so powerful it took his breath away. He began trembling inside. He got up to get a drink of water and returned to his desk almost shaking. Yes, the church has been a huge disappointment lately, but, somehow, this sense of loss was different. It was something more personal.

A couple of hours later, Steve looked up from his desk from where he was still working to see Sara standing in the doorway. Thinking it strange that she would be at the church at that time of day, he got up to hug her and thank her for the surprise visit. The look on her face, though, was unusually serious. She was pale and on the verge of tears.

"Steve," Sara said softly, as she pulled her husband close to her. "There's something I need to tell you."

Steve immediately knew that something was drastically wrong. *Not the kids!* he thought to himself.

"Steve, I just got a call from your brother. There's been an accident." Sara started to choke.

Steve began to tremble again inside and braced himself for the worst. Sara continued, allowing the tears to flow freely as she spoke.

"Your parents, Steve. They were driving home from a church conference and slid off the road because of the heavy rain they were driving in."

She paused for a moment, then continued.

"They lost control trying to get back on the pavement and slid right into the path of an oncoming semi-truck. The emergency squad said they didn't suffer."

Steve looked at her in shock. He started shaking his head, refusing to believe what she was saying.

"Steve, Honey, they're both gone."

"Oh, dear God, no!" Steve cried out, as he broke down at the news.

Sara held him tight, and they both began to sob uncontrollably together. Mrs. Hellinger, knowing that there had been unexpected death in the family from her brief conversation with Sara, came and quietly pulled the door to Steve's office closed so the couple could mourn in private. Sara had been too distraught to notice that she had not closed it behind her. The two clung to each other for what seemed like an eternity, then finally sat down on the couch still holding on tightly. The pain of this loss was excruciating. Losing one parent was hard enough, but two? And at the same time? And on top of that, Steve was losing another church he worked so hard to make successful. This was the last blow. Steve could take no more. His pioneer spirit and passion for ministry were gone for the first time in his life. He was empty.

Out of sheer habit, the two began reciting the 23rd Psalm. Somehow, it just seemed the right thing to do at that moment.

"The Lord is my shepherd; I shall not want. He makes me lie down in green pastures; He leads me by still waters. He restores by soul . . . Yea, though I walk through the valley of the shadow of death . . ."[2]

Mrs. Hellinger began to sob quietly herself as she heard the couple in the next room. Such a dear couple, who gave so much to their calling.

"Why now? Why them?" she asked God.

Pulling herself together, she did her best to wave off visitors in the office. She whispered that there had been a death in the family, and the Hansons needed to be left alone at that time. They would have to see the assistant pastor for any immediate needs.

Steve and Sara sat in silence for a long while until they could think clearly again. As they did, they began to feel the soothing presence of the Holy Spirit. He was there, like He always was, to remind them they were never alone. They were loved. The Father cared about them. He cared that they hurt. Suddenly, they both felt a renewed strength and began to wipe their eyes. Realizing that the couple was now silent, Mrs. Hellinger got up from her desk and knocked quietly on the door.

"Come in, Margaret," Steve called out.

Mrs. Hellinger opened the door. "I'm so sorry to bother you two at this time, but I wanted to make sure you were alright."

"We'll be okay. Thank you for caring. You are such a dear friend," Sara replied.

"Is there anything I can do?" Mrs. Hellinger offered.

"Yes," Steve answered. Please let the congregation know that Joseph and Marianne Hanson have gone home to be with the Lord and that their son Steven and his family will be heading out to New York this evening. Also, please call the associate pastor and have him take over things until I get back."

"Both of them?" Mrs. Hellinger was shocked. "Oh, Steve . . . Sara . . . I'm so sorry," she said, as she began to cry again.

Mrs. Hellinger wiped her eyes with a Kleenex and then walked over to hug the couple. They were now both standing.

"Just let me know if Frank and I can do anything for you. I mean that," she said after hugging them. "You know you can count on us."

"We know that, Margaret. And actually, there is," Steve said, wiping his eyes again with his handkerchief. "Would you and Frank mind taking Samson home with you while we are in New York?"

"No problem, Steve. He's such a sweet dog. We'd enjoy his company while you're gone."

"Thank you, Margaret. That means a lot to us."

"Frank and I will be over to get Samson after I close up the office in just a little while. I'll put a message on the answering machine letting people know they can call me at home later this evening if they need to contact the office about something."

"That's a good idea," Steve told her.

Mrs. Hellinger left the room to catch the phone that was now ringing in the main office.

Steve put away what he was working on and turned off the lights in his office. He and Sara then headed for the front door of the church. Margaret followed them to their cars to make sure no one bothered them as they left the building.

As they entered the parking lot, Pastor Adam spied the couple while getting out of his car and ran over to Steve to talk with him about his upcoming sermon. He did not notice that they were distraught. As he attempted to talk to Steve, Margaret told him that Steve and Sara had a family emergency, and they were not up to talking with anyone right then. He would have to confer with the associate pastor. Her comments, though, did not seem to register with him, and he began to insist that he needed to talk with Steve before he went to his office.

Margaret grabbed Adam's arm, pulled him aside, and matter-of-factly told him to leave the couple alone. Sara and Steve continued to head for their cars, got in, and drove away. As they did, Margaret waved at them and then turned to Adam and said,

"Didn't you see they were upset?"

"No, I guess not. What's going on?"

"Steve just lost both of his parents in a bad car accident today. They're going to New York. And I'd suggest that *you* behave yourself while they're gone," Mrs. Hellinger said pointedly. "You've done enough damage around here."

At that, Mrs. Hellinger turned and went back to the office to call Jonathan Wells, the associate pastor. Adam stood for a few moments in the parking lot with his mouth wide open. He knew Mrs. Hellinger called things as she saw them, and she was one individual he did not wish to tangle with. Knowing she and her husband had a little bit of money stored away, he had hoped to win her and Frank to his evangelistic vision. There was no sense rocking the boat with her right now.

Instead of going into the main office, where he knew he wouldn't be welcomed, Adam headed straight to his office in the church basement to work on his notes for Sunday.

When Steve and Sara got home, Peter was there waiting for them. His Uncle Mike had just called back to give them some flight information. He had a friend at a local airport who was willing to fly the couple and their family to New York that evening in his private plane. Peter's eyes were full of tears when he saw his parents, and he quickly ran over to hug them both. He then headed upstairs to call the community college to make arrangements to take a break from classes for a few days. Steve and Sara called Mary at her school in Ohio and asked her to get an emergency leave to go to New York for the funerals. Mary struggled to get through the conversation because she was crying so hard, but she finally managed to say that she was going to book a flight as soon as she could. She would meet her parents and brother in New York. Fortunately, when Joshua heard about her grandparents, he volunteered to drive her to the airport. He did not want her going by herself in the emotional state she was in.

Not long after the Hansons got home, Mrs. Hellinger and her husband arrived to pick up Samson. Steve and Sara quickly gathered Samson's things so he could go with them. Peter made sure that Mrs. Hellinger took some turkey hot dogs as well. Samson looked longingly at his family before he followed Frank out the door. He sensed something was wrong. He wanted to go with them, but he knew he had to go with the Hellingers instead. Samson didn't put up a fight because he liked the Hellingers and knew he would be well taken care of. Steve, Sara, and Peter all hugged him and waved goodbye as Frank and Margaret Hellinger left with their beloved canine to go home. Steve then went into his study to call his brother. He felt the two needed to talk with each other right then.

The double funeral was a blur for the most part for Steve, but he did remember the family visits at the funeral home. Steve was glad to be with old friends and family members he hadn't seen for years. He was also glad to be with his brother, Mike, who was a strong source of strength for everyone there. He and his wife Marcie had taken care of most of the funeral arrangements. Unlike many gatherings at funeral homes, this one was celebratory. Joseph and Marianne Hanson had been faithful followers of their Lord Jesus for most of their lives, and there was no question where they were now.

As the Hanson family was leaving the church after the funeral dinner, Steve and Sara looked up into the sky, and to their amazement, saw the most beautiful double rainbow they had ever seen in their lives. It had a golden cast to it. Curious as to what they were looking at, others who were also leaving the church began to look at the sky as well. Soon dozens of people were looking up at the sky and pointing. A few were taking photos with their cameras. Steve and Sara felt certain that God was telling them their loved ones were now safely on the other side of eternity. It was a statement of hope and a promise fulfilled.

"Where, O death, is your victory? Where, O death, is your sting?"[3] Steve said aloud as he stared at the sky.

Then Mike came up behind him. Putting his hand on Steve's shoulder, he began to sing the praise song, "Redeemer."[4] Soon everyone outside was joining in with them. When they were done singing, hugs and kisses were shared and people started heading to their cars to go home. Several hundred people had attended the double funeral that day. It was an incredible testimony to two lives well lived. Dr. Schaffner from the district office and his wife, Casandra, were among those in attendance. Paul Samples and his wife, Mia, came as well.

When Steve and Sara returned home a couple of days later, they found a pile of sympathy cards laying on the kitchen table and the living room full of plants and flowers from various people in the church and surrounding community. Bob and Lucie Brown had a key to their house and were bringing in their mail and other items as they arrived at the Hanson home. Sara, Steve, and Peter kicked off their shoes and sat down in the living room together. It had been a draining flight home due to turbulence, and they were glad to be back. When people began to find out the Hansons were home, many parishioners from Anderson Hills started dropping off meals for them. This continued for the next few days. In spite of the havoc Adam Daugherty had been causing, there were still many who were glad that Steve Hanson was their senior pastor.

The day after their return, Mrs. Hellinger brought Samson back home. As soon as he entered the door, he started running around the house and barking, his tail wagging in excitement. He made sure he welcomed each of his family members home by jumping up and licking them. Everyone was hugging him and rubbing his floppy ears. Somehow his presence in the house made it feel more like home again.

Several weeks went by, and Steve began to see his strength returning after the family's tragic and overwhelming loss, yet his pioneer spirit had not come back. Dealing with Adam Daugherty and his controlling spirit took the joy out of his ministry at Anderson Hills. Everywhere he looked in the church, Adam's materials were being displayed there. Adam had them strategically placed in the lobby, the hallway, the main office, and in the church bookstore. There was more of his things laid out than Steve's. Steve noticed that some of his ministry materials had been mysteriously disappearing as well. Nothing seemed too audacious for Adam Daugherty to do. To make things worse, Adam Daugherty saw this as a time of weakness in Steve and began to push harder for the board to have the congregation vote on starting his building project. In doing so, he finally won. A ballot came to the congregation and the proposal passed fifty-five to forty-five percent of those who voted. It was not an overwhelming victory because many still liked Steve's idea of taking things slower, but it was a victory nonetheless. The capital campaign would soon begin.

The following Saturday morning, Steve and Jonathan Wells were in Steve's office discussing the service for the following day, when they suddenly heard someone come in the front entrance of the building. Guessing it was Adam, and curious as to what he was up to, they wrapped up their meeting and headed to the main office door to see what he was doing there that time of the day. Carefully watching from behind the main office door, so as not to be seen, they saw that it was, in fact, Adam, and he was carrying a load of boxes in from his car to the church bookstore. The two looked at each other and just shook their heads.

After Adam finished stocking the bookstore, he left in his car. Steve and Jonathan took that as an all-clear and went into the bookstore to see what Adam had just placed in there. To their chagrin, there in the corner were stacked several boxes of Adam's capital campaign materials. He already had brochures and pledge cards printed before getting official permission from the board.

"He just doesn't stop, does he, Steve?" Jonathan remarked.

Steve just groaned.

After Jonathan left for home to work on a seminary term paper, Steve decided to go for a walk around the church property. He put on his jacket and boots and started to trudge through the wet ground. It was close to spring, and most of the winter snow had melted leaving the ground very soft in places. Right before *Hearts on Fire* officially partnered with Anderson Hills, the church had an opportunity to purchase another twenty acres from the local farmer who sold them the original ten acres. When the owner offered them a deal they couldn't refuse, the congregation jumped at the chance to expand their assets for future building projects. The total church property was now quite large. Adam Daugherty certainly considered that when setting his sights on Anderson Hills. Walking around the outermost part of the land, Steve stopped to look at the back of the church. He tried to envision what this new evangelistic complex would look like based on Adam's architect's drawings. Somehow, he just couldn't see it there.

Steve started towards the center of the property. Pausing in the open field for a few moments, he was suddenly aware of a host of angels surrounding him. In front of him, some yards away was the same angel he had seen more than once before. The agent of God, dressed in armor this time, carried a large shield and sword. His tender large brown eyes stared directly into Steve's. As he looked back into those eyes of love, Steve felt as if he knew the angel personally. Steve smiled and awkwardly waved at the heavenly spirit. The angel nodded in acknowledgment, and then he and the others disappeared. Steve stood in wonder for several minutes. What special message were these angels bringing him? Or were they just reminding him of their presence? At that moment, a cold breeze passed by. Steve pulled his hood on over his head and started walking back to the church.

As Steve walked through the wet field thinking about this new angelic visit, he was suddenly distracted by a passing low-flying bird. This caused him to turn his attention to another part of the field where a fence used to stand near the tree line. There, painted on a remnant of the old fence, was a series of occult symbols. Not noticing them before, Steve quickly surmised they had been recently placed there. Troubled by their presence, Steve took off running toward the fence, splashing through puddles of water as he went. Filling with holy righteous indignation, he shouted as he ran.

"No! In the name of Jesus, satan and your evil ones leave this place!" When he was close to the small section of fence, he jumped and knocked down a portion of the wooden barrier. Breathing heavily, Steve leaned against the remaining part of the fence and thanked God for His continued protection of Anderson Hills and the angelic visitation. Their visible presence had brought the encouragement he needed that day.

Upon returning to his office, Steve called Detective Fee at the sheriff's department. This time, Detective Fee came out personally to assess the situation. After taking some pictures of the symbols and having a police officer take a portion of the broken section back to the station as more evidence (once Steve finished praying over it), the two men started walking the grounds to see if they could find anything else. Detective Fee advised Steve to burn the rest of the fence and to let him know immediately if anything else of that nature turned up on the church property. Fee promised to have a patrol car go past the building more than once a day for at least the next few weeks. When he left, Steve contacted Pastor Jonathan and the board to tell them what had happened. He asked them to come right over to the church, if they could, to pray together over the situation. An hour later, Pastor Jonathan and a few of the board members were on their knees praying with Steve in the sanctuary. After they finished, the group went out in the field and burned what was left of the old fence. The next day during Sunday service, Steve asked the congregation to be in prayer as well. News of the unholy visitors brought deep concern to the congregants. For a brief time afterward, it seemed as if the congregation was pulling back together again because of the incident. Unfortunately, though, that unity didn't last for long.

Chapter 14

Wounded Soldiers

$\int$eve looked out of the window of his church office one weekday afternoon, a few weeks after addressing the board about Adam, to see a huge sign being erected on the front lawn of the church property. Wondering what was going on, he got up and put his warm flannel coat on and walked outside. Adam was there on the grass with three male delivery people from Anderson Hills Commercial Sign Company overseeing the project.

"What's going on?" Steve asked as he zipped his coat.

"Just a little advertisement," Adam gloated.

"For what?" Steve questioned.

"Our building project."

"Who gave you permission for this sign to be erected?"

"Well, in case you don't remember, the congregation voted to start the building project for the evangelistic outreach complex."

"Yes, I know, but no one said anything about a sign being purchased."

"Do you object?"

"Not necessarily. I would just like to be consulted when you do something like this. I am the senior pastor of this church. Does the board know about this?"

"Alex Keys does. He said it would be fine."

Steve looked at the billboard-sized sign. It read, "Future Home of the Northeast American Evangelistic Outreach Headquarters and Research Institute."

"Research Institute?" Steve asked surprised. "When was that added? I'm sorry, but you're jumping the gun here, Adam." Turning to the delivery workers, he told them, "Please put this sign in the white shed behind the church. It's unlocked. We have some things to straighten out here before it goes up."

"Steve!" a voice suddenly called from behind him.

Everyone tuned to look. It was Mrs. Hellinger.

"What is all this?" she asked, as she got closer to the men.

"It looks like Adam is getting a little ahead of himself here," Steve replied, shaking his head.

The workers looked at Adam, unsure of what to do. Frustrated, Adam gave in and told the team of men to take the sign to the shed. Quickly removing the huge wooden placard from the posts they had already placed in the ground, two of the deliverymen carefully carried the sign to its temporary storage space in the back of the church. As the sign was being moved to the shed, the driver of the truck gave Adam a confirmation of delivery form to sign, handed him a copy, and headed back to the company vehicle to wait for his co-workers. The two other men soon joined him after placing the sign in its temporary location. The driver started the engine, waved goodbye, and began to pull out of the parking lot. Steve and Adam waved back at him.

After they drove off, Adam turned to Steve and said, "The board is going to hear about this."

"Yes, they are," Steve replied. "You are forgetting how things are run around here, Pastor Adam." Turning to Mrs. Hellinger, he said, "Margaret, please get Alex Keys on the phone for me."

"Right away, Pastor," she said smiling.

Then she turned and headed back to the office. Steve followed close behind her. Adam stood alone on the front lawn, looking like a child who had just gotten caught with his hand in the cookie jar. He put the receipt for the sign in his coat pocket and headed for his office.

When Steve returned to the main office, Alex, the new board president, was on the phone. He admitted that he had given the go-ahead for the sign, believing the board and the rest of the church family would be excited about it. He thought it was already cleared with Steve and apologized for the confusion.

Steve then asked Alex about the addition of a research institute. Alex confessed that he and Adam had talked about that possibility, but it was never included in the plans presented to the congregation. He agreed that the sign should stay in the storage shed until the next board meeting. Steve asked Alex to give Adam a call and relay that message directly to him so that there would be no further misunderstanding. Soon, Alex was on the phone with Pastor Adam.

During the next board meeting, Adam did some backpedaling regarding the mammoth yard sign he had ordered, but before the meeting was over, he had the majority of the board convinced that a research center was an integral part of the evangelistic complex. The board agreed to adopt it into the building plans without going to the congregation for a new vote. Permission was then granted for Adam to put up the sign he had purchased for the church with funds from his evangelistic outreach account.

Adam then approached the group with a proposal to work with a fundraising firm he had worked with in the past, indicating that *Hearts on Fire* had used them on numerous occasions as well. Steve took issue with the proposal and suggested the group consider more than one firm before making a final decision. Adam countered with an emotional appeal and passed out letters of recommendation on behalf of the firm. He took advantage of his time on the floor by having one of the firm's representatives talk with the group via conference call to share some other fine points of their services and to answer questions. This went on for over twenty minutes. When the call ended, Adam compared their costs and services with those of some other similar firms. He told the board he did not see a need to look any further. In the end, Adam won out again. Caught up in the moment, the group voted that evening to hire the firm to handle their capital campaign efforts for the new building project.

Steve was dumbfounded by the outcome of the board meeting. It went beyond reason. Like the board at Community Church, many of them were not seeing what was happening from spiritual eyes. They were looking at Adam's proposal from the natural with human emotions. The excitement of being part of something really big had drawn them in. What started as a simple partnership with *Hearts on Fire* to build an evangelistic outreach ministry for Anderson Hills, was turning into a coup d'état of the whole church!

Before the church knew it, money was coming in from all over the area and even from various parts of the country to help with the evangelistic building project at Anderson Hills. Steve had to hand it to Adam, he certainly knew how to raise money. Adam was sending out his petitions in every way imaginable. He was even taking up more time during the Sunday services, begging for money for 'God's vision for the world.' It seemed like there was no end to his campaign. Steve and Sara wondered when he slept. Steve tried to talk with the board about Adam again, but they didn't seem alarmed. He and Paul Samples even tried to talk with Alex Keys alone about Adam's past, but he brushed it off, saying that any wrong Adam might have done in the past shouldn't be used against him now. Adam had the board so convinced they were on God's mission, nothing he did seemed to trouble them or stop him from encroaching on Steve's ministry and his authority in the church.

The final serious blow to Steve's ministry at Anderson Hills struck one Sunday when several original families of Anderson Hills came to Steve and told him they were leaving the church. They had appreciated Steve's strong yet tender shepherding leadership style over the years, and if he ever started a new ministry, they would be glad to be a part of it. But they had had enough of Pastor Adam and his constant barrage of financial pleas.

Anderson Hills had changed drastically. It was no longer a fun family atmosphere where people loved on and cared about each other and enjoyed doing ministry together. It was also no longer a place where someone could be mentored, grow in their walk with God, and be shown how to be a friend to their neighbor. Anderson Hills was more interested now in making a name for itself than helping others. The Great Commission had been turned into a fundraising frenzy, and the board as a whole had lost their way as spiritual leaders of the congregation. Jerry Simpson, Steve's only remaining strong supporter on the board, was even considering leaving the church with his family. Steve was greatly troubled by this but understood why Jerry and his family were entertaining the thought of another church family. He didn't want to stay there either.

Everything Steve did to help build the ministry at Anderson Hills seemed to be fading away. Even the music was different. Many of the new congregants were more interested in the fast-moving, rock-style music, Rick, the young music ministry leader, was playing, especially on the Sundays when Adam preached, rather than the traditional hymns or familiar praise and worship songs they used to sing at Anderson Hills. While Steve was not opposed to that style of music–some of it was good for the teens and college-age members of the church–he was concerned that there was no variety in the music selections, and the sense of worship and reverence was leaving that part of the service. It was as if the music was being performed primarily for entertainment. Some people weren't even standing and participating as the ministry team performed. And those who applauded afterward appeared to be clapping for the ministry leaders rather than for the glory of God their Creator. In sum, the worship attitude was just all wrong.

When Adam found out that some of the original families were leaving, he deceitfully argued with the board and others that those people left because Steve failed to provide for their spiritual needs. In addition, he was constantly looking for an angle to shoot Steve down in front of strategic and influential people in the church community. Adding insult to injury, Adam was having secret meetings with some of the board members concerning the capital campaign efforts without letting Steve know about them. There seemed to be no end to his schemes and manipulations.

Steve and Sara spent more and more time now praying about what to do. Steve decided it was time to fight back and delivered a strong sermon on honesty, integrity, and accountability. He also talked about spiritual blindness and manipulation. While the sermon was well received the Sunday it was delivered, many failed to connect the dots and see that Steve was referring to Adam and most of the current board of elders. Those who knew what was going on thanked Steve after the services for his bold and unhindered statements. Steve went home that day, though, feeling deflated and confused on what to do next. He was finding himself withdrawing from the ministry at Anderson Hills, and, to some degree, his friends and family as well. He was also becoming aware of deep anger growing inside. All of this scared him.

A few days later, on a Thursday afternoon, Steve and Sara received an unexpected phone call from Sara's mother. Sara's father was in the hospital. He had just had a massive heart attack. He was alert, but the prognosis was not good. Her mother wanted Sara and Steve to come right away. After praying about it, they decided that it would be best at that point if Sara flew down to Kentucky by herself to be with her parents. Steve did not feel it was a good time to leave the church but would fly down if Sara felt he was needed there or if her father passed away. Hugging and kissing each other goodbye at the airport, Sara left on the short flight to her hometown of Newton, Kentucky. It had just been a couple of months since they had lost Steve's parents, and neither Steve nor Sara was ready to lose another one. Sara prayed that God would delay what appeared to be inevitable and that somehow her father would rally, at least for a little while longer.

Back at home, after dropping Sara off for her flight, Steve sat on the living room sofa thinking about all that had transpired since Adam Daugherty had been invited to come to Anderson Hills. The thought of him strengthened Steve's growing desire to give up on the church.

Oh, how he wished his father and mother were there right then to encourage him. If only he could pick up the phone and talk with them. They always seemed to say just the right things. There had to be a reason, though, why God took them home when He did, Steve considered. It was a devastating loss. But he also knew God was in control, and that their sudden deaths could not be without purpose. The memories he had of them helped sustain him.

Remembrances, he thought to himself, a*re such a wonderful part of God's creation of the human brain. They're always there to draw on when you need them.*

God knew Steve would still need his parents' influence in his life, and so they *were* there for him even then–in his memories. Steve smiled as he thought of his parents and all the good times he and his brother, Mike, had had with them while growing up. As he allowed himself to drift further into his remembrances, Peter came down from his room and looked into the living room to see what his father was doing.

'Dad?" Peter interrupted. "Can we talk for a minute?"

Steve shook his head slightly as he let go of his daydreams.

"Sure, Son. What's on your mind?"

Peter dropped into one of the recliners.

"Well, I've given this a lot of thought, and I have come to the conclusion that it's time for me to move out into my own place. I'm sorry to bring this up now with Grandpa..."

"It's okay, Son. You're over twenty now, and I think I can safely say that your mom and I support your decision."

"Thanks, Dad," Peter said in relief. "I knew you would understand."

"Will you be living alone or with someone from school?"

"Actually, with a couple of guys from school."

"I see. Do I know them?"

"No, but I think you would like them. They're not real rowdy, and they do go to church . . . sometimes."

"Sometimes?" Steve half-smiled. "Well, I hope you can encourage them to go more often."

"Yeah. And that leads me to another thing I need to talk with you about. I probably won't be going to Anderson Hills as often as I was. At least not on Sundays when Pastor Adam is preaching. I'm sorry, but I just don't like that guy and what he has done to the church and to you."

Steve sighed and then nodded.

"You know Peter, I understand that as well. Your mother and I have still been praying about whether or not we should stay there ourselves."

Peter sat up in his chair wondering if they had made a decision yet. He was hoping his dad would say they were leaving the church at Anderson Hills. Peter decided not to ask at that time. He didn't want to interfere with their decision.

"Just make sure you go to church somewhere," Steve continued. "And please try to be around here as often as you can. Samson will be looking for you."

Peter laughed.

"Don't worry, Dad. You, Mom, and Samson will see plenty of me. And my friends too if you don't mind. . . Better warn Mom. I'll be bringing home some dinner guests now and then."

"You got it. When do you move?"

"I'd like to start this weekend. I've already signed the lease. We want to get things organized before the next semester at school."

"That's good thinking. I'll try to help you if I can. We'll see if we need to leave for Kentucky or not."

"Thanks, Dad. You're the best. Well, I guess I better start packing."

The two got up from where they were sitting and hugged each other. Steve patted his son on the back as they hugged. Then Peter ran upstairs to start sorting through his things to decide what to take with him. Samson ran upstairs behind him to see why Peter was in such a hurry. Steve sat back down and returned to his memories.

Steve talked with Sara on the phone at different times during the week. He wanted to get updates on her father and just hear her voice. Her father was holding steady. She was able to converse with him, but the doctors didn't offer much hope. Thomas Kinsey had been a coal worker when he was younger. He had suffered from black lung disease for years, but now his heart was in trouble as well. A devout man of God, he always made sure his family attended church. He had been active in the local community and his church and always enjoyed doing things for others. He was thrilled when his daughter chose to marry a man who was planning to go into pastoral ministry, a profession he had once considered himself. Instead, his ministry was helping with numerous church and local projects.

When his condition seemed to improve a little, he was glad to talk with Steve from his hospital bed in ICU. He greatly appreciated the prayers Steve prayed for him over the phone. Steve loved his father-in-law. He too had been a great father figure and a tremendous influence on his life. Thomas' wife, Elsie, had proven to be a wonderful second mother to him as well. Like Sara, she loved to volunteer in the nursing homes and was accomplished on the piano. Steve prayed that the two would continue to be around for as long as possible.

Several days later, Steve received an early morning call from Sara. She was crying softly. Thomas had passed away peacefully in the night. Her mother was with him when he took his last breath. Sara was still at her parents' house in Newton when she heard the news. Saddened by yet another loss, the two somehow still managed to help Elsie and Sara's sister, Leah, plan the funeral. Her brother, Allen, would help as well, as soon as his flight got in from Arizona. Steve was able to assist with some of the details by phone. Being involved in the plans helped keep their minds off other things as they mourned this new loss. Steve also arranged for Jonathan Wells to take over his duties while he was in Kentucky. Frank and Margaret Hellinger willingly took Samson again to their house until the family returned, and Bob and Lucie Brown once again took care of the mail and other deliveries.

Steve and Peter flew out for the funeral in Sara's hometown. Mary was able to catch a flight to Newton as well. This time Joshua Franklin went with her. He was caught up with his school work and didn't want Mary going by herself this time. Mary was glad for his company, and the couple began to talk about their future together during the flight. The two were growing closer in their relationship with each other.

After returning home from the funeral, Steve began to feel tired and at times lightheaded and nauseous. His appetite had dropped, and he found himself constantly fighting depression–something he had never done before in his life. He even found himself snapping at or criticizing Sara at times, for no reason at all. Some of their discussions were even becoming shouting matches. On occasion, Steve yelled at Samson or pushed the dog away when he tried to comfort Steve.

Mrs. Hellinger noticed some of that frustration coming out at work as well and that Steve was forgetting things. She decided to tell Sara about what she was seeing. Concerned about Steve's state of mind, Sara encouraged her husband to see their doctor. She too was feeling the pressure of everything they had been going through and decided a visit to the doctor would help her as well. The pain she was feeling inside often brought her to tears, and she knew things couldn't continue the way they were going. The mounting tension was a tremendous strain on Steve and Sara's relationship. They weren't communicating like they used to, and their prayer life together felt empty.

Steve's physician, Bruce Kelly, was a trusted friend. He had attended Anderson Hills when they first got started, so Steve felt free to tell Bruce whatever he thought he should know. After hearing what had been happening in Steve's life, Bruce told him he was going through burnout and that he needed to take a sabbatical for at least a few months. Bruce also told Steve to seriously pray about the possibility of leaving Anderson Hills. Perhaps his work there was finished. Steve had endured so much at both churches, and with his recent personal losses, his body was telling him he needed rest and a change of scenery. Bruce suggested that Steve's assistant pastor take over for a while until Steve was ready to make a decision on what he should do. Bruce prescribed a high potency multi-vitamin, a special diet, and regular exercise to get Steve's system and energy level back up to par again. In addition, he prescribed a low-strength anti-depressant, to use only if Steve felt he needed it, and suggested he see a counselor.

After the doctor visits, emotional prayer, and open discussions, Steve and Sara came to the conclusion they needed to make plans to leave Anderson Hills, without delay. Not just the church, but the city as well. They were convinced the Lord was telling them to do both. Once they were at peace with that decision, the couple decided to call an evening meeting at their home with their friends Bob and Lucie Brown, Harold and Francine Cannon, Margaret and Frank Hellinger, and Paul Samples and his wife, Mia. That night, Sara had a variety of food laid out for their guests when they arrived. When everyone had helped themselves to the refreshments and were settled in the living room, Steve told them of his decision to leave the church, and even ministry altogether, at least for now. He felt strongly that he needed a long break. Listening intently, his friends tried to convince him to just take a sabbatical. They even offered to pay for his time off. But by the end of the meeting, Steve, with the help of Sara, had convinced them that it was time for him to leave the pastorate at Anderson Hills for good, and the sooner the better. Steve wanted no more encounters with Pastor Adam. He also did not want to see the church split, and by all indications, it was very close to doing so. Experiencing two major ministry losses in the same geographical area, Steve had had enough. Seeing that Steve was firm in his decision, his friends prayed over Steve and Sara, for healing and better things to come, and then sang some worship songs with them before they left for the evening.

A few days later, Steve turned his resignation into the board. Adam feigned being sad over the news of Steve's resignation when he found out, but inside, he was celebrating. Steve then shared his decision publicly during the Sunday services that weekend. He did not go into a lot of detail but indicated that his calling there at Anderson Hills was coming to a close. He asked the congregation to remember the vision and mission of the church and to continue to be a light to the community.

Many, especially the remaining founding families, were stunned and saddened when they heard the announcement, and questions soon began to fly, many guessing that Pastor Adam's ministry had something to do with Steve's decision to leave. Steve would be leaving the church at the end of the month. Sara would finish up a few Bible studies at the nursing home and then resign from her ministry there as well. They both felt they needed to end their ministries in Anderson Hills, so they would be ready to move to a new area.

Sara was just packing up her things after Bible study one night at the nursing home when she heard someone enter the empty meeting room. She thought it was one of the nurses coming to get the wheelchair that was left in the room. Sara turned to see Officer Lester Hale at the doorway. Lester and his wife Polly, a couple in their early forties, had been attending Anderson Hills since it first started and were supporters of Steve's ministry. Polly worked at the nursing home in the business department.

"Good evening, Mrs. Hanson," Officer Hale said politely but looking serious.

"Good evening, Lester," Sara responded, surprised to see him there. "Everything ok?"

"Uh yes. Well, no . . . It's your son, Peter."

Sara became alarmed. "Has he been in an accident?" she asked anxiously.

"No, Ma'am. Nothing like that. To tell you the truth, he's been in a fight."

"A fight?" she repeated stunned.

"Yes, he's in jail."

Sara's eyes widened, and she stood there shocked and confused. Was he really talking about her son, Peter?

"Jail? Are you sure-"

"Yes, Ma'am. I am very sure. In fact, I was the arresting officer. It seems that he and a couple of friends were at *Gerald's Bar and Grill* at the edge of town and got involved in an altercation after someone said something about his father. He wasn't drunk, but he did have a couple of beers before the fight. I had to take him in on assault and disorderly conduct charges. One of his friends was arrested too."

"Oh no," Sara said, sitting down in a folding chair.

"I just got off duty a little while ago and thought I would come here and tell you personally since I had to pick up Polly from work. I didn't want anyone calling you up on the phone."

"Thank you, Lester. That was very thoughtful of you. I don't want Steve hearing about this tonight."

"I kind of thought so."

Struggling to know what to think, Sara forced herself to say, "I . . . I suppose I should go over there and bail him out."

"Would you like Polly and me to go with you?"

"No, no thank you. The station is just a little way out of town. I can handle it. I'm not sure what I'm going to say to Peter when I get there, but I will handle it," Sara said, trying to sound strong.

"Okay. Sergeant Miller is at the desk tonight. I told him you would probably be coming in. He'll help you out."

"Thank you, Lester," Sara responded. "You and Polly have been such good friends."

"You're welcome, Mrs. Hanson. We'll be praying for you tonight."

Sara nodded her thanks, and Officer Hale left the room and headed for the business office to meet his wife. Sara quickly grabbed her things and went out the side door of the home to the parking lot. She got in her car to go straight to the police station. Fighting back tears, she decided instead to sit in her vehicle for a few minutes, letting the car warm up and her mind calm down. Sara looked up at the sky and prayed for strength. As she did, she felt moved to turn on the radio. The Christian station she turned to just happened to be playing, "The Warrior Is a Child" by Twila Paris[1] – a song Sara knew very well. As the refrain played, Sara sang along softly, allowing the tears to finally flow down her cheeks. She knew God was telling her it was okay to take some time to cry.

When the song ended, she finally felt at peace. Sara turned off the radio, backed up the car, and pulled out of the nursing home parking lot. It was 8:35 p.m., and while it wasn't late, Steve would probably wonder where she was if she wasn't home by nine. Sara decided to wait until she got to the jail before calling home. That would give her some time to think about what she was going to tell her husband.

Sara turned onto the highway and headed toward the county jail, her mind on Peter. Suddenly, she was blinded by the headlights of an oncoming light gray pickup truck. It was, as she would learn later, a drunk driver coming right at her in her lane. Sara was terrified, and, immediately sensing the danger, cried out to God. Miraculously, the steering wheel was suddenly snatched right out of her hands. The next thing she knew, she had landed in a ditch on the right side of the road. Sara sat shaking fiercely inside from the incident, crying and thanking God for the narrow escape. At that moment, she thought she heard a dog barking in the field next to her, perhaps someone was out hunting, but when she looked, she saw only darkness. Travel on that road was unusually light that evening.

Realizing her predicament, Sara put her head on the steering wheel and began to pray again for help. Shortly after, an unfamiliar car came up and stopped behind her. The headlights reflected off of her mirrors until the driver of the vehicle turned the lights off. A young man with brown hair and eyes, wearing a dark leather coat and blue jeans, came to her window. Sara was afraid to lower her window very far, so she just opened it enough so she could talk.

"Good evening, Ma'am," the friendly voice said. "I saw what just happened. Are you ok?"

"Yes, I'm fine," Sara responded, still shaking inside.

"I'll see if I can help you." He took off to go around her car to access the situation.

A minute or two later, he came back to her window.

"I don't think you're in the ditch very far," the young man said. "If you'd just put the car in reverse and hit the gas when I tell you to, I think I can push you out. Just do it nice and slow when I say, 'gas!' "

"Are you sure? I don't want you to hurt yourself."

"It'll be fine, Ma'am. I work out all the time, and believe me, I've done this before."

The young man took his place in front of the car. Following his instructions, Sara was soon out of the ditch and back on the side of the road. The young man came by her window again.

"You're all set, Ma'am."

"Oh, thank you soooo much," Sara said happily. "God bless you! You're an angel from heaven!"

"No problem, Ma'am," he said with a smile and walked back to his car. Sara could hear him starting his engine. Sara thanked God for the stranger who came to help her. She then checked her side and rearview mirrors to make sure nothing was coming, so she could pull out safely. Sara looked back to get a glimpse of the young man's vehicle. She hadn't seen his lights go on but was surprised to see nothing there. A passing car's headlights illuminated the area behind her SUV long enough for her to see that his car had vanished. *Where could he have gone?* she thought. There was no way he could have pulled out around her or gone the opposite way without her seeing his headlights. Sara was full of wonder. Thanking God again for His hand of protection, and not wanting to stay on an open and empty road, Sara headed for the city jail.

When she got to the police station, Sara was surprised at how busy it was. Some people were sitting in the main lobby, waiting quietly to be waited on. Sara went straight to the main information desk and asked for Sergeant Miller and was directed to his workspace. A tall, hand-some, slightly balding man with a well-pressed uniform, welcomed her warmly as she took a seat by his desk. He was polite and sympathetic to her situation and walked her through the steps of getting her son released from jail. Sara paid the bond with the family credit card and then was escorted by a younger officer to the visitor's waiting room in another part of the building. As Sara entered the room, she noted how homey it looked. Waiting room chairs and sofas lined the walls, and a large round coffee table in the center of the room hosted a variety of magazines. Several pictures were mounted on the walls with pleasant nature scenes, and there was a large picture window looking out to the side of the building at the end of the room. Two vending machines stood next to it along with a coat rack.

Sara tried to make herself comfortable in one of the cloth-covered chairs. This was the last place on earth she thought she would be that evening, but she would try to make the best of it while she waited for Peter. There were only two other people in the room with her. The first was a woman, Sara surmised to be in her late fifties sitting quietly across from her, knitting what looked to be a baby blanket. She was preoccupied with her work and didn't even look up when Sara entered the room. Over by the large picture window was a man dressed in a dark blue suit. A briefcase sat next to him on the floor. Sara guessed him to be someone's attorney. He nodded politely at Sara and then went back to what he was reading when she came in.

Sara laid back in her chair and looked up to heaven. She prayed for the right words to say when she saw her son. She was upset, even angry, but she had to be in control when she talked with him. A short while later, Peter was brought to her in the waiting room. Sara got up to greet her son. Glad to see his mother, he approached her somewhat cautiously and embarrassed. When Sara reached out her arms, he hurried over to receive her hug.

"Let's talk about this tomorrow," Sara told him. "I'm in no mood to do that tonight."

"Yes, Ma'am," Peter replied, appreciating the hug but knowing that he wasn't going to be let off the hook that easy. He and Sara would be having a serious mother-son talk the next day. Peter collected his things from the front desk. He and his mother headed for the car, so she could drive him home to his apartment.

"Are you going to tell dad about what happened?" Peter broke the silence while Sara was driving.

"I don't know. At least probably not right away. He may be asleep when I get home. I tried calling him from the police station, but his voicemail just picked up."

Finally pulling into the parking lot of his apartment complex, Peter saw his friend had already driven his car back from the bar and grill. He was relieved to see it there. Sara swung around the apartment complex lot and dropped Peter off in front of his building.

"Thanks, Mom," Peter said getting out of the car. "This won't ever happen again. I promise."

Sara nodded.

"We'll talk in the morning. I'll come over just before breakfast."

"Ok. Good night." He closed the door of the car and headed toward the apartment building. One of his friends was already looking out of the apartment window to see which one of his roommates was coming home.

Sara sat for a minute to pray for her son and his friend, then headed for home. When she got inside the house, she found Steve asleep in the recliner in front of the television. Samson was sleeping on the floor next to him. Not wanting to wake him, she covered him with a quilt and kissed him on the forehead. Samson stirred, but she held her finger to her lips indicating he should just be still and keep lying quietly next to Steve. She turned off the TV and the lights and headed upstairs to bed. Sara knew Steve would find his way upstairs after he had rested for a while.

Sara woke up earlier than usual the next morning. As predicted, Steve had come to bed later that evening. Samson was lying on the floor next to him. Steve had gotten up in the middle of the night, realizing where he was, and went up to be with Sara. Samson woke up as well when he heard Steve moving around in the living room and followed him up to the bedroom.

Sara quickly got dressed that morning and made breakfast for Steve. She just drank some orange juice, knowing that she would be having breakfast somewhere else. When Steve came down to eat, she told him she was meeting Peter that morning for some mom and son time. Steve was not suspicious of what she was doing because she and Peter had those special times together now and then. He figured she just needed to be with him that day. Sara felt a little guilty not telling Steve the real reason for going over to Peter's apartment, but she wanted to talk with Peter first before she laid out the whole incident to his father. She knew the police report would not be in the newspaper until the evening edition, so she had some time to find out what happened first.

Steve decided to take Samson to the park while Sara was gone. Both needed some fresh air and exercise, and Steve saw it as a way to draw near to God. He always felt close to his Maker when he was out in nature. Right then, he was having trouble feeling God's presence. The pain of the last year had left him feeling distraught and at times abandoned, even though he knew he wasn't. Steve was saddened by the fact that he and Sara had left church ministry, but he also realized he needed time to heal and regroup. He couldn't imagine himself ever being behind a pulpit again, but he also knew he might see things differently after some time had passed.

When Sara arrived at Peter's apartment, he was up and waiting for her to arrive. Jumping into her car after she pulled up to the sidewalk, the two decided to go to a diner in the next town so they could have some privacy as they talked. They had been there before with Steve and Mary and liked the menu. Peter sat nervously in the booth as the waitress took their orders. After she left, Sara looked at Peter and said,

"So, what happened last night, Peter?"

Peter shook his head.

"I don't know, Mom. I just lost it. That big mouth John Willard from Community Church was spouting off and telling people that Dad was just bounced out of another church. I couldn't take it, Mom. What he said was a lie. Dad worked so hard at both churches. He was called by

God to be at each of them. He didn't deserve what he got. And we, his family, didn't deserve what we got either."

Sara nodded in agreement. Then trying to think of what to say next, she told him,

"You know Peter . . . there will always be John Willards out there causing trouble for you and those you care about, but you have to be able to handle them, especially from a spiritual standpoint."

"I know, Mom."

"Did you swing first?"

"Yeah, and I deserved to get arrested. I helped make a bit of a mess at the bar too."

"Which brings me to my next question. What were you doing at the bar?"

"Just hanging out with my friends."

"And drinking?"

"And drinking," he confirmed, embarrassed to admit it to his mother.

"Couldn't you guys have found something else to do like going camping or taking some nice girls out for the evening?'

"I guess, I should've thought about that. I just wasn't in the mood for anything else."

"I know you are hurting inside right now, Peter, and angry at a lot of people. We all are. But you can't be getting into fights like that. You were lucky something more serious didn't happen."

Peter nodded.

"My friend Parker got arrested too." He thought for a few seconds. "Are you going to tell Dad?" This was the second time he had asked his mother that question.

"No," Sara replied. Then looking him directly in the eyes, "You are."

Peter cringed but knew his mother was right.

"You are a man now, Peter. You need to talk with your father about this by yourself. I'm not going to be there when you do."

Peter nodded in agreement. His dad wouldn't be happy, but he would listen if Peter went to him.

When their food arrived at the table, Sara suggested they take a few minutes to pray together about the situation first. After they did, Peter felt some relief. Hungry, he dove into his meal. When they finished breakfast, they headed back to Peter's apartment. Before getting out of the car, Peter looked at his mother and said,

"I'll pay you and Dad back for the bail money."

"Yes, you will," his mother replied.

Peter smiled and got out of the car. He would come over to the house later that day and talk with his father. He knew it was best for his dad to hear directly from him what happened and not from another source.

That afternoon Peter went to his parent's house to talk with his father. He and Steve met in the living room and talked for a long time while Sara worked on getting supper ready in the kitchen. When their talk ended, the two stood to hug each other. Sensing from the other room that the meeting was ending well, Sara decided it was time to join the two men. Sara peeked into the living room first to make sure it was a good time to enter and then walked in with three large mugs of hot chocolate. Peter had faced his father, and his mother the night before, and found love and compassion and forgiveness from both of them. He now had the strength to accept the consequences of his behavior. It would mean making some apologies, paying for his share of the damages to the restaurant, and repaying his parents for the bail money, but at least he had his dignity back. Fortunately, because it was his first offense, the judge did not require any more jail time. His friend, Parker, received the same sentence, and the two worked hard to pay off their debts. Peter took the next term off from school so he could work full time and finish paying his legal and personal obligations sooner. Unfortunately, it wouldn't be the last time Peter would find himself in trouble because of his anger, but at least for now, he had it under control.

Sara waited until after Peter left to tell Steve about the near-miss on the highway the night before. She did not want to make Peter feel any worse about his situation than he already did. When Steve heard about what happened, he pulled Sara close to him, thanking God for

His divine intervention. He could not imagine what it would be like to be without her. There had been enough loss in his life recently, and God had lovingly spared him of one more.

Steve was cleaning out his desk at Anderson Hills Fellowship Church that next Saturday afternoon. Boxes were stacked everywhere. The joy he once had going to work every day had been stolen from him. He ached inside and was finding himself feeling angry. As he placed some of the contents of his desk in a box, he looked up to see Margaret Hellinger standing at the door. She had tears in her eyes. Steve smiled at her, and she came over to hug him.

"There are new things out there for you, Pastor Steve," she said. "I know it. The best is yet to come for you and Sara."

Steve nodded in polite agreement but was very unsure of what he would be doing after Anderson Hills. He felt like he was walking around in a thick fog, not knowing what was coming next. He still couldn't feel God at times, though he knew He was still there.

That Sunday evening, there was a quiet farewell party after the last service of the day in the fellowship hall for Steve and his family. Only those in the congregation were invited. Adam would be preaching the last Sunday of the month, so the board decided to have the reception the week before. Peter and Mary were able to break away from work and school to be there that night. They wanted to show their support for their parents at this difficult time. A number of Steve's strong supporters and founding families came to say their goodbyes and thank Steve and Sara for all they had done for Anderson Hills. Steve and Sara felt numb as they hugged and thanked people for coming. Surprisingly, Pastor Adam was one of the first to arrive. The very presence of Adam Daugherty, though, seemed to put a gray cloud over the gathering. Steve and his family tried to just ignore him. Shamelessly, he took advantage of the opportunity and was seen talking about his building project to various people at the party. Margaret and Frank Hellinger finally got tired of it and asked Adam to save his campaigning for another time. Not wanting to tangle with Margaret, Adam decided it would be best if he left. Steve and Sara were relieved when they saw him leave the room. The Hansons did the best they could to get through the rest of the going away party but were glad to finally be back home at the end of the evening.

Later, after Mary had gone to bed, Steve and Sara were in prayer for a long while in their room, Samson joining them for most of the time. Afterward, they decided to look on the internet for houses for sale in Carolton, PA, an hour and fifteen minutes north of Anderson Hills. It was a town they had visited years ago and felt moved to check out now. The Hansons had a small nest egg built up and would soon be buying their first home in years. They spotted several properties they liked for under a hundred thousand dollars. Fortunately, one could buy a nice older home in that price range in Carlton's real estate market.

Feeling assured by God that they would both find work there, and not wanting to wait, the Hansons made plans to move to Carolton as soon as possible. Sara would look for a job first, and then Steve would find one after he had some more time to rest. The church had graciously given Steve a large check to help subsidize their income for a few months until Steve was feeling better. The couple decided they would rent a small efficiency apartment in Carolton at first. They could move everything else there when they closed on their new home, which turned out to be a three-bedroom 1400 square foot gray colonial. The break from Anderson Hills would be good for them. Most of their worldly goods were soon temporarily packed into two large storage lockers owned by Bob Brown, and before they knew it, Steve and Sara were moving into their tiny apartment with their beloved beagle.

The Hansons were glad to be in a new community. Their evening walks with Samson were relaxing and helped them focus more on their future. What they were doing there, they had no idea, but Steve was sure it had nothing to do with vocational ministry. That was still the farthest thing from his mind.

Side Note...

After the Hansons left Anderson Hills, the board, and the congregation, still trying to process Steve's sudden resignation, decided to start looking for a new senior pastor. Pastor Adam was considered for the position by some, but most felt he would better serve the congregation in the position he was already in. A short two-month search later, they hired a candidate from Sara's hometown in Newton, Kentucky. He had learned about the opening when Sara called down to the local seminary to post the job description. Jonathan Wells continued as the associate pastor and handled what he could until the new pastor came to Anderson Hills. A second seminary student was hired to do some of the Sunday sermons during the transition time as well. Jonathan eventually took over the evangelistic outreach program after he graduated from seminary and was brought on full time.

Pastor Adam maintained the preaching schedule he had negotiated with the church and relentlessly continued to push his building project. By that time, he was feeling a little too self-confident, and–dropping his guard in front of people he thought he was safe with–expressed his elation with Steve leaving the church. Adam was also overly critical of Steve and his ministry and said he was a bad father to his children, pointing to his son Peter's recent arrest. As more of the members of the church and the board began to see Adam for who he really was, it quickly contributed to his downfall. Congregants were even more concerned with him after he announced a few months later, when they were more than halfway to their fundraising goal, that he wanted the new evangelistic complex named after himself. As other issues concerning Adam and his integrity eventually surfaced from a variety of sources, the board decided to contact Don Williamson, the president of

Hearts on Fire. It was finally time to end their relationship with Adam Daugherty.

Mr. Williamson was stunned when he heard the real reasons behind Steve's resignation. He did not know that Steve, and many others, had left the church because of Adam. Adam had told him that Steve left for health reasons. The president soon launched his own investigation into Adam's past, eventually finding out some of the same information Paul's friend had uncovered months earlier. When he ran into Paul Samples at a conference on legal issues in ministry, he realized he should have paid more attention to what Steve and the other board members at Anderson Hills were trying to tell him. He decided to call Alex Keys for a face-to-face meeting with the Anderson Hills Board of Elders.

After a three-hour conference between Mr. Williamson and the board of Anderson Hills, it was decided that the partnership contract between the two organizations would end that day. Adam had clearly overstepped the contract, ruthlessly damaged another man's reputation and ministry, and brought tremendous embarrassment to Mr. Williamson's organization. The money for the new complex was going to be put towards a smaller building project at Anderson Hills, which consisted of an additional structure next to their current building with an adjoining breezeway. It would contain more office space (including a large office for evangelistic outreach), a conference room, several additional classrooms for Sunday School classes, and space for possibly a small Bible institute sometime in the future. Individuals would be allowed to adjust their campaign pledges if they wished. Money already collected would stay in the building fund. So as not to draw a lot of public attention to the situation, Adam Daugherty was quietly fired from *Hearts on Fire* and summarily asked to leave Anderson Hills. His office at the church was turned into a storage room for the music ministry department. The church simply announced that Adam had been called to another ministry and that the building project had been modified. The evangelistic outreach program was still in effect but drastically scaled down. The multi-million-dollar complex Adam had pushed so hard to get was never built.

Adam Daugherty eventually found a new organization to work for in Canada and was hired to direct a program for overseas missions in African nations. There he met and married an evangelist, ten years his junior, named Misty Hayes, and became the "behind the scenes promoter" of her ministry. Two and a half years later, they separated and later divorced. They did not have any children. Adam moved on to work for another evangelistic organization in California as a promoter and fundraiser. He lasted only one year there.

Unfortunately for Adam, he still did not realize that if he had waited on the Lord and done things His way and in His timing, he would have had the evangelistic ministry to which he was called. Instead, Adam had allowed satan a foothold in his life and selfishly tried to get ahead of God by interfering with and attempting to steal the anointed ministries of other followers of Christ. His motivation was for his glory and not God's. Adam had wrongfully placed more value on his family's approval than his Heavenly Father's. He was envious of things he was not meant to have. He was also unforgiving of his family for the way he was treated, or at least how he perceived he was treated, and used his pent-up anger against others. Adam would continue on this destructive path until either God said, "enough!" or he repented and allowed the Holy Spirit to heal his heart and lead him in his original calling. He just couldn't see that he was the one standing in the way of his own success.

Chapter 15

Letting Go and Finding Forgiveness Again

elying on God's faithfulness, Steve and Sara once again experienced His hand of provision for them. To her joy, Sara was hired at a local nursing home as an activity specialist. She was given thirty hours a week, which she felt was perfect for the time being. Working with the residents at the home helped her deal with the recent loss of her father. One man, in particular, took a liking to her, and he quickly became one of her favorites. Arnold Crain was about her father's age and resembled him in many ways, even in the way he talked. He called Sara his 'second daughter' and was always available to play BINGO or be involved in some other group activity whenever he knew she was there at the home. Physically and mentally, he was in better shape than many of the other residents at Pine Grove. Even though he relied on a walker to get around, he was still very active, going on most of the outings coordinated by the activities director and the Pine Grove staff. Arnold made Sara's going to work something to look forward to each day.

Steve, however, remained at home, for the time being, deciding to wait another month or two before looking for a job. After their move from Anderson Hills, he was feeling more tired and just couldn't get his energy back. There were days when he didn't even want to get out of bed, study his Bible, or talk with anyone–friend or family member (unless it was Sara or the kids)–especially on the phone. His passion for ministry had diminished to almost nothing, and he and Sara still weren't communicating like they used to. Steve seemed so far away from Sara during this time. She was concerned but knew it would take time for Steve to bounce back. Sara didn't know how she could be a better help to her husband when she was struggling herself just to get through each week. Even so, Sara tried to be as encouraging as she could to Steve. Her quiet times with God and her work at the nursing home were her comfort, and that kept her going. The occasional visits from Peter, phone calls from Mary in Ohio, or contact from some other family member were an additional source of strength for her. They sometimes helped lift Steve's spirits as well.

From time to time, Sara would attempt to bring up what happened at Anderson Hills in her conversations with their children, to help them heal, but Peter and Mary avoided the subject whenever they could and kept their personal feelings on the situation to themselves. They knew both their parents already had enough to deal with and felt it best to find other ways to work through the variety of emotions they too were feeling at that time. Peter mostly suppressed his feelings, which unfortunately emerged unexpectedly now and then in periods of anger. Mary, however, was able to talk with Joshua and some other trusted friends about hers, giving her some release from the hurt, and a chance to deal with the emotions directly. Sara prayed that someday the four of them would be able to talk together as a family about what had happened but knew that wouldn't be any time soon.

One afternoon, when Sara was at work, Steve was home alone sitting on their bed thinking about the events of the past several years after moving to Pennsylvania. As he thought, he began to feel unusually anxious inside. He got up and paced the floor–reliving his challenges, mistakes, and failures during the last two pastorates. Suddenly, he began to experience a flood of emotions he had been suppressing for months. Startled by what was happening, he began reciting from the book of Psalms, "Why are you cast down, O my soul? And why are you disquieted within me? Hope in God; for I shall yet praise Him, the help of my countenance and my God."[1] Steve repeated this verse several times as he walked around the room. Unable to hold back his feelings any longer, he allowed them to surface, recognizing each one of them as they did. Hurt, rage, disappointment, a great sense of unfairness, loss, despair, unforgiveness, retaliation, and even hatred for another human being were distinctly among them.

Then Steve realized his anger toward God. How could a loving Father allow a man like Adam Daugherty to do so many wicked things to the church in Anderson Hills? The one he and Sara and others had worked so hard to build? His stomach tightened as the surge of emotions continued to be released from within, some he did not completely understand. The emotional pain was excruciating, but he knew the feelings needed to be released or they would continue to take their toll on his physical, mental, and spiritual health and his relationships with others.

Unable to withstand everything he was feeling, Steve turned and pounded his fists against the wall of the bedroom and shouted at the top of his lungs -

"Why God?! Why was my ministry taken away from me?! Haven't I always done what you've asked me to do?! Why two churches?! I don't understand!"

Hanging on to the bedpost, he sobbed uncontrollably for several minutes. Then, he was quiet. Still breathing heavily, Steve suddenly found himself transported to a place he didn't recognize at first.

It was a place in a warm Mediterranean climate, and he was standing outside on the edge of a large crowd dressed in strange clothing. Everyone was focused on one thing. Women were crying, children were huddled close to their parents, and men were standing and staring silently. Darkness had fallen, and the sky looked ominous. Steve pushed his way through the throng to see what was going on. When he reached the other side of the onlookers, he immediately knew where he was–Golgotha. Horrified, Steve watched the crucifixion of his Lord.

It was more brutal than he ever could have imagined. Tears flooded down his cheeks as he remembered that a follower of Jesus Christ must also suffer[2] at times, so God can be glorified and for there to be victory over demonic strongholds. He also more fully understood the tremendous sacrifice that was poured out for him, and everyone else made in God's image, that day. Forgiveness, grace, and mercy trumped unforgiveness, hate, and retaliation. Humanity's relationship with the Father had been restored.

Finding himself back in his room, Steve was overcome by what he had just witnessed. Shaking fiercely inside, he dropped to his knees, reliving the vision over and over again. Steve began to feel great shame for accusing God of any wrongdoing and for all the things he had been holding inside, especially unforgiveness. He had no right to refuse to forgive, even if the other person was not sorry.

Steve cried out to his Creator, asking for forgiveness and peace. As soon as he did, the Holy Spirit began to enfold him like a parent comforting a child. Steve knew the Spirit was praying for him[3] in words he couldn't muster for himself. Steve started to weep again and told the Great Comforter he didn't know what to pray for anymore. His passion for ministry was gone. Steve began praying "in the Spirit"[4] and continued to do so for what seemed an hour. As he did, he began to calm down. The emotions he was feeling were gone. The torment had ceased. Perfect shalom filled the bedroom. Tears of joy came to Steve's eyes.

While he was sitting on the floor, Steve thought he heard Samson come into the room. He felt something touching his arm. Appreciating the company he looked down through clouded vision and saw what appeared to be a hand instead of a paw. Wiping the tears away from his eyes and cheeks, he looked up and found himself staring into the face of the angel he had seen before.

There was no fear with this encounter. The angel's large brown eyes were filled with compassion and hope. And though the angel did not speak to him audibly, Steve knew what he was being told.

"The Father sees. The Father cares. You are loved. Do not be dismayed. You have not failed. You did what needed to be done. You will be whole again. You and Sara are the Father's pioneers, and there is still much more for you two to do. Trust Him, and don't give up." With that, the angel smiled and disappeared.

The next thing Steve knew, Samson was licking his face. The blue bandana Sara had secured around the dog's neck that morning, had somehow slipped off and was laying in Steve's lap. It was as if Samson was offering his handkerchief to Steve, so he could wipe the tears from his face. Realizing the gesture, for the first time in weeks, Steve allowed himself to laugh. It felt good. It felt healing. Finding his way back to restored health and his pastoral calling was going to take some time, but he knew at that moment he would get there. Yes, by the grace of Almighty God, he would get there.

Steve gave his canine friend a big hug and rubbed his floppy ears, which Samson happily accepted as he sat down on the floor next to his human companion. After sitting there for a while, Steve decided some fresh air and sunshine would be good, so he went to the living room and put on his jacket and grabbed Samson's leash.

"Come on, Samson," he said with a smile. "I feel like a walk."

Samson barked happily and followed Steve out the front door of the apartment. Steve looked up at the sky as he started down the sidewalk with his energetic canine friend and smiled. He could feel God's love again, and that gave him hope. For the first time in months, he told God how much he loved him too. Steve then thought of Sara. He wanted her to feel hopeful as well and determined that day he would somehow pull himself back together and help bring healing to their wounded relationship.

A few days later, Steve received a phone call from his brother, Mike, in New York. Mike had been in prayer for his brother and sensed that he should give him a call. While he too was dealing with the loss of his parents, he did not have the added loss of a church congregation. His ministry was going strong, and he and Marcie were receiving a lot of love and support from the members of their church. The two men prayed together for a long time, allowing the tears to flow freely.

When they finished, Mike told Steve about a support group he had heard about that met every week at a church about a half-hour away from where Steve and Sara were now living. It was created for ministry leaders who had suffered the same kind of hurts and disappointments they had. He strongly encouraged Steve to go. The group was called "Tears in Ministry: Renewing Lives and Callings."

"I don't know, Mike," Steve said hesitantly. "I'm not sure I want to share my personal feelings with other people in a group setting."

"Why don't you talk with Sara about it?" Mike suggested. "This could help both of you."

Steve continued to resist the suggestion, but after they talked more about the possible benefits of the group, and thinking about the angelic visit he had had a few days earlier, he agreed he would discuss the possibility with Sara that evening. When Steve hung up the phone, he still wasn't totally convinced of the share group but decided that this could be from God. He wasn't going to push the idea aside without checking it out first.

That evening, when Sara came home from work, Steve welcomed her with a hug and told her there was something he wanted to talk with her about during supper. Sara was surprised that Steve had dinner already on the table. Some evenings when she came home, he was asleep on the couch. After sitting down to eat, Steve began explaining the support group program Mike had told him about. Sara listened closely and was quiet for a moment after he finished.

Then she looked at Steve and said, "I think he's right, Sweetie. It could be very beneficial for both of us. We can't go on as we have. We aren't connected like we used to be, and that makes me sad. We're both hurting, and healing is going to take some time. We haven't even found a new church family yet. And don't forget, we'll be closing on our house next month. Those sessions could help get our spirits up before we move again."

"Well, we could go to one meeting," Steve responded a little more persuaded. "Just to see if we like it."

"Yes, and if we don't, we don't have to go back. We can just sit in on that first session to observe. Why don't I call the pastor in charge of the program tomorrow and get some more information on their support sessions?"

"Okay," Steve sounded more encouraged. "This appears to be from God."

The next day, Sara called Mt. Hope Church and talked with Pastor Martin Deem. He led the inner healing ministry. Pastor Deem explained that people from a variety of ministry backgrounds came to the group, some traveling from as far as two hours away. He had seen great healing in most of those who had gone through the group sessions over the years, and the majority of them had returned to some kind of professional ministry within a year or two after joining the group. He gave her the time and date of the next meeting, which just happened to be that Friday, and told her that he looked forward to meeting her and Steve. Sara put down the phone feeling encouraged about attending the group. She sensed that something was about to change in their lives, and it would be for the better.

Steve and Sara arrived at Mt. Hope a few minutes early that Friday evening. It was a large old gray stone church with beautiful vintage stained-glass windows. They were greeted with a warm smile and handshake by Pastor Deem, who met them at the side door when he saw them coming up the walk. He was a man in his late forties, medium build, and a little on the heavy side. Like them, he had on business casual clothes. They both liked him immediately and were glad they had come.

"Just feel free to listen this first time," Pastor Deem told them. "I want you to be comfortable with the group before you jump in. I will introduce you, though, so everyone knows who you are and why you are here this evening."

Steve and Sara agreed and followed Pastor Deem down the well-lit hallway to the meeting room where most of the group had already assembled. The room was warm and cozy with a fireplace at one end of it. There were a couple of sofas, a few comfortable-looking recliner chairs, and a number of padded folding chairs in the room as well. All of the furniture was arranged in a circle, so everyone could see each other. Steve counted fifteen other people in attendance as he looked around at those standing and sitting down with their coffee and cookies. Some smiled as Steve and Sara entered the room. Others just nodded politely, probably feeling as uneasy as they were at that moment.

Pastor Deem offered the Hansons some refreshments, closed the door, and took a seat near the front of the room. He welcomed everyone and opened the session with a word of prayer. His words were soothing to Steve and Sara as they listened to his radio announcer-type voice proclaim words of health and healing over all of those there. They could feel the presence of God in the room.

Following the prayer, Pastor Deem introduced the newcomers to the group. Everyone smiled and welcomed Steve and Sara to the session. As they did, Steve and Sara began to feel a kinship with the other participants. Then Pastor Deem asked everyone to introduce themselves, which they did, taking turns going clockwise around the circle. Pastor Deem reminded everyone of the rule that everything said in a session was to stay in the room, and all indicated they understood and would honor the rule.

Pushing back the gray framed bifocals on his nose, he began…

"Okay. Tonight, Bob and Tracy said they would like to share their story with us."

The young couple, both in their mid-twenties, sitting to his left, looked at each other, took a deep breath, and smiling nervously, started sharing their ministry experience. As they did, Tracy, who had short brown curly hair, held on tightly to a box of Kleenex in her hands. Everyone could tell that sharing their story was a difficult thing for them each to do. Rob, a tall athletic-looking man with sandy-colored hair was nervously playing with his note cards as he spoke. At different points, someone in the group would say things like, "You're doing good."

"We hear you." "We understand." This helped the couple move forward and stay focused on their story.

Up until a couple of months ago, Rob and Tracey Alexander had been co-music ministry leaders at a church of around a thousand members about an hour east from Mt. Hope. Music was their life, and ministry was their passion. They had met at a Christian college, each majoring in music ministry. Both had spent many years preparing for their calling in life and were ecstatic when they were hired together at a church to lead the music ministry. For the first two years, all went well, and they built a strong and dedicated music ministry team. But one day, out of the blue, the church leadership decided to bring in some new musicians to add to the current mix of people already on the ministry team. The couple was involved in the interviews and gave their input on the candidates, but for some unknown reason, were not allowed to help make the final determination of who would be added to their team. To their chagrin, the new vocalist and two musicians that were chosen had starkly different philosophies on worship ministry from what they and the others on the ministry team currently embraced and practiced at the church.

Before the couple knew it, the entire music team was in conflict. As it turned out, the three new members were children of some very influential people in the congregation, who soon took issue with the music leaders when their adult offspring's ideas were not being accepted and implemented the way they thought they should be. As time went on, more trouble erupted as various members of the team and the congregation took sides on various music-related issues. Bob and Tracy did their best to compromise whenever they could, but they soon found they were no longer able to do the kind of ministry they had done in the past.

After almost a year of emotional turmoil, the church's board and the senior pastor finally stepped in and sided with the new members, and the young couple was encouraged to resign from their positions at the church. Believing it better to leave than to continue to fight a losing battle, the couple decided to hand in their resignations. When they left, three of the lead singers and the drummer left the ministry as well. The couple was deeply wounded by the situation and disillusioned about ever being in ministry again. Their music ministry had been well respected and received at the church until the new music ministry members were added to the team. Why were they now considered trouble-makers?

To top it off, Tracy was expecting their first baby. Joyful as they were at becoming new parents, they had hoped to share that moment with their former church family. Now they had no real church family to claim. They were applying to other churches for music ministry positions, but nothing had come about yet, and they were unsure of how to explain their recent resignation from the other church. They didn't even know if they could get good letters of recommendation from the leadership of that congregation.

Steve and Sara listened closely to the young couple, recognizing some similarities in their situations. After the music ministry leaders finished sharing, they were met with encouraging words from other members of the group. Pastor Deem thanked Bob and Tracy for telling their story and asked everyone to come over and surround the pair laying their hands on them as he prayed for their inner healing. Ascertaining they were ready and willing to forgive those who had hurt them, he anointed them with oil and prayed for God to heal their inner wounds and begin to prepare them for their next assignment with a fresh anointing.

When the pastor stopped praying, some of the other members began to pray over the former ministry leaders as well. The Holy Spirit's presence in the room was powerful and unmistakable. After the prayers ended, members of the group hugged and kissed the young couple. Steve and Sara hadn't gone up but watched from their seats. Both wiped their eyes after witnessing the emotional scene. When everyone was once again seated, Pastor Deem went on to deliver a short presentation on dealing with hurts from a Biblical perspective. When he finished, one of the members led the group in a closing prayer.

The group adjourned for the evening and people started gathering their things and putting on their jackets to go home. Steve and Sara went over to the young couple and thanked them for sharing their story. They encouraged them to keep looking for another church and let them know they would be in prayer for them. The young couple smiled and thanked them for caring. Pastor Deem then came over to Steve and Sara and asked them to stay for a few minutes after the meeting. Soon, everyone was filing out of the room, some stopping for a minute to shake the Hansons' hands. Finally, Steve and Sara were left alone with Pastor Deem.

"So, what did you think?" Pastor Deem asked carefully, as he came over to them. "Want to come back?"

Sara and Steve looked at each other for a moment and then both nodded affirmatively.

"I'm not sure I am ready to share yet, but we will come back," Steve said, trying to be as honest as he could.

"Oh, no pressure there, Steve," Pastor Deem replied quickly. "We're very patient here. The Spirit will let you know when it's time. It could be weeks or even months, but I'm confident that you will find the strength to share your story. That's an important part of inner healing."

Pastor Deem grabbed a couple of copies of a book he gave to all the new members of the support group, from one of the end tables. It focused on inner healing and forgiveness after sustaining deep wounds in ministry.

"Here's a little gift from us at Mt. Hope," he said as he handed them the books.

"Thank you," Sara said, smiling as she received it.

"And if you folks would ever want to come and talk with me or one of our counselors alone, you can do that too," Pastor Deem offered.

"Thank you, Pastor Deem. We will pray about that," Steve replied.

Pastor Deem gave them each a hug, and Steve and Sara left the building to head for their car. They were both convinced at that point that they were meant to be there that night and were to continue to come back until they felt strong again.

As the weeks passed, Steve and Sara returned to the group every Friday evening, feeling the Holy Spirit doing a fresh work inside of them each time. They soon found themselves talking more to each other again, and even started looking around for a church family, which they found in a small independent church on the other side of town. Steve's energy level was coming back, and the gray cloud was lifting, so he decided to begin looking for a job. Within a couple of weeks of submitting applications, he was hired by a local contractor to put up wallboard in new homes. Steve enjoyed working with his hands when he was younger and was happy to have the opportunity to do it again. The job was relaxing, and his supervisor was encouraging, always expressing great appreciation for Steve's careful and thorough work. Best of all, his supervisor, Gerald Riley, was a believer. The two had many good theological discussions together. This too impacted Steve's healing process and helped build his confidence.

In addition to the support group sessions, Steve and Sara decided to start going to private counseling sessions with Pastor Deem and his associate, Connie Malone, a licensed family counselor. It was during those sessions that the Hansons realized just how far they had drifted apart. They had each been struggling with emotional trauma, making it difficult to function normally or enjoy each other's company as they had in the past. The couple recognized that it was wrong to keep their feelings to themselves. They had to talk about them with each other. They also had to face the hurts, work harder at forgiving the past events, and move on. They needed to apologize to each other and to those they might have offended during the spiritual challenges[5] of the last ministry. God still needed them. And He needed them strong and whole.

Steve and Sara soon found themselves making friends with many of the people in their support group. The Hansons listened with empathy and compassion to story after story every week, each one a little different, but devastation and loss were the common themes in all of them. One of the women, a former youth leader, had been sexually assaulted by her pastor. A male pastor had an office manager who was constantly undermining his authority. He couldn't fire her, because no one would let him, even though she had been confronted several times on the issue. Another pastor was recovering from a heart attack because of the stress from his congregation fighting over the building plans for the new church. The plans had been changed five times and still, no one was satisfied. People were leaving the church in droves, and he wasn't sure he wanted to go back himself. In addition, one ministry couple shared how they were being shunned by both church and family members because they took an unpopular stance on a particular "hot button" theological issue.

Hearing those stories helped Steve and Sara remember they weren't an isolated case, and that others in ministry were hurting as well. Yet over and over, they saw that life and beauty could still come from the ashes[6] of injustice, devastation, and burnout.

Throughout the weekly sessions at Mt. Hope, Pastor Deem emphasized the importance of prayer and spending time in the Scriptures each day, even if the group members didn't feel like it at times.

"There is great power in prayer, especially when you pray in the Spirit," he kept telling them. "And the word of God will heal and build you up, so you can continue to do combat with the forces of evil."

He also told them to guard their relationship with the Lord, because it was the most important and precious relationship they would ever have. They must not allow satan to come between them and God, reminding them of how the enemy had successfully damaged the first God-man relationship in the Garden of Eden, thus bringing about the whole human calamity we still deal with today. Since Christ had repaired that relational break, through His sacrifice and resurrection, the new bond must be prized above all others and clung to–no matter what happens in their lives or ministries.

Pastor Deem went on to warn the group not to become bitter. Bitterness stifles a ministry and leads to the unforgiveness of others, often leading to depression and various kinds of physical ailments. Hurts must be dealt with and released, not harbored or nursed.

"The Lord has forgiven all our offenses. We have no right to hold anything against a group of people or another individual, no matter what they have done to us or anyone else. Instead, Jesus told us to, 'Love your enemies, do good to those who hate you, bless those who curse you, pray for those who mistreat you.'[7] To do so, not only cleanses us inside but preserves the intimate relationship we have with God, the One who provided a way for us to be forgiven."

Pastor Deem also said that it was essential to forgive oneself for past mistakes. Those must be let go, so the enemy cannot use them as a stumbling block in the future. Any remembrance of those mistakes should only strengthen our resolve to do better the next time not tear us down.

"And most importantly, we must forgive God, even though He has not done anything wrong. Our anger against God only hurts our relationship with Him, and keeps us from moving forward the way we should."

Complete forgiveness in those areas was the key to complete healing[8] and getting back into ministry full force.

Pastor Deem then emphasized how much God loved each member of the group and was always there to bring comfort and restoration. Despite what they had suffered, God had never abandoned them. Unfortunately, suffering often comes at the hand of other believers. That was probably the worst kind of suffering in ministry because those people are also a part of the Body of Christ. It is something every church leader should be prepared to face in any ministry situation because the enemy will use whatever means he can to cause division in a church family. How they respond to those attacks will speak volumes to others. And yes, sometimes the best response in those situations is to leave. But that decision comes with much prayer, and often fasting, and being open to doing what the Spirit is leading you to do.

As they listened each week to Pastor Deem and the other group members, Steve and Sara's confidence grew, and they decided it was time to share their story with those who had suffered as they had. What helped them decide was when Pastor Deem shared his own ministry story where he too had suffered great hurt and disappointment in ministry, vowing at one time that he would never return to pastoral ministry again. God had used that experience to inspire him to help others rebuild their lives and reboot their ministry callings. Steve and Sara greatly admired his courage and tenacity to get back in the saddle again. Yes, God could make all things new again. It happened for Pastor Deem, and it would happen for them as well!

When Pastor Deem announced one Friday evening that the Hansons were going to speak, Steve began to feel his mouth becoming dry. He kept taking sips of water from a water bottle, just to get started. There was a resistance inside of him, but he knew he couldn't give in to it. Sara was nervous as well but felt freer to talk than Steve did. Taking turns at different points of the story, the couple shared what happened to them. They started at the point when they left Ohio, how they were warmly welcomed at Community Church, and then later were essentially starved out of that same church, so the sin of a seemingly respected minister would not be uncovered. They went on to tell the group how the Lord told them to start a new church in the same area, which was hugely successful for a few years. But later, a partnership turned the ministry into something unexpected and very ugly. They also talked about how the loss of three parents came at a time when they were struggling with so many other attacks from the enemy. In addition, Steve and Sara shared how they felt after leaving the second church and moving to their current home, and how prayer and God's reminders of His love and presence had kept them going through everything, in spite of the deep soul wounds they had sustained.

Steve and Sara closed by telling how the situations affected them as a family and how God was helping them deal with that. And yes, they had chosen to forgive those who hurt them. When they finished, there was not a dry eye in the room. Everyone thanked them for sharing. Pastor Deem came over and anointed Steve and Sara with oil and invited everyone to come and pray over them. The presence of God was wonderfully evident in the room at that moment. As Pastor Deem led the prayer, the Hansons both began to cry. Others joined in the prayer, and the presence of God became stronger.

When the time of prayer ended and everyone sat back down, Steve told the group that while they were praying, he had a vision of God crying over the hurts he and Sara had sustained.

"He cries for all of us," Steve added.

At that statement, the whole group was in tears again. Steve went on to say that God never said the ministry was going to be easy. In fact, He told His disciples to "count the cost."[9] Then making his comments applicable to the whole group, he explained that they were all at a new crossroads in their lives. They had paid some of that price, and now they would each have to decide if they would continue to be faithful and move forward again, or let satan win. Would they forgive and allow themselves to be healed and reenergized, or become bitter and stagnant, unusable for God's purposes?

"For the first time in a long time," Steve said, choking back the tears, "I can honestly say, I am willing to pay the price again."

Sara smiled proudly as she reached for Steve's hand, squeezing it to show her support and agreement. She was feeling the same way. Tears were beginning to fill her eyes as well.

"I don't know what the Lord has in store for us next, but I am feeling His peace this evening," Steve said, smiling back at Sara.

Everyone in the room, now over twenty members, started to clap. That evening, the joy of vocational ministry was restored to the Hansons.

Steve and Sara left Mt. Hope that night feeling like they had experienced a significant breakthrough. The passion and energy were returning, and they knew God would be calling them again to another ministry. And somehow, they seemed better prepared this time. God had shown them so much about faith, trusting Him, and even more about forgiveness than they fully realized before.

"Let's call the kids tomorrow," Steve said, as they were driving home. "I think it's time to get them to talk a little more about what has happened over the past several years. It certainly has affected them too."

"We can try," Sara responded. "They are still a little guarded about saying anything to us. I know they're still processing some things themselves."

Steve nodded. Then suddenly he spotted something of interest on the right side of the road, and a look of pure delight spread across his face. He slowed down, signaled, and pulled into the parking lot of an ice cream stand, finding a spot towards the back of the building.

"I feel like ice cream," he announced.

Sara looked at him surprised and then giggled.

"I do too! A chocolate sundae would be especially nice right now," she said, feeling more like her old self again.

"Let's make that two," Steve replied, putting the car in park. "Come on!"

The couple got out of the car and raced each other to the ordering window, like they did when they were dating. No one else was in line at that time.

"And let's not forget Samson," Sara called out as she ran. "He'll love it!"

"He sure will," Steve called back, picking up speed and reaching the ordering window first. "I win!" Steve shouted proudly.

Sara arrived just seconds after, laughing. The young woman behind the window, wearing blue jeans and a company T-shirt, just stood staring at them as she smacked her gum in her mouth. Radio music was playing in the background. She waited as the two studied the outside menu. The couple was trying to decide if they wanted to get something else and which size to get.

"May I help you?" she finally asked, raising her brows and tapping her brightly polished fingernails on the counter.

"Uh yes, I'd like to buy two medium chocolate sundaes with walnuts on top," Steve said. One for me, and one for this beautiful woman standing next to me."

Sara broke out in laughter.

"Oh, and would you fill another bowl with just vanilla ice cream? And put a lid on it? It's for our dog."

Sara laughed again.

"Got ya," the young woman replied, rolling her eyes and turning to go fill their order.

Steve and Sara both burst out in laughter once more. When the order was ready and paid for, the couple sat down at a picnic table for a few minutes to enjoy the cool treat. Then they decided to head back to their neighbor's house to pick up Samson. He would be excited about getting some ice cream, even if it was a little soupy by the time they got there.

The next morning while the Hansons were finishing their breakfast, there was an unexpected knock on the apartment door.

"Maybe that's the realtor with our final closing costs," Sara said, hopeful as she went to the door. To her surprise, as she opened it, Lisa Wright, from Anderson Hills, was standing on the front porch.

"Lisa!" Sara exclaimed. "What a wonderful surprise! I can't believe it's you! Come in! Come in!"

Lisa entered the small apartment smiling. She had a colorfully wrapped box of candy tucked under her arm.

"An early house warming present for the two of you," she told Sara, as she pulled the gift out and handed it to her.

"Oh, thank you, Lisa. I love candy. Especially chocolate. It is chocolate, right?" she asked with a mischievous grin.

"It is," Lisa confirmed laughing.

The two hugged each other, and Sara led Lisa to the living room area where they could sit down and visit.

Steve smiled from the kitchen table when he saw their friend come into the living room area of the apartment. Lisa was doing some shopping at the area mall and thought she would take a chance and come over for a visit. Samson had just woken up from his nap, and, recognizing an old friend, he jumped to his feet to welcome her. Steve got up to greet his friend and hugged her.

Lisa sat down in a recliner and began to share that she was now going to a new church in Anderson Hills and that she was seeing her doctor friend almost every weekend now. She was still at the nursing home and leading Bible studies there. She also mentioned that she and Mrs. Hellinger had been having lunch together once a week and that Margaret was filling Lisa in on what was going on at the church, both good and bad.

"Margaret really misses you guys," Lisa told them. "She said to tell you that she and Frank are going to come up to help you move next week when you close on your house."

"That will be great!" Steve replied. "Bob and Harold and their wives are coming up as well. Why don't you come and bring that doctor friend of yours?"

"I was hoping you would say that," Lisa smiled, slightly blushing. "We would love to come. It will be like old times again."

"What a wonderful blessing!" Sara joined in.

Lisa looked at Steve and Sara. "You know. There's something different about you two. You look refreshed. There's a peace about you I haven't seen in a long while."

"God has been doing a work in us," Sara confided. "We're much better now than we were when we left Anderson Hills."

"Praise God!" Lisa replied, before taking a cookie Sara offered her. "He is faithful."

Steve and Sara went on to tell Lisa about the support group they were going to and how God was bringing them inner healing and helping them forgive all that had happened. They were still rebuilding, but the passion for ministry was returning. Lisa was overjoyed to see her friends on the rebound. At that moment, she was so thankful that God had placed them in her life. They had done so much for her. And now, seeing how they were being restored after some very challenging times, she began to feel closer to them than ever before. She also felt strengthened in her decision, some time ago, to return to church fellowship.

Lisa stayed for an hour and then said she had to be on way her way to finish some shopping. She wanted to be home early because James was coming over that evening to take her to an outdoor concert. It was mid-summer, and she loved being outside in the warm weather. Kissing and hugging Steve and Sara goodbye, Lisa was soon on her way back to Anderson Hills.

Later that afternoon, Steve and Sara decided to call their children. They tried Mary first, and just happened to catch her when she was studying in her room. They told Mary about their breakthrough and shared that they had concerns about her and Peter regarding how they were handling the hurts and disappointments over the past several years. Mary, for the first time, told her parents a little about the anger she had been feeling. She went on to say that Joshua had been a good ear and that she had also talked with a couple of close friends and the campus chaplain more than once. Mary was glad to hear her parents sounding stronger and promised to continue seeing the chaplain if she needed to do so in the future.

When the subject of her brother came up, Mary was a little hesitant but confided in Steve and Sara that Peter had been in trouble again. He didn't want his parents to know, but Mary decided that it was important that they did. This time Peter had gotten into a fight with another student in the student center's lounge at the community college. He had reacted again to a comment someone had made about his father. Peter swung at the other student but missed. Instead, his fist smashed into a plastic panel of one of the pop machines. When he had pulled his hand free, Peter turned and pushed the other student backward. The two young men then began to wrestle, falling on and flipping over the furniture. Some of the girls in the room got up from their chairs and started screaming for them to stop. A few of them ran down the hall to the campus police office, and soon, a couple of officers came running into the lounge to pull the two combatants apart, one blowing a shrill sounding whistle.

Both young men were subsequently suspended for two weeks. Dr. Neil Wilson, the president of the college, threatened to suspend Peter from school for the rest of the term but gave him an alternative instead. Peter had to agree to attend weekly anger management counseling sessions for the rest of the quarter. This would be provided by a campus counselor. Dr. Wilson knew Peter had been in trouble for fighting before and wasn't about to let Peter off lightly. Peter was later given a bill for the damage he did to the pop machine panel. The other student was given a firm warning against ever provoking a fight again and told he would face more serious consequences if he became involved in another altercation.

After their conversation with Mary, Steve and Sara called Peter. They did not say anything about what Mary had told them when they talked with him on the phone but decided to wait until Sunday afternoon to broach the subject, after hearing he was coming over for a visit. Seeing God at work, the Hansons recognized the wisdom in waiting. It would be far better to discuss the situation with their son in person.

Steve and Sara happily hugged their son when he arrived at their apartment the next day. He too noticed something different about their demeanor while talking with them. After telling him what had transpired through going to the support group meetings, they decided it was time to ask Peter about what had happened at the college. At that point, the conversation became tense.

"Mary had no right to tell you guys about that!" Peter seethed, as he jumped up from his chair in disgust. "She promised she'd let me tell you myself."

"And when were you going to do that?" Sara asked pointedly. "Didn't you stop to think that we might hear it from someone else first?"

Peter looked the other way and started pacing around the room. Samson, sensing the change in mood in the room, went over and licked

Peter's hand. Peter started to relax as he felt the wet sticky tongue on his fingers.

"You and Dad have been going through a lot the last several months. I didn't want to worry you," Peter said, trying to defend his decision. He had calmed down, but tears were starting to form in his eyes, which he quickly wiped away with his hands.

"Well, we appreciate that, Son, but fighting is a serious matter," Steve responded. "You are taking on a lot of responsibility when you decide to strike another individual in anger. We've talked about this before. You could have really hurt someone or gotten seriously injured yourself. You could have also found yourself doing some serious time in jail. Peter, you're a walking time bomb. You can't keep doing this! Didn't you learn anything from the last time?"

"I know, Dad," Peter responded. "I'm going to an anger management counselor at the school. I promised Dr. Wilson I would finish all of the required sessions."

"We're glad to hear that, Peter, but is that counselor talking with you about forgiveness? Deep inner healing?" Sara questioned.

"A little, I guess. I suppose you are asking if this person is dealing with the spiritual aspects of my life. Some, but she's not trained in that."

"Perhaps you should see someone who is," Steve said gently.

Peter sat down in a recliner. He was quiet for a minute as Samson came to sit on the floor by his feet. He finally nodded in agreement.

"I don't know what's happened to me. I was never like this before."

Sara got up and went over to Peter and stroked her son's head. "We've all been hit pretty hard. Your dad and I understand what you're feeling. But it's how we handle those hurts that really matters. We know some counselors who can help you deal with your hurts at a deeper level. Would you consider talking with them too?"

Peter looked at his mother. Her eyes were soft and pleading. He knew his parents cared about him. He was very blessed to have been born to this family.

"Yeah, Mom. I'll go," he said quietly.

Sara kissed her son on the cheek and gave him a big hug. Then looking down at his hand she asked if he had injured it when he broke the plastic panel.

"No, just a couple of scratches. My hand went through so fast, I didn't really feel anything."

Steve then suggested they all pray together at the kitchen table. Holding hands there, the three went before God's "throne of grace"[10] and asked the Father to bring healing and wholeness to their son's life, and that Peter would release his anger so that God could use him more powerfully in this life.

After the prayer, Peter's parents convinced him to finish out the term at the community college, but also look into going to a four-year college in Ohio that was an hour's drive from where Mary and Joshua were going to school. This would give him a better chance at a fresh start. Steve offered to take time off from work to drive Peter there, so they could look over the campus together. Peter was happy to take his father up on his offer, and the two decided to take a day in the next couple of weeks to go. Peter would call the college on Monday to make an appointment to talk with a recruiter and tour the school. Peter left his parents' apartment once more feeling loved, affirmed, and forgiven.

That Wednesday, Sara and Steve went to the closing of their new home at a local bank. Receiving the keys from their realtor to the home, the two went right over to their neighbor's house to get Samson. After getting him into the car, which was already packed full of some of their things, they were on their way to another new start. As soon as Steve unlocked the front door and Samson entered the hallway of the cozy colonial, their furry friend began to run around and bark excitedly. He knew he was home. Steve and Sara laughed as they watched their little companion run from room to room to see what his new abode looked like, sniffing as he went. The next thing they knew he was bounding up the staircase to check out the bedrooms on the next floor. Shaking their heads, Steve and Sara began looking around their new purchase and talking about where they would be putting their furniture. They would load up what they had left in their apartment the next day and bring it over in a small U-Haul they had rented. Thursday evening would be their first night in their new home, situated in a warm setting and surrounded by a neighborhood of houses of varying styles. They felt comfortable being there, having already met two of their neighbors and were looking forward to meeting more.

Saturday was moving day. Mid-morning, Bob and Lucie Brown, Harold and Francine Cannon, Frank and Margaret Hellinger, and Lisa and Dr. Lin pulled up in front of the Hansons home in separate cars. Following close behind, was a large moving van, which pulled into the Hansons' driveway. Soon there were hugs and handshakes and joyful conversations. Samson came running down the stairs from the spare room after the visitors were all inside the house. He was excited to see his old friends again. After lunch, Paul Samples and his wife, Mia, showed up to help as well. The professional movers brought in the furniture while the rest worked on putting the smaller things away. Steve and Sara had sandwiches, potato chips, cookies, and hot and cold drinks available for the group to enjoy throughout the day. At one point, a couple of people from their church fellowship brought in some hot casseroles, and their pastor called on Steve's cell phone to wish them well in their new home.

That evening, when the professional movers had gone and everything had been placed in the house, the group joined together in the living room for some pizza and dessert. Then they followed Steve through the house, anointing the doorposts of all of the rooms and outside entrances and praying as they went for God's protection over the household. Twenty-five minutes later, they ended up in the living room. Bob Brown prayed a special blessing on the Hansons and on whatever God had in mind for them to do next. When he finished, the group stood unusually silent for a couple of minutes. As they did, a soft breeze drifted quietly through the house, and the Hansons could feel the presence of the Holy Spirit settling in their home. Along with feeling His presence, there was a sense of a new calling on the horizon, not only for the Hansons but also for the others in this special group of friends. No one could say what their role would be, or describe the calling in any way, but everyone sensed that they were all connected in some way for some new and special purpose. Perhaps for more than one purpose. However it worked out, they knew all things would be revealed to them in God's time.

After Bob Brown's moving and heartfelt prayer, Steve and Sara's friends got ready to leave. There were hugs and kisses goodbye. Waving to the group from the front porch as each car pulled away, Steve put his arm around Sara's waist and drew her close to him.

"Well, Mrs. Hanson, are you ready for a new adventure?" he asked.

"You betcha, Mr. Hanson," Sara replied smiling, happy to have her husband back to his normal self again.

Steve kissed his wife on the cheek, and the two went back into their new home to take a break for the evening, full of God's peace and joy. There was a strong feeling of hope for the future again.

Chapter 16

Restoring the Fire. Rebuilding

*W*hen Steve returned from work late one February evening, he found Sara in the living room talking excitedly on the phone. Samson came running to greet Steve as he was taking off his ball cap and winter jacket. Steve reached down to rub Samson's head and ears and then headed for the kitchen. Sara spotted her husband just in time and covered the phone receiver long enough to ask him to come into the living room with her. Steve went in and sat down next to Sara on the floor as she resumed her conversation. Sara covered the phone receiver again.

"Lisa's getting married," she whispered.

"Oh? Who's the guy?"

Sara playfully pushed him on the upper arm while Steve snickered softly.

"Steve is home now, Lisa. . . . Okay. Here he is." She handed the phone to Steve.

Taking the phone receiver, he said smiling, "Hellloooo Lisa! How are you this fine day?"

"I'm wonderful, Steve," Lisa replied at the other end. There was enthusiasm in her voice. "As a matter of fact, I'm fantastic! James and I are getting married!"

"Wow! Congratulations to both of you! When's the big day?"

"Well, that's going to depend on when we can get our minister to do the ceremony."

"Have you asked him yet?"

"That's what I'm doing right now."

Steve smiled, realizing she was referring to him. "Lisa, I would be honored. Where were you planning on having the wedding?"

"We were thinking about the state park lodge near Carolton. They have a beautiful meeting hall in the main lodge, big enough for a good-sized wedding. All of our family members are traveling from either out of state or overseas, so it doesn't matter where we have it. We'll have the reception in the lodge's smaller meeting room. . . . Will the last Saturday in April work for you?"

"Uh, yes ... I think I can manage that. We're not tied up the last Saturday in April are we, Sara?" Sara shook her head, smiling over at her husband. She could hear everything Steve and Lisa were saying from where she was sitting.

"Wonderful! I'll confirm with the lodge and order the invitations tomorrow. James and I will come over sometime soon to talk with you about the details. Would next weekend work?"

Looking at Sara again, she nodded in agreement. "Next weekend should be fine," Steve replied.

"Thanks, Steve. Looking forward to seeing both of you."

"You're welcome, my friend. Looking forward to seeing you and James as well. . . . Oh, and give James my congratulations."

"I will."

"I'll hand you back over to Sara now. I'm sure you two have lots more to talk about."

Steve gave the phone back to Sara and got up to see what was in the oven for supper. Samson followed close behind him, hoping to get some kind of snack or taste of what they were both smelling. To Samson's delight, Steve opened the refrigerator first and pulled out a turkey hotdog, and placed it in the dog's bowl. It was gone almost as fast as it was given to him. Steve then went over to peek into the oven. There he saw a large meat and vegetable casserole baking inside.

"Hmm… looks pretty good," Steve observed. "Smells good too."

Just as he was closing the oven door, Sara came into the room, eager to talk more about the upcoming wedding.

"Steve, this is exactly what we need."

"I know, Hon. It will be great. I'm looking forward to it," he said, with one eye on the timer on the stove.

"Lisa asked me to help with the music. She also said something about having some Scripture read in Chinese. Some of James' family just speak Mandarin."

"That's a good idea, but I'm not sure I can help them out there," Steve said, a little hesitant.

"Oh, don't worry about that," Sara laughed. "His youngest sister is going to cover that part."

"That's good. I don't think I can learn Mandarin in just a couple of months."

Sara shook her head and grinned at Steve. Just then the oven timer went off. "Time to eat!" she announced.

Both Steve and Samson were ready for whatever came out of the oven. They were starving. Soon, Steve and Sara were enjoying their meal. Sara had scooped a little of the casserole into a bowl for Samson to enjoy, which he happily consumed while the couple talked. Sara suggested that the two of them drive down to the lodge sometime soon and take a look at the layout for the wedding. Steve agreed it would be a good idea. It would also make a nice outing for them.

The following week, on their day off, it was unseasonably warm, so Steve and Sara loaded a picnic lunch and Samson in their car and headed for the lodge, just a few miles south of Carolton. They decided to get an early start since it was such a nice day. Traffic was light, and the two easily found the lodge, based on the directions they were given. The outside of the huge log structure was rustic yet unique in architecture. When they went inside, they were greeted by a park ranger who volunteered to show them around the building and the grounds, after she found out why they were there. Going through the lodge first, they went from room to room discussing how the chairs and tables could be set up. Samson waited in the car, which they parked in a shady area with the windows lowered partway. When they were done with their tour, they let Samson out of the vehicle and looked for a place to have their picnic. Steve spied a picnic table next to a nearby stream and suggested they go there.

Sara was soon spreading a blue and white checkered table cloth over the table and began pulling the food out of the cooler she and Steve had packed that morning. Samson stood next to the insulated container, eagerly waiting for his share of the meal. As a soft breeze drifted through the trees, the Hansons worked together to set the table for their meal. The warm sun felt good on their faces. The sky was blue, and fluffy white cumulous clouds were scattered here and there across the great expanse above them. Even though it was still winter, it felt like springtime. It was a perfect day to be out in nature.

"You know," Steve said, laying back on one of the table's benches to watch the sky just before the meal was ready. "When I was little, Mike and I enjoyed looking for cloud pictures."

"Me too," Sara replied, as she finished unwrapping the food she was laying out. "Mom and Dad had us kids do that when we were traveling someplace in the car. It kept us occupied and out of each other's hair," she laughed.

"Look how the sun is shining through that group of clouds over there!" Steve said, pointing towards the eastern part of the sky. "It's almost like seeing the light of heaven. A stairway to eternity."

Sara turned her head to get a better look. "And you can almost *feel* heaven too."

The two sat and watched the light streaming down from the sky through the thick clouds until the billows moved on, giving the couple a sense of supernatural peace. Just then, Samson came over to them from where he was sitting and nudged Sara.

"Okay, Boy. Time to eat."

"I'm ready," Steve said, as he sat up and led the couple in a brief prayer of thanks. Samson sat quietly beside them as he prayed, and got up quickly to look for his food once Steve said "amen." While they were eating, Steve looked up at the sky again and quickly felt the presence of the Holy Spirit. He could tell Sara was feeling His presence as well. At that moment, each was given a sense of a new call, and they knew God would be revealing their next assignment to them soon. But for the moment, they were glad just to be together enjoying God's creation. It had been a while since the two had had some time alone in their favorite place on earth, the woods.

Like Sara, Steve was looking forward to Lisa and James' wedding. Several months before, he would not have agreed to perform the ceremony. He wouldn't have been ready. So much had happened since that time. Pastor Deem's group had impacted his and Sara's lives in huge ways. This upcoming wedding in essence symbolized a new beginning not just James and Lisa. It was a fresh opportunity for the pioneer couple to strike out again, to clear the way for yet another new ministry.

Encouraged with new hope and purpose, Steve and Sara struck out on a long hike through the woods after lunch. They were both wearing their boots in anticipation of the muddy trail, which turned out to be fairly dry most of the way down the slightly rugged path through the thick forest. Samson ran and romped ahead of them, sniffing and exploring as he went. The couple held each other's hand as they strolled down the park trail. There was no need to hurry, they had the whole day off. They talked about the possibilities that lay ahead for them and what might be coming for Lisa and James. They felt blessed to be a part of their friends' lives and to be asked to play a major role in the April wedding ceremony.

That evening, when they returned home, Steve took his telescope outside to gaze at the stars. It had been stored in the hall closet since they moved into their new home. Steve felt it was time to use it again. As he adjusted the focus on the optical instrument, he thought about how his focus had been recently adjusted as well. Once more, Steve stood in awe of God's magnificent creation. Somehow, it looked more wonderful than ever before. He also marveled at how God had brought him and Sara so far since coming to Carolton, following a long hard season in ministry. Things were being made new again for them in more than one area of their lives.[1] As he searched the sky for the constellations, Steve's thoughts turned to Lisa and James. They too had experienced great hurt and loss in their lives, but God made things new again for them as well. How incredible God looked to Steve that evening. As he continued looking at the sky, Steve's heart soared and he began to sing.[2] His favorite praise and worship songs took on new meaning, and Steve found himself falling in love with his Savior once more.

Steve stood at the front of a large assembly room in the state lodge looking out over a sea of friends and family of the bride and groom. Much preparation had gone into that special day, and he knew he and his family would enjoy the celebration. It felt odd at first to be standing in front of an audience once more, but after a few minutes, it felt natural again. Sara, dressed in soft lavender and wearing a corsage, was playing the piano. Peter, wearing a light gray tuxedo, accompanied her on the guitar, and two of James' nieces, both wearing long violet dresses, played the violin. At exactly 2:00 p.m., while Sara played their entrance music, four groomsmen began to line up in the front of the hall on the right side before Steve. James came in last behind them. All were wearing dark gray tuxedos and shirts to match the bridesmaids, who were yet to come. James' wore a light gray suit and an ivory shirt.

With all of the men assembled, Steve nodded his head and the ring bearer and flower girl, each four years old, started down the aisle. Everyone smiled as the two preschoolers walked slowly side by side through the middle section of the myriad of chairs, each child dressed in light gray outfits with purple accents. The ring bearer was James' nephew, and the flower girl was Lisa's niece. When the two children took their places at the front of the room, the music changed and the bridesmaids, one being James' daughter April, made their way down to the front as well, lining up on the opposite side of Steve. Each was wearing a different shade of lavender and carrying a bouquet of mixed spring flowers. The room itself was filled with flowers (real and silk) from both the United States and Taiwan, including various colors of orchids, lilies, roses, chrysanthemums, and tung and cherry blossoms. The hall looked like a botanical garden and smelled heavenly.

Soon the cue was given for the bride to come down the aisle, and Sara began to play a wedding processional. Everyone stood as Lisa and her father, a man in his early sixties and also in a dark gray tux, started making their way to James, who was smiling from ear to ear as he watched his bride approach him. People of several nationalities nodded and smiled at Lisa as she went by with her special escort, some women wiping their eyes, including her mother, who was dressed in mauve. As Steve watched Lisa moving toward the front of the room, he thought she was the most beautiful bride he had ever seen, outside of Sara. Her striking full-length designer ivory gown was purchased for her by her future sisters-in-law on a recent trip to Taiwan. Her dark hair was pulled up on top of her head in a delicate braid and a long veil, matching her train, cascaded behind her. Both dress and veil were embroidered with roses and other floral designs. She was carrying a colorful spring bouquet and was smiling broadly at James. When they reached the wedding party at the front of the room, her father gave her hand to James, and the pair grasped each other's hand tightly. Steve smiled like a proud parent himself as he started reading through the wedding service. He was wearing a black suit, ivory shirt, and lavender tie, blending in well with the wedding party.

At various points in the ceremony, James' younger sister would read some of the Scripture in Mandarin Chinese and then in English. His two older sisters and his daughter sang traditional wedding songs in Mandarin. They also sang a couple of wedding songs in English. When it came time for the couple to say their vows, they each recited what they had written just for this special occasion. Beautiful wax candles with wax flowers were used to light the unity candle, which was equally ornate, towards the end of the service. When Steve pronounced them man and wife, the new couple kissed and then hugged each other. At that point, a great cheer rose from the audience, which made the couple both laugh and cry. Steve reached over and hugged them both, then they turned and headed down the aisle to the back of the room where they and their attendants formed a receiving line. Soon the ushers were guiding people through the line and into the reception hall.

The wedding reception was incredible. Every kind of popular Asian and American food imaginable was available to the guests. While everyone ate at the colorfully decorated tables, an American and an Asian band took turns playing the music. Mary and Joshua had come in for the wedding from Ohio and were frequently seen holding hands as they spoke with those they knew in the crowd of guests. When it came time for the bride to throw the bouquet, Mary caught it. And to everyone's joy, she announced her engagement to Joshua Franklin. A surge of happiness filled the room once more at the news of another nuptial.

Mary and Joshua let Steve and Sara know that they would wait at least a year and a half until Joshua was finished with his degree and had started work full time. He was already working part time with a local newspaper and was promised a full-time job when he had his degree. Mary would continue to go to school to become a literature teacher, and they would wait to start a family until after she secured her first teaching job. At some point, she wanted to get her Master's degree, so she could teach at a community college. Frank and Margaret Hellinger came over to hug and congratulate them. They both had been helping serve the wedding cake, which had been masterfully created in a breath-taking Asian floral design. James and Lisa, the Samples, Cannons, and several others from Anderson Hills came over to wish them well too.

The reception went on for three hours, and then the new couple decided it was time to change their clothes and head for the airport.

Twenty minutes later, they emerged from the dressing areas in their traveling clothes. They continued making the rounds around the tables until it was time to leave for their flight. Before they headed for their car, they gathered their things and went over to thank Steve and Sara for playing a big role in their special day.

"It meant so much to us for you to do the ceremony, and for Sara to lead the music," James told Steve and Sara.

"We were honored to do it," Steve replied. "God's blessings on both of you."

"Thank you both," Lisa said, giving Steve and Sara each a hug. James followed with a hug for each of them as well.

The newlyweds then headed for their car, already packed with their suitcases to go to the airport. There they would catch a flight to Taiwan where they would be enjoying their honeymoon. James had a small apartment near Taipei he used when he was in Taiwan visiting family members who still lived there. The guests lined the park lodge's driveway to applaud and throw rice and birdseed on the bride and groom before they drove away in their car. Steve and Sara had their arms around each other as they waved goodbye to their friends. While they did, they thought of their own wedding day and the excitement of the new life they embarked on together at that time. As James and Lisa's car disappeared from sight, Steve and Sara and some of the newlyweds' other close friends and family started packing the wedding presents into a van owned by one of James' sisters and her husband. They would deliver the gifts to the couple's new home in Philadelphia. Steve and Sara would miss spending as much time as they had with Lisa and James but knew they were not too far away from them to visit.

After the wedding, life continued as usual. Steve's workload increased a few more hours a week hanging wall board, and Sara continued her 30 hours a week job at the nursing home. They both still wondered what was coming next for them but tried hard to give their best to the jobs they had while they waited on the Lord. Neither of them was working full time, but they made the money they needed to keep things going.

Unfortunately, they had no health insurance when they left Anderson Hills. They were, however, able to join a Christian health share organization, which was a good backup for any major medical needs. At that point, there was no immediate need for medical coverage. For that, they were very grateful.

Spring passed quickly and before they knew it, summer was upon them. One morning, Steve walked out in the backyard after breakfast to enjoy the warm summer morning. Feeling the sunshine on his face, he soon found himself in prayer, asking the Lord what he and Sara should be doing. Suddenly, Sara came to the back door and called out to him. Jonathan Wells, Assistant pastor at Anderson Hills was on the phone. Amazed, Steve quickly walked inside to take the call on the land line in the living room.

"Well hello, Jonathan! This is a pleasant surprise!"

"Good morning, Pastor Steve. It's good to hear your voice, too."

"So how are things at Anderson Hills?"

"Good, good. Actually, that's why I called. Pastor Burt O'Neal, our new senior pastor, asked me to give you a call."

"Oh?" Steve responded a little surprised.

"Yes. We're finishing up the new addition next week and were wondering if you and Sara, and hopefully Peter and Mary, would be available to come to the dedication celebration we are having the second weekend in August. Burt would also like to have you speak during the service for a few minutes that morning. We're just having one service that day, so everyone can be together."

Steve was suddenly quiet. He wasn't sure what to say.

Picking up on the reason for the silence, Jonathan said, "I know what you're thinking Steve, but really, it would be a good thing if you all came. There are still some of the original members here, and they'd love to see you. Pastor Adam is long gone, and we're under some terrific leadership now. He would have called you himself, but after hearing what happened to you and Sara, he thought I would have a better chance of getting you to come than he would.

Steve broke his silence.

"I don't know, Jonathan. Sara and I will have to pray about this. There was a lot of hurt when we left. People we thought were our friends were working against us. So many lies. So many deceptions. I'm not sure we're ready."

"I understand. Don't forget, I saw it all happen. Perhaps I should call you back in a few days. That would give you and Sara a chance to think and pray over the invitation."

"Thanks, Jonathan, I appreciate that. I also appreciate being asked to come and speak."

"No problem, Steve. I'll get back to you this weekend."

"That would be good. Thanks for calling."

When their conversation ended, Steve turned to Sara, who was standing close by.

"They want us to come to Anderson Hills later this summer for the dedication service for the new addition to the church."

Sara stepped back and leaned against the wall in the hallway and looked up at the ceiling. She exhaled loudly as she did. "What are you thinking we should do?"

"I don't know. It took so much to leave that place. I just don't know if I'm ready to go back and face some of those people again, especially a few of the board members."

"I know." Sara was silent. "I guess we need to pray about this."

"Yeah."

"Maybe we could talk with Pastor Deem and the group," Sara suggested. "We haven't been going as regularly as we were, but I'm sure they would be glad to see us again"

"That's a good idea. I think I'll give him a call right now and let him know what's going on."

Steve pulled out his cell phone and dialed Mt. Hope. A short time later, Pastor Deem was on the phone. Steve told him about the phone call he just had from Jonathan Wells. Pastor Deem encouraged the couple to come to the next meeting that Friday evening. He assured them that the group would want to know about their next challenge and would gladly join them in prayer over the invitation.

When Steve and Sara arrived at Mt. Hope, they were greeted with many warm hugs. They found that a couple of new people had joined the group since they'd last been there. After introductions were made, Pastor Deem opened with a word of prayer and then told the group that Steve had something he wanted to share with the group. Steve stood up with a forced smile and some hesitancy and told the members about his recent invitation to go back to Anderson Hills for a dedication celebration. He filled in the newcomers a little bit on his situation there so they would understand his dilemma.

"I just don't know that I can. And I know Sara has her reservations as well."

Sara nodded in agreement with the group.

After some words of encouragement from various group members, Pastor Deem finally spoke up.

"You know, Steve and Sara, even though this invitation has you two in somewhat of a quandary, perhaps it is God's will that you return right now. Maybe you won't be able to take on your next ministry assignment until you have finally closed the door in your mind on the last one. I sense that you're still hanging on to some unresolved feelings, and I would like to see you be set free of them, so God can use all of you, your whole being, in the next call."

Steve looked at Sara, and after a few seconds, the two agreed. It was hard to admit, but there were still some hurt and unforgiveness lingering inside of their hearts, perhaps in more than one area. Pastor Deem asked everyone to come up and pray over Steve and Sara. As before, the presence of God was very evident. When they finished, the two were in tears. Yes, this visit to Anderson Hills was something they knew they had to do. Not just for the church members, but their children and themselves. The next day, when Jonathan Wells called, Steve said that he and Sara were planning on going to the celebration, and he would be glad to address the congregation. They would be in contact with Peter and Mary to see if they would go as well. Jonathan was elated and told them he would let the senior pastor know. Steve was going to be given fifteen minutes to deliver a message to his former church family.

When the conversation ended, Steve began to wrestle with what he was going to say, but he knew in the end, God would supply the words. Over the next several weeks, Steve began to slowly construct a positive sermon of hope and purpose for Anderson Hills. Beginning first with the history of its inception to its full realization. He would then tell how God, even after some unfortunate turmoil, still had a wonderful plan and purpose for the congregation, and that he and Sara were proud to be among the founders of the original church plant. To him, the new building signified God's continued blessing on the congregation.

On the day of the dedication, Steve and Sara anxiously got ready to head to Anderson Hills. When they were both dressed, they went into the living room and knelt on the floor, praying for strength and grace for the day. As they stood back up, they knew God would show them that grace and mercy and that He was pleased with their decision to go. The two were quiet on the trip down. Both lost in their thoughts of their former life there. Sara broke the silence by reminding Steve that Peter and Mary and Joshua would be meeting them at the church. If anything, they were looking forward to seeing their children. When Steve finally pulled into the drive at Anderson Hills, his stomach began to tighten, but Sara, sensing his tenseness put her hand gently on his arm.

"It will be okay, Steve," she said reassuringly. "God is with us, and we'll have friends and family close by."

Steve nodded as he parked the car towards the back of the parking lot. They were a little early, but the parking spaces were already filling up. Some people were even parking on the church lawn. Looking around, he could see that the local newspaper was there, just as they had been when the church was first built. The radio and television stations, though, were nowhere to be found. Steve took Sara's hand as they walked toward the church office, briefly getting a glimpse of the new addition as they walked by it. Similar in architecture to the original construction, the addition was connected to the main church building by a screened-in breezeway. Inside, the couple was to meet with Pastor Bart and Pastor Jonathan before the service. As they entered the church doors, Frank and Margaret Hellinger were there to greet and escort them to the office.

"So glad you two decided to come," Margaret said, as she hugged each of them tightly.

"This isn't easy," Steve whispered to her, as he received her hug.

"I know," Margaret whispered back. "You won't be alone today."

Steve smiled, encouraged by this thought. Frank gave each of them a hug as well, and then the Hellingers led the way to the church office.

After meeting with the two pastors in the main office, Sara went with the Hellingers to join Mary, Joshua, and Peter in the sanctuary. The former music minister, Rick, was still there. He and his group of musicians were playing prelude music before the service. What they were playing, though, was a little different from what he used to do when Pastor Adam was there. Sara concluded that Pastor Burt must have had some influence on him. As Sara waited for the service to start, she was greeted by various people in the congregation. Some kissed and hugged her. Some gave only polite acknowledgments. It felt strange being in the sanctuary again after all that time, and Sara was starting to feel uneasy about being there. Mary, noticing how uncomfortable her mother was feeling, took her mother's hand and held it smiling. Sara squeezed her daughter's hand in a gesture of thanks.

It was not long until the sanctuary was filled. The overflow was directed to some of the Sunday School rooms, where closed-circuit TVs were set up for them to watch the ceremony from there. When the service was about to begin, the three pastors came into the sanctuary from a side door and took their seats in the front row of the pews on the left-hand side of the room. Sara felt a great sense of pride as she watched her husband take his place with the other ministers. As the service started, Pastor Burt led the congregation in a time of worship. He then told the congregation that this was a special day in the life of the church and that their founding pastor had returned to bless them with some words of encouragement. He asked first, that his family would stand. As they did, there was polite applause. After that, he introduced Steve and took his seat in the front row of the pews. Polite applause went up again.

Steve stood nervously at the podium looking out at the congregation. As he scanned the group, he spotted both friend and foe. Unable to speak at first, he grabbed the water bottle he had placed behind the lectern. Saying a quick prayer, and taking a sip of water, his nerves began to settle and the words began to flow. Seeing Sara and his family sitting a few rows back from the front gave him even more confidence. Starting with a brief word of thanks, Steve went on to deliver his message. As he did, suddenly he felt a gentle hand rest on his right shoulder. He wanted to turn to look but dared not to do so. Somehow, he instinctively knew that it was the Lord Himself standing behind him.

Joy began to well up inside of Steve as he gave an encouraging and deeply heartfelt message. When he reached the end of his notes, the hand lifted and great applause went up in the sanctuary. Many began to stand, which took him and Sara and their children by surprise. But what was even more miraculous, at that very moment, Steve was also hearing Heaven's applause, which quickly drowned out what was taking place in the natural. For a few wondrous seconds, Steve was transported to a place of marvelous peace and acceptance. Suddenly he realized he was in the presence of the Father. Though he couldn't see Him, Steve felt His indescribable love and was lifted in ways he never could have imagined. A host of angels and "a great cloud of witnesses"[3] were also surrounding him, clapping and cheering him on. And for the first time, Steve could feel compassion filling his heart towards those who had harmed him and his family, and a fresh new pride of being a child and servant of God Almighty overtook him. Even though the applause from the natural audience touched Steve's heart, it was the supernatural applause that kept him awestruck for a while more. He had heaven's approval when he had thought he had failed so miserably at Anderson

Hills. When the applause ceased in both realms, he stepped down from the stage and took his seat in the first row. The service continued with special music and other presentations. Steve looked up at the cross that hung on the front wall of the sanctuary and thanked God for the privilege of being the first leader of that church family.

After the service, everyone headed to the new building addition for a brief dedication ceremony and a blessing, which included the anointing of the building with oil by the senior pastor. Steve and Sara were given the honor of cutting the huge red ribbon, and then the congregation flooded into the building for the reception in an enormous multi-purpose room, with basketball hoops at either end. A massive covered dish meal was laid out on a large number of tables for everyone to enjoy, and soon, Steve and Sara found themselves at the front of the line.

When they finished their meal, Steve and Sara forced themselves to move around the large assembly room to talk with as many people as they could. To their joy, Harold and Francine Cannon were there, along with Paul and Mia Samples. Lisa and James Lin were also there enjoying the festivities. Steve and Sara greeted all of the board members who had ever served at Anderson Hills. Most of them responded warmly to them. Jerry Simpson and Angela Camp, whom they had not seen since they left Anderson Hills, were there with their families and were excited to see their former pastor and his wife. They both expressed their heartfelt thanks for them coming to the celebration. However, a few of the board members, who had supported Pastor Adam, were noticeably cold and distant towards them. Steve and Sara surmised later that they were either feeling guilty over what happened, or they were still burning a torch of allegiance for Pastor Daugherty. In any case, it didn't matter. They prayed those people would one day realize what really happened at Anderson Hills.

After the reception, when many of the parishioners and visitors had gone home, Steve and Sara decided to go out into the field behind the church to look at the new addition from the far side of the property. The two felt a stroll and some fresh air would be beneficial before they said goodbye to the pastors and headed back to Carolton. It had been an emotional day, and they needed to break away from the crowd for just a little while. They let Mary and Joshua know they were going for a walk, in case someone was looking for them, and then struck out on a brief hike.

As they followed the property line, there was a strong sense of God's presence all around them. When they reached their selected point of observation, they were stunned to see an angel, the one Steve had encountered before, standing in the field between them and the church. He was smiling and began walking towards them. Not sure how to react, the two moved closer to each other and held hands as the huge commanding-looking being approached them. Steve and Sara quickly sensed a gentleness with the strength they saw in this angel, and oddly, despite his size and build, their fear faded away. It was almost like greeting an old friend.

When the angel came within a few yards of the couple, he suddenly stopped and looked up towards heaven. Without thinking, the two looked up at the sky as well. As they did, a pure brilliant stream of white light pierced the heavens and descended to where they were standing, gently pouring over them. They closed their eyes, overwhelmed by God's magnificent presence. When they opened them, the angel was gone. Someone else was standing in the field instead. Steve and Sara instantly recognized Him as the Lord Jesus. The two were astounded, unable to move or speak. They stood quietly, captivated by His beauty,[4] majesty, and marvelous glory. Their hearts filled with joy. Smiling at them, with His eyes full of love and tenderness and robe and tallit flowing in the breeze, Jesus walked closer to them and began to speak.

He said gently, "Don't be afraid." When Jesus came to where they were standing, He placed a hand on each of them. Their knees began to weaken, but His smile quickly brought strength back into them. He told Steve and Sara how very pleased He was with their faithfulness over the last several years, amidst all the pain and turmoil. Their work in this church plant was being celebrated in heaven. Steve and Sara were never meant to stay at Anderson Hills. They and their children were only there to establish the foundation for a strong fellowship of believers, and help clear the way spiritually for the current pastor. That was why they had been asked to build the church quickly. He reminded them that they were God's pioneers — His special frontline forces, breaking ground and clearing the way for new things to take place. Because of Steve and Sara's obedience, the new senior pastor and assistant pastor, Jonathan Wells, would have many years of a powerful life-changing ministry at Anderson Hills. The toughest job had been done for now. Certain strongholds had been removed.

The Lord also told Steve and Sara their time at Community Church was to prepare them for their last assignment in Anderson Hills and help wake up the Nordstown parishioners to what was going on in their place of worship. That congregation had been in denial for too long and needed to be shaken up, so their spiritual eyes would be opened, so demonic strongholds could be destroyed. Unfortunately, it would take yet another ministry couple in the future to help bring that task to completion. The husband of that couple had visited their home a few years earlier. He had come to Steve in the dark of night for help. Steve and Sara immediately understood Jesus was talking about a young man named David, whose destiny was miraculously changed that day. Even though they had not heard from David since that evening, they had always believed God was going to use him powerfully for His kingdom.

Led by the Holy Spirit, the forthcoming Community Church ministry leaders and the pastors of Anderson Hills would help bring about a major change in the community at large by leading other area ministers in eradicating witchcraft and other diabolical practices from the county for good. Steve and Sara sensed that they too would be playing some kind of role in that extraordinary movement of God.

Steve and Sara were then told that a new door was about to open for them, something they had been waiting on for a long time.

"Use what you have learned," the Lord said. Softly touching each of them on the face, He said, smiling again, "Receive this gift." Then, He too disappeared.

The couple stood silently, yet expectant, with the light sent from the Father still streaming down on them. A moment later, they began to feel oil being poured over their heads. Its sweet fragrance was of fresh roses, like Sara grew in her flower gardens, yet richer. As the oil began to run down their faces, a warmth rushed through their bodies. It was a healing balm. They dropped to their knees, lifting their eyes and hands towards heaven in submission, and worshipped God. An incredible sense of empowerment from the Holy Spirit swiftly rushed through them, just like it had when they first went into ministry together. They began to pray with the help of the Spirit. With that, came a feeling of fulfillment for the work they had done and a release from any lingering unforgiveness. After a few minutes of this incredible anointing, the light faded and returned to heaven, and they found themselves alone in the field, refreshed and renewed.

Aware of their surroundings again, Steve and Sara thanked God for using them at both Anderson Hills and Community Church. They were humbled to have been chosen; it all made sense now. Yes, they had sustained many injuries during intense battles but were not mortally wounded. The two had learned so much–far more than they could have learned in any classroom. They knew they had the strength now to handle the new assignment that was coming because the Spirit had just given it to them. His newly imparted unction stirred inside of them. They marveled at what had just taken place as they lingered in the field a while longer, remaining on their knees. They didn't want to leave. The encounter was just too precious, too holy. After several more minutes passed, Steve felt prompted to look at his watch.

"We better get back and say goodbye," he told Sara. She agreed, and the two got up and walked back to the church, holding hands again. There was no visible sign of the anointing oil that had just been placed on them, but they knew, in their spirits, it was still there.

"There they are," someone called out, as the couple approached the new building addition. "We thought you two ran away." It was Pastor Burt. Everyone standing there started to laugh.

"Hope you don't mind. We were just taking another look at the church from the field," Steve said, at a loss for words. "We didn't mean to be gone so long. We just needed some time alone."

"Oh, no problem, Steve. Glad you got a chance to do that. I often go out there myself to get away. Sometimes, I can even sense the presence of angels in that field," he said, knowingly winking at them.

Steve and Sara looked at Pastor Burt, immediately understanding that he too had experienced angelic encounters in the property behind the church.

"We just wanted to give you something," Pastor Burt went on. "As a token of our appreciation for coming today, and for all you have done for Anderson Hills."

"You didn't have to do that, Burt," Steve said, as he watched Pastor Burt pull a white legal-size envelope from his coat pocket.

"We wanted to, Steve. Please accept our gift," he said, pushing the envelope into Steve's hand. "This is from our hearts. If it weren't for you two, I wouldn't be here today. For that, I am personally and eternally grateful."

"Thank you," Steve said, as he closed his hand on the envelope.

"Thank you, Burt," Sara said, and reached over and hugged him. She was glad he was the new leader. He was an excellent choice. One only God could make.

Steve and Sara went on to say many more goodbyes and receive lots of hugs from those still at the church. But before leaving, Steve asked Pastor Burt and Pastor Jonathan if he could pray over them and the rest of the ministry team in the new addition. He felt it was something the Lord wanted him to do. They eagerly accepted his offer and assembled the group in the large meeting room in the new addition. There the ministry team knelt. Standing with Sara by his side, Steve prayed and pronounced a blessing over the group and their ministry at Anderson Hills. With hands held up towards heaven, the ministry leaders received what Steve declared over them through the inspiration of the Holy Spirit. Tears came to everyone's eyes as the imparting and a blessing was given, and an endowing supernatural blanket of light fell on them. At that moment, Steve was finally able to emotionally release the ministry God had temporarily entrusted to him and Sara to those God had called to take over. Complete closure had just taken place, and the mantle had been passed. When the light faded, Steve and Sara hugged each other, knowing they had once been a part of something very special. The ministry team then stood, full of new passion and excitement for the ministry they had been entrusted with. Wiping their eyes and thanking and praising God, they soon were hugging each other and Steve and Sara.

After expressing their thanks for a wonderful day, Steve and Sara headed for the parking lot. They were glad they had come. Their work there had not been forgotten. They were happy for the opportunity to symbolically turn the ministry over to Pastor Burt and his ministry team. The two would have missed out on a tremendous blessing had they chosen not to return to Anderson Hills Church Fellowship that Sunday.

Getting into their car, Steve and Sara waved goodbye to everyone still there at the church. Full of peace, they were leaving confident that God's perfect will had been done for that congregation. Peter and his new girlfriend, Leah, and Mary and Joshua had been waiting for Steve and Sara in the church parking lot. When they saw the couple's car starting to leave the church property, they were soon close behind them in their vehicles.

The family had decided to meet at a new restaurant halfway between Anderson and Carolton for a couple of hours before everyone had to go their separate ways. As Steve and Sara drove down the road in the lead, curious, Sara decided to open the envelope Pastor Burt had given them. Steve had handed it to her after they got in the car, knowing at some point, she would open it for them.

"Mind if I open the envelope now, Hon?"

"No, go right ahead."

Sara slid open the top of the envelope with her fingernail and pulled out a check. Oh my," she gasped in surprise. "It's a check for a thousand dollars!"

"You're kidding," Steve said with surprise. "Wow! I never expected that. To be honest, I didn't expect anything when I agreed to come today."

"Me neither. But it certainly will come in handy."

"That it will, Babe," Steve agreed, as he gripped the steering wheel tighter, thanking God for the unexpected financial blessing. He looked in his rearview mirror to make sure their entourage was still following close behind and continued toward the restaurant. As they drove, Steve and Sara Hanson also thanked God all had gone well that day and for the special time they were about to spend with their children. They sensed that two weddings, instead of one, were on the horizon, and they wanted to get to know their future in-laws a little better while they had a chance.

The restaurant was busy that evening. The group managed to secure a wide curved booth near a large picture window, so they could better pay attention to when it was starting to get dark. The young people spoke excitedly as they dreamed out loud about their futures. Steve and Sara, still fairly young themselves, listened intently, even though they were growing tired from the long day in Anderson Hills. The service at the restaurant was slow, but it didn't matter. They were all together, at least for a while, enjoying each other's company. When their time together came to an end, everyone hugged, headed to their cars, and continued on their separate ways home. It would be a little while before they would see each other again, but it would not be long before some major changes would come to all of their lives, changes that would richly bless them all and their relationships with each other.

Chapter 17

A New Start

$\int$teve was outside mowing the lawn behind his house when his cell
phone rang.

As soon as he felt the phone vibrate in his back pocket, he stopped
the engine of his antiquated, but still usable, mower to take the call.
Steve was surprised to hear the voice of Dr. Michael Schaffner from the
district office on the other end.

"Well, hello, Dr. Schaffner!" Steve replied. "This is a pleasant surprise.
It's good to hear your voice."

"Good to hear yours as well, Steve."

"So, to what do I owe the honor of this call?"

Dr. Schaffner started to laugh. "Well Steve, I've been talking a lot
with Paul Samples and the regional board of directors the past several
weeks, and with much thought and prayer, we have developed a position we would like you to seriously consider filling for us."

"Sounds interesting," Steve said, walking over to sit down on a lawn
chair on his back deck. "What kind of position?" he asked, as he wiped
the perspiration from his face with a handkerchief.

"First of all, let me tell you that it's full time. And there will be
benefits."

"Okay, that's a good start."

"Steve, we've decided to create a mentoring and support department
for the district for both new and veteran pastors and ministry leaders.

As you know, people in those positions often encounter situations that are extremely challenging, both emotionally and spiritually. We need to do something more than we are doing now to help support our church leadership in the district during those times, so they don't feel abandoned or alone, or get burned out."

"I'm with you," Steve responded in agreement.

"So, we're looking for someone who's been in the trenches, so to speak," Dr. Schaffner continued. "Someone who can lead a department that will help meet the needs of individuals going through those difficult times in ministry. In other words, we want to keep good pastors and ministry leaders going, and we believe you are more than qualified to be the one in charge of that service."

Steve smiled. "Wow. That sounds tailor-made. When would this position start?"

"How about the last week of September?"

Steve was taken aback. What an incredible opportunity!

"You know, as tempted as I am to say 'yes' right away, I want to talk with Sara and pray about this to be sure."

"I expected that. Do you suppose you could give me an answer within the next 72 hours?"

"Yes, definitely!"

"That would be great Steve. We will be in prayer at this end as well. I look forward to hearing back from you soon."

"I look forward to talking with you too. Thank you, sir. Goodbye."

"Goodbye," Dr. Schaffner returned. "Have a good day."

"You too."

Steve sat stunned for a couple of minutes. This felt right. But he needed to have confirmation. He didn't want to accept it too quickly. Yet the possibility of a new ministry was exciting. The fire inside was burning once more, and he couldn't wait to get started. Unable to contain his joy any longer, Steve jumped from his chair and went running into the house.

"Sara! Sara! Where are you, Babe?!"

Sara was upstairs getting ready to go to the nursing home. She did not have to be there until eleven that morning, but since Steve was busy with the lawn, she thought she would go ahead and get dressed for work. Sara came running out of their bedroom when she heard Steve calling her. She feared something bad had just happened.

"Here I am, Steve!" Sara called down from the top of the stairs. "Is everything ok?"

Steve stopped at the bottom of the stairs to catch his breath as he hung onto the banister. "Oh, Baby. Something wonderful just happened. We need to pray about this right away."

"What is it?" Sara asked, starting to get excited. She felt the Spirit telling her that a new opportunity had just opened up for them.

"Come on down to the living room, and I'll tell you all about it." Sara dropped the plastic hanger she had in her hand and went racing down the stairs, eager to hear what was going on.

The two sat down on the living room couch as Steve filled Sara in on what he had just been offered by the district office. When he finished telling Sara about Dr. Schaffner's proposal, she threw her arms around Steve and held him tight.

"I feel good about this, Steve. This is from God. I know it is. Remember, the Lord told us we were going to use what we learned."

"Yes, He did. Let's pray about this position right now. This is just too good not to be true. We need confirmation. And let's pray about what your role will be in this as well. The Holy Spirit gave a fresh anointing to both of us."

"Yes, He did!" Sara said, even more, thrilled over the prospect.

The two knelt together beside the sofa. Holding hands, they thanked God for the opportunity that was just presented to Steve. He really wanted to call Dr. Schaffner and say 'yes,' but he also wanted to be sure that God didn't have something different in mind for him, so they prayed for a clear discernment of God's will. As they prayed, Samson came into the room wagging his tail and laid down next to them. He knew something important was being talked about and remained still until they were finished. When they said "amen," Samson got up and snuggled next to Sara. Steve kissed his wife on the forehead, gave her a big hug, and quickly got up from the floor.

"Got to finish the lawn now," he said with a big smile, and energetically headed back outside to complete what he was doing and to think some more about the job offer. Sara smiled back and shook her head as she watched her husband leave the room, whistling as he went. It was so good to see him happy about being in ministry again. Now full of energy herself, Sara ran back upstairs to finish getting ready for work. She too was thinking about what just transpired. The two had prayed for confirmation, and so they would wait for it to come.

After Sara left for work, Steve decided to call his brother once he finished the lawn. Mike was working on some sermon notes when his phone rang. When Steve told him about the offer from the district, Mike told his brother that he had had a dream about him the night before. He said he saw the district superintendent handing Steve something that looked like a contract. Steve reached for the agreement, and when he had it in his hands, the dream ended. He said he felt that something new was coming for Sara too. He had planned to call Steve later that day to tell him all about it but had gotten busy with his notes for Sunday. Steve sat amazed as he listened to his brother relay his dream to him. This position just had to be God's will. Later that day, he received yet another confirmation.

After lunch, Steve got into his old midnight blue truck with a matching cap to drive to work. He bought it from a man on his work crew, shortly after getting the job with the contractor, so he would have a way to go to work. He also used it to transport some additional materials needed at the various job sites he worked at, and as a place to store his work tools. Just as he was about to pull out of the drive, he received a call from a private number. When he answered, it was James Lin, calling from Philadelphia.

"Well hello, James. This is a pleasant surprise. You just caught me before I left for work. How's everyone doing?"

"We're terrific, Steve. I still can't believe I'm married again. God couldn't have given me a better wife. April is here now too for a visit, and the two women are having a ball together. As a matter of fact, they're downtown right now shopping. I don't expect them back for hours."

"Oh, that's great to hear, James. What a blessing. They've really become close in such a short time."

"Yes, they have. I'm very thankful for that." James paused for a second and then abruptly changed the subject. "I'm sorry to bother you, Steve. I know you're probably ready to leave for work." James went on, "But there's something I must tell you."

"Oh really? Everything okay?"

"Oh, indeed. Everything's great. This may sound kind of strange, but Lisa and I both had the same dream last night, and we felt compelled to let you know about it right away. It was about you, Steve. Something good, I might add."

Steve was quiet for a moment.

"I see," he managed to say. "Please tell me about it."

"It was very short but very clear," James started to share. "There was a man in the dream who seemed to be an important church leader, and he was handing something to you that looked like a contract. You took it and signed it and gave it back to him. Then the two of you shook hands. Sara was there next to you looking on."

Tears began to form in Steve's eyes, and he was quiet for a moment. He wiped his eyes and told James about the offer he had that morning from the district office and that his brother Mike had had a similar dream about him the night before.

"It looks like the Lord wants you to take that job, Steve," James told him. "And right away!"

"It appears so, my friend. This is incredible. Thank you so much for calling me. You just confirmed for the second time what God wants me to do."

"No problem, Steve. I'm glad I caught you at home."

"Say hello to Lisa and April for us. Let's try to get together some-time soon."

"You're welcome, Steve. And yes, we would very much like to get together with you two soon. God bless you both! Say hi to Sara for us!"

"I certainly will. And blessings to all three of you as well! Bye now."

"Goodbye."

Steve sat in his truck for a few minutes, reviewing the events of the morning, and decided to call Gerald Riley, his supervisor, to see if it was okay if he could be at the worksite an hour late. He told him he needed to take care of some family business and would explain more when he got there. Steve wanted his brother in Christ to know what had taken place but didn't want to take the time to do it then. Gerald agreed, and Steve pulled out of the driveway and headed towards the nursing home where Sara worked. He needed to talk with Sara in person. This was something that couldn't wait. It was too important, especially since they had just prayed about it together.

Steve entered the lobby of Pine Grove Nursing Home and went to the receptionist's desk to see if Sara could be paged. Molly Perkins, a young sprightly redhead in her early twenties, who was popular with both the patients and the residents, was on duty. She was a great PR person for the facility, and Steve always appreciated her friendly pro-fessionalism whenever he and others came into the building. As usual, she was wearing a bright-colored outfit and had her long auburn hair pulled back in a ponytail tied with a satin ribbon.

"Sure, Steve, I can do that," Molly replied cheerily, exposing the braces she had on her top teeth. Dialing up the department Sara was working in, she asked if someone could take over for Sara for a few minutes, so she could take care of some immediate family business. In just a few minutes, Sara came rushing down the hall to meet Steve. Fortunately, there were two volunteer aids in the activity room, so it was easy for her to break away at that moment. When she saw Steve, she was a little confused because it was not like him to have her paged like that. Seeing his smile, she knew something else good had just taken place. Not wanting to keep her from her work, Steve quickly led her over to the other side of the room where two overstuffed sofas had been arranged in front of a stone fireplace and told her about the two phone calls and the dreams Mike and James and Lisa had about him and the job. He mentioned that she was in one of the dreams as well.

"This confirms it then, Steve. This is definitely from God!" Sara said without hesitation. "I'm so excited! I just knew God had done something special when you called me downstairs this morning."

Full of joy, Steve swept Sara off her feet and swung her around in a circle. Then they hugged and kissed as he put her down.

"Must be good news," Molly said while smiling from the front desk.

"The best," Sara replied. "God's best."

"You betcha," Steve added. "Well, I better get to work. I'll call Dr. Schaffner before I leave here and tell him I'm taking the job. He'll be blown away. I'll tell you about it when we get home. "Thanks, Molly!" Steve said, turning to the receptionist. Steve and Sara kissed each other goodbye, and Steve left for work, whistling as he went out the door.

"You're welcome, Steve," Molly called after him.

"Yes, thank you, Molly," Sara added. "I'd better get back to work too. I'll see you later and tell you all about it then."

"Ok," Molly said. "See ya!" Molly waved as Sara hurried back down the hallway towards the activity room. They were playing BINGO, and most of the residents had joined the group, hoping they would be the winner for the day. The grand prize was a gift card to a popular local restaurant.

Before leaving the nursing home parking lot, Steve called Dr. Schaffner at the district office and told him what had transpired in just a short time. Dr. Schaffner was amazed at how quickly the Lord confirmed the calling to Steve and asked him if he and Sara could come up to his office that coming Saturday afternoon, right after lunch, to talk more about the position and for Steve to sign a contract. Paul Samples would be e-mailing him a pdf file on it later that day. Steve said they would be there and thanked Dr. Schaffner for the new assignment. He was glad to be back with the district again.

When Steve arrived at work he explained to his supervisor, Gerald, what had just happened. He was excited for Steve. Gerald told Steve if he brought his new contract to him the following Monday, he would arrange with the owners for Steve to be able to leave the company with just a two-week notice. That would give Steve time to prepare for the new job before he officially started with the district, and the construction company time to find a new worker.

"You're a pastor, Steve, and you need to be doing a pastor's job," Gerald told him.

Steve thanked his friend for his understanding and worked with new energy and enthusiasm the rest of the day while putting up wallboard. Gerald had to tell him to slow down a couple of times or he would be way ahead of the painters. Steve just couldn't hold back his excitement and joy. God was ready to move again in his and Sara's lives, and he was more than ready for it.

Sara arrived home around 6:00 p.m. that evening, and Steve was not far behind her. He was anxious to talk with her again. When he got home, Steve told Sara that he had talked with Gerald and would be able to finish up his job with the construction company in two weeks. Everything was falling in place for them. Going into the living room, they knelt by the sofa again to thank God for the new calling. Holding hands, they expressed the deep gratitude they were feeling for the new position and asked for divine guidance for Steve as he oversaw this new ministry. When they finished, the two decided to go out to dinner to celebrate. They even took Samson with them, because they were going to a drive-in restaurant. Samson happily jumped into the car when he realized he was going to be a part of the celebration too.

Shortly after Steve and Sara returned home that night, they called Mary and Peter to let them know about Steve's new job. Both siblings were excited to hear their father was going back with the district. The district had always treated Steve and his family well and were very supportive of him during some very hard times. The two promised to be over for a visit soon, which gave their parents something more to look forward to.

That Saturday, Steve and Sara got up at 6:00 a.m. to get ready to go to Dr. Schaffner's office in Pittsburgh. It would be at least a two-hour drive there, and they wanted to take their time and enjoy the ride. Both were thrilled about the job and were ready to leave early for their trip. The neighbor across the street promised to come over and make sure Samson had plenty to eat and the opportunity to go outside a couple of times while they were gone. Seeing everything was covered for the day, the two got in their car and started for Pittsburgh.

As Steve and Sara traveled, they put a cassette in their tape player and sang several praise songs while driving along the countryside. Stopping at a roadside café for lunch, they enjoyed their meal outside under an umbrella table. Throughout the trip, they talked about the new position and how it would change their lives for the better. Before they knew it, they were pulling into the parking lot of the district office in Pittsburgh. It was situated in a large complex of office buildings on a busy side of the city. The two-story brick structure looked impressive among the others standing close by. The district shared a building with three other Christian organizations, so they were able to afford to have a nice facility.

It's been a while, Steve thought to himself as he got out of the car. But it still felt like being home. Steve had received his ordination papers through the district office over twenty-one years before.

Steve and Sara were met at the front door by Paul Samples. He had worked hard to help develop a position that not only would be a great benefit to the district's many pastors and ministry leaders but would also help Steve get back into ministry again. As Steve and Sara walked down the hall of the first floor, they looked at and commented on the new decor that now graced the building. When they arrived at Dr. Schaffner's office, they were greeted by a distinguished-looking man in his late fifties with graying black hair, dressed in business casual.

Happy to see them, Dr. Schaffner warmly shook their hands and offered them some refreshments of coffee and apple coffee cake upon entering his office.

After Steve and Sara sat down in some comfortable chairs, Dr. Schaffner explained Steve's position in a little more detail to the couple. The job would involve some travel, but Steve would be able to have an office in Carolton. The district would cover office rent, utilities, phone, and internet service, and pay the office help. Expanding on what he had mentioned to Steve on the phone, Dr. Schaffner told him and Sara the district wanted to offer ongoing mentoring for new pastors and ministry leaders and counseling services for those who have gone through serious ministry wounds. Steve said he would ask Pastor Deem to help him set up a program for the district, similar to his at Mt. Hope. Dr. Schaffner indicated that the district would pay for consultation fees if Pastor Deem's group agreed to help them get started and assist in interviewing and hiring counselors for their site.

A review of his contract showed that Steve's income would be in the high-forties, with benefits and a small expense account to cover travel costs. Along with the duties already discussed, as director of the new department, he would also do some public speaking, present training sessions at district conferences, and be a guest speaker at seminaries that district pastors and ministry leaders often attended. In addition, the district wanted him to be a consultant for new church plants in their region. This excited Steve even more.

As they continued to discuss Steve's position, Sara shared that she had an idea for starting a support service for pastors' and ministry heads' spouses. Dr. Schaffner liked the idea immediately and told her he would check on some funding, so she could get paid to handle that part of the ministry. Surprised at his offer, Sara told him that if the Lord didn't tell her differently in the next couple of days, she would gladly accept his ministry offer.

When all of his questions were answered, Steve was handed a pen, and he eagerly signed his contract. He thought of Mike's and James and

Lisa's dreams as he did. When he handed it to Dr. Schaffner, he felt like he and Sara were embarking on a new chapter in their lives. The prophetic was now a reality, and he thanked God for the speedy confirmation and the new chance to be in ministry again. He was now in effect a "pastor's pastor," and that greatly pleased and humbled him. The search would be on now for an office and an office manager. Little did Steve know that he would not have to look far to find the perfect candidate for the office manager's job.

On the way back home that day, Steve and Sara decided to invite the Browns, Cannons, and Hellingers over to fill them in on Steve's new job and to see if they could enlist their help in some way with the new program. The following Thursday, all of those friends gathered at the Hanson home, expressed their desire to help. Margaret Hellinger spoke first. She felt her work at Anderson Hills was finished. She had just stayed there long enough to help the new pastor transition into his position there. If Steve was interested in her being his new office manager, the current assistant office manager at Anderson Hills could easily take over her job, and Pastor Burt could hire a new office assistant of his choosing. In addition, Frank was doing much of his work at home now, so the Hellingers didn't mind relocating again. They had already discussed it before coming over. Steve readily accepted her offer and looked forward to working with her once more. Bob, Harold, and their wives volunteered that night to help with any events his department might be doing that coming year. Steve and Sara were elated that they would once more be working with such cherished friends.

Steve and Sara were able to find office space in a building on the east side of town. The owners, two retired medical doctors, were looking for some new renters. It was an older building, built in the 60s. But it was solid and still in good shape, and the rent was more than reasonable. When everything was said and done, the new district department had a five-room suite, which consisted of the main office, where Mrs. Hellinger would work, Steve's office, a conference room, a smaller office for Sara, and a large storage room. They also had access to a conference room and two smaller offices down the hall, at no extra charge, for meetings and counseling sessions. The office was near the interstate, so it was easy for Steve to get to when he had to travel to another part of the state or the district as a whole. The new team couldn't have found a better situation. God had worked out all of the details for them.

Steve's last two weeks soon ended with the building contractors. To show their appreciation for his good work while he was with them, the company had a small farewell party for him with pizza and cake. Everyone in his crew was there, along with the president of the company, who gave Steve a bonus check for always going the extra mile. He also gave Steve a small silver hammer, with an inscription on the back, which included a Bible verse, to thank him for his service. It was a bitter-sweet moment, and Steve hated to say goodbye, but he was anxious to move on to his next calling.

The end of September arrived before he knew it, and soon the Carolton office was buzzing with activity. It was like old times again having Margaret Hellinger run the office. She was in her element once again. Her husband, Frank, came in from time to time to help with mailings and other jobs that needed to be done. Sara continued working at the nursing home for a while but cut down to just a couple of days a week as her responsibilities at the office grew. The nursing home hired another minister's wife to take over the hours she was no longer able to work. Eventually, Sara had to stop working there altogether and just went to the nursing home for personal social visits.

One fall October evening, Steve and Sara were just finishing supper when they heard the land phone ring. Samson went running to the telephone in the hallway to let them know it was ringing. As always, he beat them to it. Patting Samson on the head, Steve picked up the receiver. Sara was not far behind. It was James and Lisa.

"Well hello, friends!" Steve answered happily when he heard their voices.

"Who is it?" Sara asked eagerly.

Steve covered the receiver and told Sara it was James and Lisa. Then he told the couple he was going to put them on speaker so Sara could hear them as well. Sara smiled. When their voices came over the intercom, Samson began to bark and run around excitedly, realizing who was on the other end. Sara grabbed his collar and told him to calm down. When she rubbed his floppy ears, he began to relax.

James and Lisa had important news to share with their friends and couldn't wait to tell them all the details. They felt called to become medical missionaries in China. The two would be working in a clinic that was already established by James' family and a colleague of his, who currently lived in China. James' family, and some other benefactors, would be donating money to expand the clinic, which was situated in a poor rural area in southern China. They wanted to help more people in the region and add more medical services.

Steve and Sara talked with the Lins for over a half-hour about their plans for this ministry outreach. James and Lisa were still in the process of working things out to go there. James' daughter, April, was going to school to become a physical therapist and would be joining them later. She was dating a man nine years older than her who was finishing dental school. He too felt called to join the efforts at the clinic and would start going over to China with them as soon as he graduated from dental college in another year.

"This is an incredible opportunity to serve the Lord," Lisa told her friends. "He has confirmed this venture several times to us. We won't be there all year, though. We'll go every other quarter and be here every other quarter. That way James can keep his practice going in Philadelphia without selling out to his partners. His associates will take over while he's gone. His friend in China has another doctor friend who will be at the clinic in China on opposite quarters. And of course, I'll be working as a nurse in both practices. It works out well for everyone. At some point, we may stay there longer. We're just taking it one step at a time."

"It sounds like a great opportunity to serve the Lord and others," Steve responded. "We're so happy for you two."

"Yes, we are," Sara joined in. "When will you be going over?"

"Our first round will be this winter after the holidays. We're still working out our visas," Lisa told them. "That will give me some time to learn some more Mandarin," she giggled. "Fortunately, I have two wonderful teachers."

"Actually, Lisa's been picking it up pretty fast," James put in. "And her accent is almost perfect."

"That has to be God," she responded. I was never very good at learning or speaking foreign languages before. Of course, I never really had a reason to learn one until now."

"Please keep us posted," Steve said. "We want to be in prayer for you two. We'd also like to come over to Philadelphia right before you leave to pray over and anoint you for service there."

"We'd appreciate that very much," James responded. "We're not sure yet how free we will be to share the Gospel while we're there. But at least we can show them the love of Christ and give them some good medical care."

"Amen," Steve responded.

"You know," Lisa said. "Before I met you two, I had just about given up on the Church. If it hadn't been for you and Anderson Hills, I probably wouldn't be where I am right now. Thank you so very much."

"Thank you for saying that Lisa," Sara replied. "That means a lot to us."

"Yes, it does," Steve responded. "More than you know."

The couples ended their conversation with a group prayer, each pair praying for the other couple's ministry. Samson sat nearby as they interceded on each other's behalf. Like always, he never moved from his spot when he knew they were talking to God.

Three months later, Steve and Sara were waving goodbye to their friends at the Philadelphia International Airport. Neither James nor Lisa would have ever dreamed that they would someday be heading to China to practice medicine in a clinic for the poor, but there they were, hand-in-hand, pulling their carry-on suitcases behind them, and heading to a plane that would take them to a whole new adventure. At that moment they both felt very blessed. Steve and Sara wondered how they were going to connect with these friends in ministry in the future, as they believed they would, but time would tell how that would come about.

The following spring, Steve and Sara received phone calls from both of their children. They were each planning to get married the next year. Mary and Joshua were getting married first in the chapel on their college campus in Ohio. Mary wanted her Uncle Mike to do the ceremony, so her father could walk her down the aisle. To her, that was more important than having him conduct the ceremony.

When that day came, Steve enjoyed the new role and vantage point. He had always seen the bride come down the aisle from the front of the room, but now he was walking beside her. Steve thought Mary was just as beautiful as her mother had been when they got married. As he and his daughter walked past the crowded pews of smiling faces, it seemed like just yesterday that he was teaching her how to ride her bike and write her name. Today, he was giving her in marriage to a man he and Sara knew would be a perfect mate for her. *Where did the time go?* Steve thought.

Tears formed in Steve's eyes as he placed his daughter Mary's hand in Joshua's. Turning to join his wife in the front left-hand pew, he pulled his handkerchief from his back pocket to wipe his eyes. Sara was already blotting hers when Steve came over to sit next to her. The couple at the front of the church glowed as they looked into each other's eyes, eager to start their new life together. Like James and Lisa, they too had written their vows, and when it came time to exchange rings, they announced that the wedding rings had been made by Joshua's aunt, who was a jeweler. The rings were unique in design and complemented each other, sliding on easily to their fingers when they were exchanged. When Mike pronounced Mary and Joshua man and wife, everyone in the room cheered. The couple kissed and hugged each other and then hugged Mary's uncle. As they started to leave the front of the sanctuary, they stopped to hug and kiss both sets of parents before going down the aisle and heading to the college's cafeteria for the receiving line and reception.

Shortly before the celebration ended, the couple changed clothes and left for their honeymoon in Canada. They had reservations to spend the night at a hotel on the Canadian side of Niagara Falls. The next day, they would move on to some other well-known vacation sites. Steve and Sara watched their baby girl drive off with the man of her dreams. They knew she would be happy with Joshua, and they were thankful. He had a good job, and so would she, as soon as she graduated from Christ's College.

To the joy of their families, Peter and Leah married two months later. Steve performed the wedding this time, and Sara played some of the music on an electric keyboard. Mary was the maid of honor. The couple decided to be married at the lodge, just below Carolton, where James and Lisa had exchanged their vows. Theirs was a small wedding with just close friends and family, but it was just as beautiful as Mary and Joshua's wedding because, like them, the newlyweds were deeply in love with each other, and with God. Steve and Sara agreed that Leah would be good for Peter. She was a teacher for disabled children and was kind and patient. She encouraged Peter to go to counseling for his anger issues when he needed it most. He now had a good handle on the problem and was making great strides forward. He realized how powerful forgiveness can be in healing past hurts. Peter and his new wife planned to work with troubled teens at their local church after he graduated with his degree in social work. They wanted to make a positive impact on their community for the Kingdom of God.

That evening after Peter's wedding, Steve and Sara sat quietly together on the living room couch, thinking about their two children. So much had happened since they were first married, and now their children had each started their own married lives with someone very special.

"You know," Steve said, stroking Sara's hair as she rested her head on his shoulder. "We could be grandparents in the next couple of years."

"I know," Sara replied. "I'm going to have to get used to the name "Grandma" though. It sounds kind of old."

Steve laughed. "But you'll be a young grandma."

Sara smiled. "Yes, that's true, isn't it? And you'll be a young grandpa."

"Yes, I will," Steve responded, grinning at his wife.

"To tell you the truth, I'm looking forward to grandbabies," Sara said thoughtfully. "It gets kind of quiet around here sometimes. It would be nice to hear little feet running around the house again." Just then Samson jumped up on the sofa and onto Steve and Sara's laps.

"Speaking of little feet," Steve chuckled.

"Oh, we didn't forget about you little one," Sara said, rubbing Samson's floppy ears. "You're going to be with us for a long long time."

"Yes, you are," Steve agreed. "The grandkids are gonna love you."

Samson barked in apparent agreement, making Steve and Sara laugh.

Chapter 18

God's Pioneers Once Again

Oone Saturday afternoon late that summer, Peter, Mary and their spouses and the Hellingers were at Steve and Sara's house for a barbeque picnic. After everyone had eaten their fill and sat and talked for a while in the backyard, the group decided to play a couple of games of volleyball. Then they went around to the front porch to have some homemade ice cream. While they were enjoying their dessert, Samson, who was working on his own bowl, suddenly looked up and became transfixed on something across the street. Noticing his unusual behavior, Mary watched him with great interest, wondering what he was looking at. Then with no warning, Samson jumped off the porch and darted across the yard, barking as he went. There on the other side of the street was three-year-old Tony Russell. He had been chasing a large yellow plastic ball in his front yard and was about to run out in the road where the ball had rolled. Without hesitation, Samson dove across to the other side of the street to save Tony from being hit by a speeding black pickup truck, now bearing down on them.

Realizing what was about to take place, Mary froze at first. Then, instinctively she got up quickly and jumped onto the front lawn, ready to run out to the road. Mary started to yell for the truck to stop, but there just wasn't time to get the driver's attention. He was focused on the road, and his vehicle was moving too fast. The others in the group looked up from their conversations when they heard Samson bark and saw Mary get up hurriedly. Before Mary could do anything else, there was a loud noise. The truck had hit something. Startled, everyone on the front porch jumped out of their chairs, joining Mary on the front lawn, to see what had just taken place. In the meantime, they could hear the pickup truck screeching to a halt partway down the road. Fearing the worst, Mary screamed hysterically, "Tonyyyy!" "Samsonnnn!"

When the dust started to clear on the other side of the street, everyone saw the boy laying on the front lawn of his home crying and his mother frantically running towards him, screaming his name as she went. Samson had made contact with Tony just in time, as he entered the road, and pushed him safely back into his yard. But Samson was not so fortunate. He had been hit. The driver of the truck was not able to avoid him but quickly slammed on his brakes when he realized what had happened, tires screeching on the pavement, and was soon parked alongside the road, a short way from the site of the accident. He hastily jumped out of the vehicle to see what he had hit. The Hansons and their company ran out to the road to see what had happened as well. The group was soon overcome with emotion. Mary and Leah started to cry. Their husbands tried to comfort them as best they could. They all were concerned about the boy and Samson. When Tony's mother reached her son, she hurriedly looked him over, asking him if he hurt anywhere, and then scooped him up in her arms. She had seen Samson push him back into his yard and knew the truck had missed Tony.

A man in his early thirties with blonde hair wearing gray and white utility work clothes ran up to the group. The name "Kevin" was embroidered on his shirt just above his right pocket.

"I'm so sorry," he said, choking out the words. "I didn't see anyone run out in front of me. I should have been driving slower."

After he caught sight of Tony's mother holding her son close to her, he breathed a sigh of relief. The little boy did not appear to be hurt. His mother, Stacy, was crying but was grateful her son was alive and safe.

"It was a miracle," she kept saying. "Thank you, Lord. Thank you for saving my Tony! You are so good!"

As she continued to hold her son, Stacy rocked him from side to side to comfort him, stroking his hair and kissing him on the face and forehead. Stacy Russell had been in the backyard hanging up sheets to dry in the sun and didn't realize Tony had wandered off with his ball. She came running when she heard the truck's tires squeal and her son crying, terrified of what might have happened. The man went over to make sure Tony hadn't been injured and then apologized to Stacy for his carelessness.

"We both should have been watching," she confessed.

As the two talked, Frank Hellinger announced he was going back to the house to call the police and tell them to send an ambulance. He then took off sprinting across the street.

"I don't understand," the man said confused. "What did I hit?"

"I believe you hit our dog, Samson," Steve said, going over and putting his hand on the driver's shoulder.

The man jerked slightly as Steve touched him. He could tell the man was visibly shaken and was observably sorry for what had just taken place.

"I'm Steve Hanson," Steve told the stranger, extending his other hand to him.

"I'm Kevin Lash," the man replied, as he nervously reached out to grab Steve's hand. "We should see if we can find your dog. He's probably still alive. I'll pay for the vet bill."

"Some of us can start searching for him. I suggest you stay right here and wait for the police."

Kevin nodded and went back to talking with Tony's mother. He apologized to Tony for almost hitting him. Tony smiled and then shyly turned to his mother, giving her a big hug. Seeing that Tony did not appear to be injured, the Hanson family and their friends started looking around the area of the accident for Samson, but couldn't find the dog anywhere close by. They didn't want to go too far until after the police arrived. Peter found the red bandana Samson had been wearing that day lying beside the road, yet there was no evidence of the dog or even a drop of blood on the pavement. When they examined Kevin's pickup truck, there was only a slight dent on the front right-hand bumper. There were no other signs of a hit. Out of desperation, Peter looked at the tires, and even under the frame of the truck to see if there was any trace of the dog. Nothing. The whole group was perplexed as to what had happened to Samson. Did he run off into the woods? Why? Was he hurt? Dazed? Surely he would find his way back home if he was able. Frank and Margaret decided to go search the nearby yards.

Daniel Rodriquez, another neighbor, had witnessed the accident from his living room picture window and called the police as well. His house was right next to Stacy's. He came running out of his home to let the group know the police and emergency squad were on the way. He also wanted to see if Tony was alright.

When the police cruiser arrived, two officers jumped out and rushed right over to the mother and her son. After checking on Tony and talking with Stacy, the officers called their dispatcher to let her know the little boy appeared to be fine, but they were going to have the paramedics make the final determination. While they waited, the witnesses filled the officers in on what had happened. The police then took statements from Kevin and Stacy Russell. When they had all the information they felt they needed, the officers cited Kevin for speeding and reckless driving, but no other traffic violations were noted.

A couple of minutes later the ambulance arrived and the paramedics were soon looking Tony over to make sure he wasn't injured. When their examination indicated he was fine, and knowing he wasn't hit by the pickup truck, the emergency squad driver called into the firehouse to let them know there was no need to transport the child to the hospital. They had advised Tony's mother to have him seen by his doctor should he start to complain of any discomfort. The team received permission to leave the scene and return to base. Before they left, the paramedics gave Tony a small stuffed Teddy bear and told him to stay close to his mother and let her get the ball if it went into the street again. Tony nodded and said he would.

The police decided to stay for a little while to help look for Samson but had to give up on the search when they received a call from their dispatcher. There had been another accident on the edge of town. Leaving the scene and waving goodbye to the group, the officers sped off in their cruiser, red and blue lights flashing as they pulled away. Mr. Rodriquez, who was part of the search party, felt it was time for him to go home, but promised to keep an eye out for Samson. Stacy and Tony promised to keep an eye out for the dog as well and headed back to their house, so Stacy could call Tony's father at work and let him know what had happened.

Distraught over not yet finding Samson, Steve and Sara, and their family and friends decided to spread out and do a more thorough search of the area. Over an hour later, when he was nowhere to be found, the search party headed back to the house to get something to drink and regroup.

As they walked back, most of them were wiping their eyes. Kevin, at that point, felt he should leave for work. He had stayed as long as he could. During the search, he called his place of employment on his cell phone and let them know he had been involved in an accident and would be late for the second shift. He was told to stay as long as he was needed at the scene. Kevin thanked the Hansons and their friends for being so nice to him and promised to drive more safely in the future. That was a wake-up call for him, and he wasn't going to forget it. Steve shook his hand again, and after sharing his contact information with the Hansons and saying goodbye to the group, Kevin was back in his truck and heading for the expressway. The Hansons and their company gathered on the front porch to talk about where they should search next.

Tears began to flow from Sara's eyes as she picked up the bowl Samson had been eating from just before he took off running across the street that afternoon. Steve put his arms around her to give her some comfort. Soon everyone was wiping their eyes again. After refreshing themselves and saying a brief prayer, the group set out again, two of them in cars and the rest on foot. They continued looking for Samson until dark, even in the nearby woods, whistling and calling his name as they went, but finally, they decided it was time to stop. If he was still alive, he would certainly find his way back home. However, they realized then their cherished little friend was probably not coming back. Where he had gone was a mystery. Samson had first come to the Hansons unexpectedly and now left unexpectedly. It just didn't make sense. At that moment, they could not imagine life without Samson, but they knew God saw their hurt and would somehow help them through this difficult loss.

The next morning, Steve and Sara woke with a terrible emptiness. But even though they knew Samson likely didn't survive the accident, they wanted to search the neighborhood one more time. They weren't ready to give up yet. Walking for blocks, the couple stopped now and then to talk with some of the neighbors, asking them to watch for their dog. They even checked with the local animal shelter, but no one had seen Samson. Making sure they covered all of the bases, the two also placed posters around town, requesting people to contact them if they saw or found the Hansons' beloved canine.

After lunch, Steve and Sara thought it would be a good idea to go a little deeper into the woods near the Russells' home to see if, by chance, a confused Samson wandered off to nurse his injuries. Perhaps, he went there to die. It seemed unlikely that he could have gone so far without being seen, but anything was possible, and they were still intent on finding him, alive or not. As they entered the woods, they asked God to show them if he was there.

Walking through the thick woods for several minutes, Steve suddenly spotted something metallic on the ground glistening in the sunlight. Pointing it out to Sara, the two headed over to where it was lying. Sara bent down to discover that it was the buckle of a dog collar. Picking up the collar to examine it more closely, she and Steve immediately recognized it as Samson's.

"He was here," Sara said hopefully. "Maybe, he is alive!"

"Let's look around," Steve responded, also feeling hopeful.

The two began to search through the foliage of the immediate area with new energy, but no Samson was found. They decided to split up to cover more ground, but still, there was no trace of him. After two more hours, they knew it was time to go back home. The search was over.

When a week had passed and no news of Samson's whereabouts had come to them, the couple concluded that they had to fully accept the fact that he was gone. Perhaps if he had died, someone found and buried him. Convinced there was nothing else they could do, Steve and Sara gathered up his things in the house, put them in a box, and stored the container in the garage. They just couldn't bring themselves to throw anything of his away at that time.

A few weeks after the accident, Steve and Sara were at their church to help with an outdoor event to welcome new residents to the area. Peter and Leah and Mary and Joshua were with them. Still heartbroken over the loss of Samson, they thought the family time together would help lift everyone's spirits. The Hanson family was assigned to run the main concession stand in the churchyard. The day was hot, approaching 87 degrees mid-afternoon, but their stand was situated in a small tent under some trees, which made the heat more bearable. The air-conditioned church, just yards away, gave them a cool place to take breaks when they needed them.

Throughout the day, the family handed out free hotdogs, chips, cookies, and pop. Towards the end of the event after the supper hour, they decided to take a break before cleaning and packing up their area. While sipping on cans of cold pop and enjoying a drop in temperature, a man in his mid-forties wandered up to their serving table. He had brown hair and a beard, deep blue eyes, and was wearing jeans and a T-shirt. He also had a red bandana around his forehead for a sweatband and was carrying a small U-Haul storage box.

"Good afternoon folks," the man said cheerfully, as he entered their tent smiling. "Would you be interested in a puppy? I don't normally do this, but I felt compelled to bring this little fella to your tent when I was driving by the church. It's a beagle pup. A good hunting dog or family pet."

The family members looked at the man and then at each other. They were stunned. How could he have known?

"I don't believe we've met before, I'm Steve Hanson," Steve finally said, extending his hand to the stranger. "And this is my wife Sara and my son and daughter, Peter and Mary and their spouses, Leah and Joshua. Welcome to Carolton Fellowship! Would you care for something to eat or drink? It's all free."

The man smiled broadly as he shook Steve's hand, and then nodded at the family members.

"Nice to meet you all. I'm Gabe. Gabe Browning," he said. My wife and I live over on Post Road. And no thanks on the food. I just ate." Setting the box on the table, he said, "This here is little Levi. He's the runt of the litter and the last one I have to give away. Would you like to hold him?"

The Hanson family members sat speechless, not knowing how to react. Then Sara slowly got up and walked over to the box to look inside. There at the bottom, sitting on an old towel a tiny puppy looked up at her with soft friendly eyes. He was similarly marked like Samson, but decidedly different. Immediately, her heart was captured, and she reached into the box to pick him up and hold him in her arms. As soon as she did, the whole family was surrounding her and wanting to hold him too. The puppy seemed to enjoy all the attention he was getting.

"You know," Gabe said. "It's great what you people are doing here at this church. I can feel the presence of God."

"So can we," Steve said smiling at the stranger. "So can we."

At that moment, Steve knew this was a gift from God and that they had acquired a new member of the family. "I guess little Levi has found a new home," he said with a grin. He's just what we needed right now."

"Wonderful!" Gabe replied. "My wife, Berta, will be pleased. There's just no room at our place for more than two dogs. I can tell he'll be loved. Keep the box and towel. You'll need something to take him home in."

After being thanked profusely for his gift, and invited back to the church for Sunday service with his wife, Gabe left the concession stand and headed for his motorcycle with a sidecar. Suddenly he turned around. "I forgot to give you something" he called to them. "Be right back." He walked over to his sidecar and retrieved a small bag of puppy food and took it over to the Hansons. Then saying goodbye once more, he left on his bike, waving as he left the parking lot.

As the Hanson family watched Gabe go down the street, Steve remarked, "God cares about every detail of our lives, doesn't He?"

"Yes, He does," Sara replied coming alongside him, thanking God in her heart for this new little blessing.

Dr. Michael Schaffner, from the district office, stood in front of a small crowd of fifty-some ministry leaders and church delegates in a breakout session at the denomination's annual conference, shortly after Steve opened the Carolton office. It was held at a large district member church near Pittsburgh, PA. He was there to show support to Steve and his program and to introduce Steve to the group. They had come to hear Pastor Steve Hanson's presentation on spiritual warfare in ministry. Steve sat in the front row of chairs with his notes in his hands as his superior and trusted friend gave an opening prayer and a brief introduction to his presentation. When the applause came, Steve stood confidently and walked over to the podium. He was smiling broadly, excited about being there to share his message and experiences with those in the room. Steve could feel the presence of God all around him. He had come so far since leaving Anderson Hills. Steve shook Dr. Schaffner's hand first and then faced the audience. Dr. Schaffner took a seat in the front row of chairs next to Paul Samples, who was also there to show his support for Steve and his program.

"Good morning," Steve began, after opening his notes. "I am here today to talk with you about a subject that is very important to me because I lived it. Unfortunately, though, it is a subject not discussed enough among many church leaders today. And even more sadly, not in great detail in many of our seminaries and Bible colleges. I am talking about the spiritual conflicts we as Christian leaders, both vocational and laity, encounter daily in our ministries. These spiritual battles cause great pain and confusion to many church and Christian organizational leaders and their members, often because they don't have a good understanding of what they are dealing with. They are the kind of battles that damage and often split Christian communities and fellowships. We as humans are primarily trained to handle conflicts in the natural, but I am here today to tell you that we need to be handling those encounters first in the supernatural. That is where we can have true victory over the powers of darkness.[1] That approach will help us be more successful in what we deal with in the natural realm."

"As you know, most men and women leave seminaries and Bible schools full of hope and passion for the Gospel. Their hands are gripped tightly to the plow, and they are ready to take on the world.[2] And while that is a good and necessary attitude for a new ministry leader to have, he or she can soon become frustrated or disillusioned if they are not prepared to handle the many spiritual issues that come their way. In reality, the ministry is not always exciting and fruitful. It's hard work and requires a strong resolve and commitment. Along with the successes, breakthroughs, and mountaintop experiences, there will always be challenges, hurts, and disappointments along the way, so we must be ready to take on both the good and the bad in our respective callings as they come to us. And I can tell by the nods of some of you in this room, you know exactly what I am talking about."

"My mission, then, for this seminar, is not to discourage you or anyone else from being in ministry because we must all submit to the call of God on our lives. I am here today to paint a more realistic picture for you, so you can become better equipped and stand stronger in battle when the spiritual attacks come. And they will come. You cannot escape them. Sometimes they are small conflicts, but often they are all-out battles or wars, which can be tremendously overwhelming to the new or uninformed ministry leader."

"I am first going to share some stories of some things other ministry leaders and I have encountered during our years in ministry. Then I will talk about what we learned from our experiences that will help keep you resilient and moving ahead in your divine assignments, despite what you might face in them."

Steve went on to tell what happened to him and Sara at both Community Church and Anderson Hills Fellowship Church, careful not to divulge too much information, especially names of people and organizations or the places where they took place. With permission, he also shared some of the stories he had heard while going to Pastor Deem's support group. In addition, he shared how the support group at Pastor Deem's church had helped him and Sara heal emotionally, forgive, and regain their passion for ministry again. When he concluded the first part of his presentation, Steve asked for and answered questions. Then he went on to his PowerPoint presentation, which focused on important points to know and remember when dealing with combative spiritual issues while in church or Christian organizational ministry.

- **"First and foremost,"** Steve told the group, **"Fully recognize the fact that a supernatural world runs parallel with our natural world.** Angels and demons are real. The Bible is clear on that, and I know it to be true from my own experiences. Spiritual battles rage around us even though we can't see them. Thus, as I mentioned earlier, when we encounter a conflict of any kind, we need to know how to deal with it in both the natural and the supernatural simultaneously. To help you do that, I would like to encourage you to memorize Ephesians 6: 10-20 and Psalm 91 and recite them often. Also, mentally put on the armor of God every morning. That is critical. This puts us in the right frame of mind to fight the battles with satan and his demons. As you know, satan, once an anointed cherub, was expelled from heaven when he tried to put himself above God.[3] With his rebellion, a third of the angels fell with him.[4] It is these forces of evil that war against us in our personal and professional lives. They are the enemies of our souls and we must be able to resist and fight against them continually."

"When the Apostle Paul penned his letter to the early church in Ephesus, he understood the pressure and influence of their surrounding pagan culture and the spiritual impact it had on them and their faith in Jesus Christ. Demonic influences were everywhere in the city at that time. Thus his emphasis on daily preparation for spiritual battles[5] was exactly what that group of early believers needed to hear. Unfortunately, not all of them heeded his advice and fell prey to the lies and deceptions of the enemy."

"Later in the book of Revelation, we find that this same church had somehow lost its focus and allowed certain pagan ideas and practices to come into their fellowship.[6] This is what happens when we lower our guard and neglect to wear our full spiritual armor. The enemy is always looking for a way to get church communities to compromise the Scriptures and what they as believers know to be true. And that critical error, my friends, can quickly lead a church family to some very dangerous territory."

- **"Remember what Christ accomplished for us on the cross.** His sacrifice broke the power of sin and darkness on our lives. And because of that, we have been empowered and given authority to do battle with the enemy of our souls, who comes to steal, kill, and completely destroy, whenever he and his workers of evil come against us. As you know, blood represented life to the

Jewish people, and so through Christ's blood sacrifice, we have life abundantly.[7]"

- **"Be on guard of the enemy every day.** To do that, be fully equipped. Make sure your relationship with God, Father, Son, and Holy Spirit is strong, vibrant, and growing. Strive for higher levels of intimacy and spiritual connectedness with Him. Know the One you serve and live for. Find time to be alone with God and commune with Him. Reach out to Him, no matter what happens to you or those around you. Talk with Him continually. While He was on earth, Jesus often went off by Himself to pray to the Father.[8] And when you talk with God, listen. Listen to what He is telling you and be obedient to follow His instructions closely. He sees things you don't. He is omniscient, all-knowing. So rely on His counsel to you."

"So, my friends, 'be sober, be vigilant; because your adversary the devil walks about like a roaring lion, seeking whom he may devour.'[9] A spiritual attack can come at any time and in any form, but know that God will always be with you. And if you are prepared for those storms, you will weather them so much better."

- **"Don't do spiritual battle alone.** Often you need the engagement of others in a particular spiritual war or conflict. If they don't join you, you may not see the breakthrough you are praying for. This, unfortunately, is where the Church as a whole has fallen down at different points over the centuries. The Body of Christ wasn't functioning like the early church during those times. Instead they were fighting each other over theological and power issues. They should have been pulling their spiritual arsenal together and fighting against the darkness together."

- **"Trust God, no matter what is happening around you, and be faithful to Him.** Do so, 'with all your heart and lean not on your own understanding; in all your ways acknowledge Him.'[10] Keep your eyes on Jesus. Don't let go of that childlike faith you had when you accepted Him as your Lord and Savior. Remember, Peter started to sink when he focused on the waves around him instead of Jesus."[11] God is always faithful to us. He's not going to let you drown. All you have to do is grab onto His hand."

- **"Understand how much God loves you and those you serve in ministry.** He has a plan for all of our lives and wants to see those plans fulfilled. God sees you, not as the world sees you, but as His child, made in His image, with all the gifts and talents He has given you."

- **"Be well versed in the word of God, the Bible.** Read and meditate on the Scriptures daily. Continually ask God for new insights. Now that might sound like a given to you, but I want to tell you, it's easy to get busy with ministry stuff and slack off on the study. Did you know that in Jewish thought, studying the Scriptures is considered one of the highest forms of worship? So worship the Lord each day in your study of the Bible. You need that! Make it a scheduled priority! I suggest at least ninety minutes a day. If you have to get up early in the morning, do it! If you're doing a lot of traveling, listen to the Bible on tape. Just get that study time in. Being consistent in your study of the Bible will pull you closer to God, make you stronger in a spiritual battle, and develop you into a better teacher and preacher of the Word."

- **"Be careful what you fill your mind with.** With the age of computers now at hand, we find ourselves inundated with a tremendous amount of information. While a lot of that information is good, as believers, we must be discerning as to what and how much of that information we will allow to influence our thinking. That goes for other things as well, like certain books, magazines, movies, television shows, music, etc. We don't want the enemy to steal or distort our Biblical perspective."

- **"Praise and thank God,**[12] **no matter what happens in your life, and find refreshment for yourself often.** I would like to encourage you to regularly read through the Psalms. Also listen to praise music whenever you can, especially those songs based on a Psalm or some other Scripture. Sing along, even if you weren't blessed with a great voice. Lift your hands heavenwards as you sing. In addition, listen to respected pastors, theologians, or Christian leaders on TV or radio, to obtain new insights. Read some of their books. Continue to refresh yourself daily, so you can do battle with complete sureness."

- **"Work on keeping a positive attitude.** Don't let others or situations bring you down. And laugh! Laughter is always great medicine.[13] Use humor in your sermons, group presentations, and staff meetings. Making others laugh also reduces tension among group members and often opens doors to friendships. In addition, it triggers positive chemical reactions within your body, helping to keep your immune system and overall health in good condition."

- **"Before starting a new call or divine assignment, deal with those things that may still be lingering in your past.** Unresolved issues or secret personal sins can greatly hinder your ministry. They can also surface at any time without warning. Take care of them quickly, so they don't become a stumbling block to you or those you are serving and leading. In other words, don't take your emotional or spiritual baggage into ministry with you!

Examine yourself, with the help of the Holy Spirit, and see what needs to go. Ask God to completely free you of that luggage, because it could be exposed in a way you won't like. If you know you are struggling in a certain area, seek out those who are trained to help others be delivered of spiritual strongholds. Deliverance ministry can be helpful to everyone.

- **"Before starting at a new church or fellowship, ask if there are any unresolved issues the ministry is still dealing with.** While you may or may not be told there are such issues, it's good to ask. That will help prepare you for what you might be walking into."

- **"Before you accept a new assignment, make sure your family (if you have a spouse and children) is on board with your decision.** Family unity in this kind of decision is essential. You need their support. Continually work on family relationships and make sure you pray and read the Bible together. Don't neglect them. Spend time with them. Go on vacations and family outings with them. Talk together at the dinner table, and listen to them. That will make a big difference when challenges come to you and your ministry. You don't want to be fighting major spiritual battles at home at the same time you are fighting them in your church or organization. Also, involve your family in your ministry in some way. They are a part of your calling too!"

- **"Make sure your calling has been confirmed to you by God before taking it on.** If it isn't your true calling, you won't be accomplishing what God wants you to do for the Kingdom, and you probably won't be as effective in it either."

- **"Always be led by the Spirit and use the spiritual gifts and stand in the authority God has given you.** The Holy Spirit is our teacher and friend.[14] He is not a thing or a force, but the third person of the Godhead. He was sent to guide and direct our steps. He also equips us with spiritual gifts[15] to use in our callings. Recognize and utilize those gifts in your ministries, and encourage your church family or fellowship to do the same. Together, you will build a strong ministry."

"And stand in the authority God has given you. Through God, we have power over evil.[16] Learn how and when to use that authority. Remember when King David was just a young shepherd, he was able to overthrow a giant because he spoke on behalf and by the authority of Almighty God.[17] Those giants we encounter may not topple immediately like Goliath did, but they will eventually come down as long as we are persistent and stand committed with other believers when in spiritual battle."

- **"Delegate responsibility whenever possible, so you are not overextending yourself.** That frees you up to pay attention to what's going on in the big picture of your church or organization. Give that delegated responsibility to members who are known to be faithful and Godly men and women, and gifted in the area or areas they are assigned."

- **"While you serve God and others, remember to take care of yourself.** Yes, ministry is about serving, but you need to take care of yourself as well. Make sure you have a day off each week to take a break and be with family and friends. You must have that break, especially from work-related spiritual conflicts, so that you can reboot and regroup. In some cases, sabbaticals or long-term absences may be helpful and or even necessary after you have been in a position for a while. A steady diet of problems and spiritual assaults will wear you down and weaken your resolve. Our bodies can only take so much stress. Don't let continuous attacks affect your health or your church/

congregational or family relationships. In other words, take preventative measures!"

- **"Study spiritual warfare.** Get books and tapes on the subject if that is not something you fully understand or know a lot about. Some authors to consider are Neil T. Anderson and Chuck Ingram.[18] Talk with others who have had extensive experience in that area and can give you some pointers. Go to a conference or take classes on the topic. An informed person is a wise person. Spiritual wisdom in this form will help you choose your battle plan and keep you standing on your feet when the attacks come."

"If you have not read it yet, I would also like to encourage you to read *A Pilgrim's Progress,* written in 1678, by John Bunyan.[19] It is a classic Christian novel in allegory form, which expertly combines both the natural and supernatural together in one story. Anyone studying spiritual warfare can glean valuable spiritual insights and instruction from that writing."

- **"Ask God to make you a strong discerner of spirits.** Watch for red flags, no matter how small, that come to your attention concerning others and what is going on around you. Compare those things that are spiritual with the spiritual.[20] Try to spot trouble when it enters the doors of your church or organization. And listen to those who try to warn you about spiritual attacks. Prayerfully consider what they are saying. They may be seeing something you aren't."

"In addition, be careful who you align yourself or your church or organization with. Watch for smooth talkers or those who are constantly bearing gifts to influence you and others. While some might be genuine or well-meaning in their actions, you'll know the manipulators and troublemakers by their obvious fruits.[21] Do your homework and research on those individuals before you grant them leadership roles in your church family, fellowship, or Christian organization. Act responsibly before you help create a situation that could get out of control. In sum, watch for divisive or manipulative people who have an agenda. Satan is the great divider and he will use those people to do just that in your organization."

- **"Speak up when it is important to speak up.** When something doesn't feel right, say so. If you worry about who you will offend, you may not get a chance to speak out later. You could also be giving evil a stronger hold on a situation. By remaining silent, you might even find yourself out of a job."

- **"Amid a spiritual battle, pray fervently 'in the Spirit'[22] and fast whenever you can.** Together, these two things will strengthen your position in spiritual warfare. Encourage others involved in a situation you are fasting over to fast as well, whenever possible or necessary. The book of Esther has an excellent example of how fasting can help bring about breakthrough. Queen Esther, along with her maids, Mordecai, and the Jews in Shushan, fasted for three days before she took on a huge spiritual challenge.[23] And as a result of their prayers and fasting, there was a tremendous breakthrough for the Jewish people."

  "And just a quick comment on fasting. . . There are of course many ways to fast. A medical condition may prohibit you from skipping meals, so consider other forms of fasting if you need to, like giving up something for a specified period of time. God will honor those sacrifices as well."

- **"Anoint your home, study, church, and organization facility with oil.** Declare those buildings to be the property of Almighty

God! Take authority over all unclean spirits that may try to enter your home or place of work or worship. Understand that you are a child of God, and you have been given the right and privilege to represent Him on this earth. You have the authority to tell the powers of darkness to leave. That's part of why you're there in a particular ministry. So, be bold!"

- **"Pray for the members of your church or organization and the leadership and/or ministry team, and encourage them to pray.** Have them pray for you and your ministry as well. In addition, have people outside of the church pray for you and your congregation/organization. Model prayer to others. Inspire your congregation or group to 'pray without ceasing!' "[24]

- **"Be a teaching church or organization.** Offer Bible studies on a variety of topics, including controversial ones. Keep people in your congregation or group informed on what the Bible says on all of those things. Refer to the vision and mission statement of your organization often. And mentor others in their walk with the Lord and Christian leadership. Remember, every believer is a member of a royal priesthood.[25] Being a follower of Jesus Christ means more than a ticket to heaven. It is active involvement in the Kingdom of God."

- **"Encourage those you lead to fill their hearts and minds with God's truth.** Satan wants to control people's minds. He is the father of lies. Jesus used the Scriptures to combat what satan was trying to tell him in the desert.[26] Remember that the Word of God is 'sharper than any two-edged sword.'[27] It is a powerful weapon in your hands. So pick up your sword and stand for what you know is right!"

- **"Watch for false doctrine, philosophies, and anti-Biblical worldviews.** Don't allow them to come into your organizations! Many today want to hear what makes them feel good[28] but you and I know that what they need to hear is the truth of the Bible. Truth is not relative ladies and gentlemen. There is only one truth, and that is what we must continue to teach and preach to others. Do not let truth be compromised, especially to fill up the pews in your church. You will be respected for holding the line."

- **"Never let yourself feel you are alone in ministry and don't try to go it alone.** This can lead to burnout, depression, and other serious health issues. It can also injure your relationship with God. You need to have your wits about you when you are in the midst of a storm or spiritual struggle, so keep your connection with God strong! Also, keep your relationships with trusted Christian friends strong! In other words, have a support group. Reach out to them when you are under attack. Receive wise counsel from respected veteran Christian friends and colleagues. And as far as the district goes, you can now utilize our new support program. I will be explaining that ministry to you very shortly."

- **"Understand that you can be wounded in battle.** The Bible tells us that if we belong to Christ, we will experience suffering in this life. We are not promised an easy road. In other words, you will not always leave a ministry situation unscathed... And just so you know, it's okay to cry. God understands the pain and disappointment we feel. The important thing is to get back up again. And always forgive. That is key. When a ministry leader suffers great hurt, it is very tempting for him or her to want to hang on to the bad feelings or retaliate in some way, but be aware, the enemy uses that unforgiveness to try to keep you and others at odds with each other, and from moving forward together in unity. Pray for those who hurt you, so you don't become bitter.[29] Bitterness will only drive a wedge between relationships. You must let it go! That of course does not mean you cannot defend yourself in a bad situation. It is how you respond that makes the difference."

"To hang on to unforgiveness is sin. And since Jesus died for all sins, we have no right to hang onto any ill feelings towards another human being, no matter what he or she or they have done to us. You must forgive, even if your offender is not sorry, so God can use you effectively in ministry. If you cannot forgive, you haven't fully grasped what Christ accomplished for you at Golgotha. Unforgiveness is like a virus. It consumes you and leaves you paralyzed. Know that something bigger is going on when you are in a spiritual battle. Look beyond the hurt, and don't let satan steal your joy in the Lord! Remember, 'our struggle is not against flesh and blood.' "[30]

"Work on inner healing along with forgiveness when you have been deeply hurt. Don't wallow in self-pity. Seek counseling if necessary. Do not stay angry with others, yourself, or even God. Be encouraged, God sees all trespasses against you. He will deal with unrepentant individuals in His way and in His time. Be reconciled whenever possible with those who have injured you. In short, forgive yourself for your mistakes, forgive others for their wrongs against you, and forgive God, even though He has not done anything wrong. This will bring you peace when you do. God is the great restorer and He can make you completely whole inside again when He sees you are willing to forgive. And when you do forgive, let God fill that space you just emptied with love, a love that overflows and touches others. A love that will not allow you to hang on to or reclaim those negative feelings ever again."

"To add, don't make a decision to give up on ministry altogether after you have suffered great pain. You may not be in the right frame of mind to do that. Wait on the Lord and your healing. God will let you know when you are ready to do ministry again."

- **"Be an example to others in all that you say and do.** Be the same person of God both inside and outside of your church or organization. People are watching you. Don't compromise your witness or beliefs, because others could in turn compromise theirs, and likely open the doors to spiritual influences you don't want in your church or organizational family."

- **"Finally, be prepared to leave a place of ministry calling if necessary.** You may be a pioneer like Sara and I have been. Be open to God's direction. Don't hang on to a ministry that is no longer yours. Know that something fresh and new awaits you just around the next corner. A ministry could be suddenly taken from you, but don't let that devastate you. It just might be God's plan. Remember, God's ways are not our ways. And don't be discouraged if you didn't accomplish everything you wanted to while you were there. Just because you don't see the fruits or outcome of your labor before you leave a place of calling, doesn't mean that you didn't accomplish what you were sent there to do."

- **"In sum, you may never encounter great spiritual battles like we described today, but you will always have spiritual struggles, pushback, and discouragement.** Whenever you enter unchartered areas with unbroken strongholds you will likely have some resistance, so it is essential to be ready for any size attack. Listen to and rely on the Spirit to clear the way and get you through those circumstances."

"In addition, understand and implement deliverance ministry at your church or organization. Pray against spiritual bondages. This sets people free from demonic forces so they can live out the life God meant for them to live. Realize the authority God has given you here on earth. You should never do ministry in fear because God loves you and wants you to have victory over darkness and be successful in your calling. His love for you is perfect and His "Perfect love casts out fear."[31] Walk then in bold confidence, and in the power, strength, and love of Almighty God as you do ministry!"[32]

As Steve moved through his final points, he was suddenly aware of a familiar face in the back of the room. A young man in his twenties was sitting in the middle of the last row of chairs, with people on either side of him. He was wearing Dockers and a dress shirt and tie. Steve searched his mind to place where he had met this man. Suddenly it came to him. It was David, the young man who had come to his home in Anderson Hills one night a few years ago to find Christ. When the two made eye contact, the young man smiled at Steve, and then he knew for sure. The man had the same peaceful look on his face he had the evening he received Christ. Steve smiled back in recognition, slightly nodding. Trying to stay focused on his closing remarks, he forced himself to return to the pull-down screen to point out something in the next PowerPoint slide. Steve couldn't wait until the end of his presentation to talk with this young man again. Joy filled his heart. God had done something wonderful in David's life! *Wait until I tell Sara!*

Steve ended his PowerPoint presentation with a description of the services his support department through the district offered to pastors and ministry leaders. He then prayed for the group, thanked them for being there, and dismissed them to go on to their next session. Several people from the audience quickly came up to Steve to ask questions and make appointments with his office. Dr. Schaffner and Paul Samples both smiled as they watched Steve interact with them. A few of the attendees were seminary students. Steve genuinely had a servant's heart and a personality others were drawn to. He cared about those new leaders and wanted them to be successful in their callings. As he greeted each person he kept looking around to make sure David was still in the room and that he hadn't imagined him being there. When he saw David taking his place in the line of people, he breathed a sigh of relief.

After several people had briefly conversed with Steve, David, who was last in line, walked forward. He had so much to tell Steve, but time was limited. He knew he and Steve had to go on to another session. The two reached for each other and hugged tightly, wiping their tears when they pulled away. They talked for a few minutes and then exchanged contact information. Steve invited David to come over to his house that weekend. David promised he would call that evening. He and his wife, Mariam, were anxious to meet with Steve and Sara. They had some important things to share with them. When David left the room, Steve quickly filled Dr. Schaffner and Paul in on how he had met David. They were both anxious to hear about the upcoming visit. Then picking up his briefcase, Steve and the others left the room and headed for their next presentation.

Side Note...

The district support program, overseen by Steve and Sara, quickly proved its value to the churches in its region. The ministry leaders utilizing its services were richly blessed because a couple of veteran pioneers, and their friends, obediently agreed to break ground again and give the new program a try. Soon, representatives from other districts in the country and different denominations were visiting Steve's office in Carolton when they learned how successful his program was. The district program would soon be duplicated in other parts of the state and country, bringing much-needed support to many ministry leaders.

That evening when Steve got home from the conference, he found Sara sitting in front of the computer in the family room. She had not gone with him this time because she and Mrs. Hellinger were manning the Carolton office. They had been receiving so many phone calls from people from other districts and denominations, either wanting to know about their services or asking to speak to a counselor, they felt that keeping the office open was more important than all of them going to the conference that year. Frank Hellinger stayed behind as well to help answer the phones and to run errands.

"Hi, Honey," Sara said when she saw Steve coming into the room. She got up from her chair to greet him. Placing his topcoat on the sofa, Steve hurried over to Sara. They hugged and kissed each other, and then Steve sat down on a folding chair beside the computer desk. At that moment, little Levi came running into the room, glad to see Steve back home. Steve smiled and rubbed his floppy ears as the dog greeted him. Steve was thankful for his presence there. Like Samson, he was a good watchdog and a great companion for Sara and him.

Then turning his attention back to Sara, Steve announced, "You'll never guess who was at the conference today."

"Who?" Sara asked while opening a saved file on the computer for Steve to see.

"David."

Sara stopped what she was doing. "David? . . . Our David?' she suddenly realized. "The one who came to our house that night in Anderson Hills?"

"Yes. And I've invited him and his wife to come over this weekend. He's calling tonight."

"He is? Oh my goodness, Steve, this is so incredible! I can't wait to see him, and hear his story! And he's bringing his wife?! Wow!"

"Yes, it's going to be an exciting reunion. . . . Oh, yeh. He uses the name Philip Rogers now. People in his situation sometimes change their identities. His wife's name is Mariam."

"I understand. I can't wait for his phone call!"

"I thought you'd be excited about it."

The two hugged again and began to plan for the weekend. Then they turned their attention to what Sara wanted to show Steve on the computer. Their daughter, Mary, had started working on a novel focused on spiritual warfare in Christian ministry. Motivated by her family's story, and several other ministry leaders' experiences she knew about, Mary was writing the book to help other pastors and ministry leaders, especially those who were new to vocational ministry, deal with their own spiritual battles. Mary also found it personally healing and therapeutic to write about these experiences, especially since she had lived many of them firsthand. Her husband, Joshua, was her editor. She had just sent her parents the first few chapters of the book to get their input.

"It's going to be a great novel," Sara proudly told Steve. "She's including some of our story in it. Sit here and see what you think," she said, offering the leather desk chair to Steve. "I'll get you something to eat."

"Ok," Steve said, loosening his tie.

Sara got up from her chair so Steve could get a closer look at the draft, now appearing on the computer, then went to the kitchen to get him the sandwich she had made for him earlier that evening. Curious as to how the book started, Steve pulled off his suit coat and tie, sat down by the computer and began to read the file. Little Levi laid down next to him.

"... It was moving day. A seasoned pastor and his wife, their teenage children, and playful beagle were on their way to a new calling. A new adventure. ..."

Steve skimmed through the pages of the opening chapter. Suddenly, he wasn't tired from his long trip. As he read, his mind flooded with memories of the past several years.

"This is great!" he told Sara when she returned with his sandwich. He was excited his daughter had chosen to take on this project. "This is going to help a lot of people in ministry. It sounds like Mary is drawing from a lot of sources. I can't wait to read the next chapter."

"Me too," Sara agreed, as she munched on some potato chips and sat down on the folding chair next to him. "I'm glad she's writing about this. It needs to be discussed more. I bet we could advertise it on our district website when it's finished."

"That's a good idea," Steve responded. "A lot of people will be interested in reading it."

As they went through the starting chapters and pondered the book's possible impact on Christian leadership in ministry, Steve and Sara couldn't help but think about their beloved canine friend, Samson. Mary had written his character into the story as well. Samson had played a big role in many years of their church ministry. Little Levi had filled the gap he left in their lives, but as they thought of Samson, they could almost hear him barking next to them, letting them know he was still there. And in a way, he was.

Endnotes

Chapter 1

[1]Luke 10: 1-24

[2]"Days of Elijah," a worship song. Words and music by Robin Mark (1994/1996).

Chapter 2

[1]Titus 1: 6, NIV (Read verses 6-9)

Chapter 3

[1]Ephesians 5: 3-15

Chapter 4

[1]1 Thessalonians 5: 5

[2]Revelation 12: 9

[3]Acts 26: 18

Chapter 5

[1]"The Battle Belongs to The Lord," a worship/praise song recorded by the Christian music group Petra (1989). Words and music by Jamie Owens-Collins (1984).

[2]Ephesians 6: 12, NIV

[3]Matthew 6: 9-13, NIV. The Lord's Prayer. Also see Luke 11: 2-4.

[4]Doxology to the Lord's Prayer. Found in the 1662 Book of Common Prayer (BCP), printed in England and other sources. There are some variations of this doxology.

Chapter 6

[1]Psalm 91: 4, NIV

[2]Philippians 4: 13

[3]Proverbs 15: 13, 17: 22

Chapter 7

[1]Zachariah 2: 5, NIV

[2]Ephesians 4: 29; Proverbs 18: 21

[3]Luke 14: 28, NKJV (Read verses 25-35)

Chapter 8

[1]The Gaither Vocal Band. A Gospel singing group. Many of the group's songs have been written by Bill and Gloria Gaither.

[2]Luke 2: 1-20

[3]Luke 8: 17, NIV

Chapter 9

[1]1 John 4: 1

Chapter 10

-None-

Chapter 11

[1]2 Kings 6: 16-17; 2 Chronicles 20: 15; 2 Corinthians 10:3-5; Matthew 14: 22-33

[2]Psalm 46: 1, NIV

[3]"It Is Well with My Soul." A Christian hymn by Horatio G. Spafford (words 1873) and Philip P. Bliss (music 1876)

Chapter 12

[1]Job 41: 1-34; Psalm 74: 13-14; Isaiah 27: 1

[2]Judges 6: 12

[3]Matthew 9: 37, NIV

[4]Esther 4:14, NIV

Chapter 13

[1]Acts 5: 34-39, NIV

[2]Psalm 23: 1-4, NKJV

[3]1 Corinthians 15: 55, NIV

[4]"Redeemer," a worship/praise song. Words and music by Nicole Coleman-Mullen (2000). Based on Job 19: 25-27.

Chapter 14

[1]"The Warrior Is a Child," a worship song. Words and music by Twila Paris (1984).

Chapter 15

[1]Psalm 43: 5, NKJV

[2]Romans 8: 17-18; Matthew 10: 38; Philippians 1: 29; 1 Peter 4: 19

[3]Romans 8: 26

[4]Ephesians 6: 18, NIV. Also see Jude 1: 20

[5]James 5: 16

[6]Isaiah 61: 3

[7]Luke 6: 27-28, NIV

[8]See books listed under forgiveness and inner healing by R. T. Kendall and other authors in "Resources."

[9]Luke 14: 28-30, NKJV

[10]Hebrews 4: 16, NKJV

Chapter 16

[1]1 Peter 5: 10; Psalm 51: 12; 1 John 5: 4

[2]Isaiah 40: 31

[3]Hebrews 12:1-2, NIV

[4]Psalm 27: 4

Chapter 17

-None-

Chapter 18

[1]2 Corinthians 10: 3-4

[2]Luke 9: 62

[3]Ezekiel 28: 14; Isaiah 14: 12-15; Revelation 12: 9

[4]Revelation 12: 4, 9

[5]Ephesians 6: 10-20

[6]Revelation 2: 1-7

[7]John 10: 10

[8]Matthew 14: 23; Mark 6: 46; Luke 6: 12

[9]1 Peter 5: 8, NKJV

[10]Proverbs 3: 5-6, NKJV

[11]Matthew 14: 22-33

[12]Psalm 34: 1-3

[13]Proverbs 17: 22

[14]John 14: 26

[15]1 Corinthians 12: 1-11

[16]Matthew 10: 1, Mark 6:7, Luke 9:1; 1 John 2: 13-14, James 4: 7

[17]1 Samuel 17: 38-51

[18]See books on spiritual warfare listed under "Resources"

[19]*The Pilgrim's Progress: From This World to That Which Is to Come,* an allegory/novel written by John Bunyan in 1678. Various publishers. (Originally printed in London, England, for Nath.Ponder in 1678.)

[20]1 Corinthians 2: 13-16

[21]Matthew 7: 15-20

[22]Ephesians 6: 18, NIV. Also see Jude 1: 20

[23]Esther 4: 15-16

[24]1 Thessalonians 5: 17, NKJV

[25]1 Peter 2: 9

[26]Matthew 4: 1-11

[27]Hebrews 4: 12, NKJV

[28]2 Timothy 4: 3

[29]Hebrews 12: 14-15

[30]Ephesians 6: 12, NIV

[31]1 John 4: 18, NKJV

[32]2 Timothy 1: 7

Resources

Spiritual Warfare/Angels/Deliverance

Anderson, Neal, T. *Victory Over the Darkness: Realize the Power of Your Identity in Christ.* Minneapolis, MN: Bethany House, 2000.

Anderson, Neal, T. *The Bondage Breaker.* Eugene, OR: Harvest House Publishers, 2006.

Collins, Hakeem. *Unseen Warfare: Rules of Engagement to Discern, Disarm, and Defeat the Works of the Enemy.* Shippensburg, PA: Destiny Image Publishers, Inc., 2021.

Evans, Tony. *Winning Your Spiritual Battles.* Eugene, OR: Harvest House Publishers, 2011.

Ingram, Chip. *The Invisible War, Updated and Expanded: What Every Believer Needs to Know, About Satan, Demons, and Spiritual Warfare.* Ada, MI: Baker Books, 2015.

Meyer, Joyce. *Battlefield of the Mind: Renew Your Mind Through the Power of God's Word.* New York: FaithWords/Hachette Book Group, 2017.

Sheets, Tim. *Angel Armies: Releasing the Warriors of Heaven.* Shippensburg, PA: Destiny Image Publishers, Inc., 2016.

Stark, Emma et al. *Lion Bites: Daily Prophetic Words that Awaken the Spiritual Warrior in You.* Shippensburg, PA: Destiny Image Publishers, Inc., 2022.

Forgiveness/Inner Healing

Hamilton, Adam. *Forgiveness: Finding Peace Through Letting Go.* Nashville, TN: Abingdon Press, 2012.

Hutchings, Mike. *Supernatural Freedom from the Captivity of Trauma: Overcoming the Hindrance to your Wholeness.* Shippensburg, PA: Destiny Image Publishers, Inc. 2021.

Kendall, Robert, T. *Revised and Updated Total Forgiveness: When Everything in You Wants to Hold a Grudge, Point a Finger, and Remember the Pain—God Wants You to Lay it All Aside.* Lake Mary, FL: Charisma House, 2007.

Kendall, Robert, T. *How to Forgive Ourselves Totally: Begin Again by Breaking Free from Past Mistakes.* Lake Mary, FL: Charisma House, 2007.

Kendall, Robert, T. *Totally Forgiving God: When It Seems He Has Betrayed You.* Lake Mary, FL: Charisma House, 2012.

Seamands, David, A. *Healing for Damaged Emotions* (Updated). Elgin, IL: David C. Cook, 2015.

Sheets, Dutch. *The Power of Hope: Let God Renew Your Mind, Heal Your Heart, and Restore Your Dreams.* Lake Mary, FL: Charisma House, 2014.

Calling/Leadership in Ministry

Blackaby, Henry T., Brandt, Henry, and Skinner, Kerry L. *The Power of the Call.* Nashville, TN: Broadman & Holman Publishers, 1997.

Blackaby, Henry and Blackaby, Richard. *Spiritual Leadership: Moving People on to God's Agenda.* Nashville, TN: Broadman & Holman Publishers, 2011.

Blanchard, Ken, and Hodges, Phil. *The Servant Leader: Transforming Your Heart, Head, Hands, & Habits.* Nashville: TN, J Countryman, 2003.

Blanchard, Ken, Hodges, Phil, and Hendry, Phyllis. *Lead Like Jesus Revisited: Lessons from the Greatest Leadership Role Model of All Time.* Nashville, TN: W Publishing Group/Thomas Nelson, 2016.

McNeal, Reggie. *A Work of Heart: Understanding How God Shapes Spiritual Leaders.* San Francisco, CA: Josey-Bass, 2011.

Malphurs, Aubrey. *Being Leaders: The Nature of Authentic Christian Leadership.* Grand Rapids, MI: Baker Books, 2003.

Printed in the USA
CPSIA information can be obtained
at www.ICGtesting.com
JSHW080328220823
46969JS00001B/3